JANE'S WORLD AIRCRAFT RECOGNITION HANDBOOK

First published in the United Kingdom in 1979
This edition published in 1982 by
Jane's Publishing Company Limited
238 City Road, London EC1V 2PU

ISBN 0 7106 0202 2

Designed by Judy Tuke

Computer typesetting and origination by
Method Limited, 8 The Broadway, Woodford Green, Essex

Printed in the United Kingdom by Biddles Limited,
Guildford, Surrey

Contents

ACKNOWLEDGMENTS

In preparing this book I have received help from a number of sources: John Blake has prepared all the sketch drawings, and the silhouettes have been supplied by Pilot Press and Michael Badrocke. I am also grateful to Michael Taylor and *Jane's All the World's Aircraft* for the supply of many of the photographs. Derek Ballington kindly produced the test sillographs. Finally, my thanks go to my wife, Lin, for her patience and for again typing much of the manuscript.

RECOMMENDED FURTHER READING

Jane's All the World's Aircraft
Jane's Pocket Books:
   Major Combat Aircraft
   Commercial Transport Aircraft
   Military Transport and Training Aircraft
   Light Aircraft
   Helicopters
   Home-built Aircraft
   Air Forces of the World
Frederick Warne: *Observer's Book of Aircraft*
Ian Allan: *Civil Aircraft of the World*
   Military Aircraft of the World

PICTURE ACKNOWLEDGMENTS

Thanks are due to John and Michael Taylor, Stephen Piercey (*Propliner* magazine) and Barry Wheeler (*Joint Services Recognition Journal*) for their picture-research efforts.

INTRODUCTION

Aircraft recognition is as important today as it ever was, for military and civilian observers alike. This volume is intended as a primer for students of the subject, and is not a standard collection of aircraft types by country and manufacturer with full data. There are a number of excellent volumes of this type and a list is provided on page 6.

The aim has been to satisfy the needs of three types of recognition student:

Armed service or auxiliary personnel worldwide to whom recognition is vital for survival in war.

Those who have an interest in aviation and wish to learn how to recognise aircraft from scratch.

The knowledgeable enthusiast in service or civilian life who requires quick answers, either to check judgement or for revision.

The initial "teach-in" section provides an introduction to the subject and includes a glossary, without which the newcomer would be lost in a world that has built up its own exclusive jargon.

The essential elements of airframes are illustrated, together with an explanation of the breakdown of the book into fixed-wing aircraft and helicopters of various distinctive types. The emphasis throughout is on shapes and not manufacturers or designations, and all groups are assembled on the basis of similarity in general configuration. After all, when an airborne object comes into view, the observer on the ground wants to refer to a shape to find out what it is. Is it jet or propeller-driven? Are its wings straight or swept? Are the engines on the wings?

The 480+ aircraft shown in the reference part of the book have been selected as most likely to be seen round the world. There is a limit to the number of aircraft that can be illustrated and those omitted include several "one-offs", types not due to fly or appear in service for some time, aircraft of which only a handful are flying, and ultra-lights and homebuilts.

Both military and civil machines are included, as it is impossible, even for the serviceman, just to study warplanes. Confusion can always arise if the observer has not covered all the significant types. In the early stages of the Second World War an axiom was adopted by those who were either unable or unwilling to learn recognition. Aircraft were divided into three categories: receding and presumed friendly; approaching and presumed hostile; and Lysanders. That the ultra-distinctive Lysander should be regarded as the only readily recognisable type is an indication of the very low standards that prevailed until recognition was really taken seriously and proper teaching methods were evolved. Faulty recognition in war has led to untold casualties which could have been avoided.

Black-and-white silhouettes have been used throughout the reference section of this book, as the detailed three-view silhouette remains the best method of encapsulating the shape and main features of any aircraft. Line drawings just do not give the same emphasis to recognition outline, although they can be useful once the student has become reasonably proficient.

All sorts of so-called mnemonic aircraft-recognition systems have been invented; one such is "WETFUR", standing for Wings, Engine, Tail Unit, Fuselage, Undercarriage and Radiator. In practice these methods are completely useless, as recognition depends on the aircraft's total appearance and there is usually little enough time to look for individual features, let alone reciting sets of letters. Mnemonics have no place here.

Long-winded descriptions of the aircraft with a mass of complex data also leave little impression on the recognition student and only serve to confuse; they too have been omitted.

Additional information such as designation systems, code-name lists and general characteristics are very important, both for reference and to add to the general picture. They have therefore been included.

After the basic details on each type there is a list of the similar designs with which it might be confused. This has been done to stimulate interest and comparison. Some students may decide that aircraft X is much more like aircraft Y. If this comes after careful study of a number of silhouettes and photographs, then the individual's recognition knowledge will have been significantly extended.

Introduction to new edition

Since the first edition of *Jane's World Aircraft Recognition Handbook* a number of new aircraft have emerged and many others have moved from the prototype or pre-production stages to full production and service.

The text has been revised throughout, and 69 new silhouettes and over 100 new photographs, together with additional features, have been incorporated. The question "should it go in or not?" has remained the same. Are there sufficient numbers of a particular type flying over a wide enough area of the globe to warrant inclusion? A number of old aircraft are still familiar to many people, while some prototypes are not yet on the line and fly only over a limited territory.

Over the past three years some well known types have finally left the scene, including the Comet airliner, Vulcan delta-wing bomber, the Gannet carrierborne AEW aircraft and the CL-41 Argus maritime reconnaissance aircraft. Others have been so reduced in numbers that they have to be excluded on the grounds of limited visibility.

The book is inevitably larger, with many nations tending to keep all or part of their old equipment while continuing to acquire new aircraft; this is particularly true of the Soviet Union.

Quick-reference symbols

At the top outside corner of each page in the following chapters you will find a quick-reference symbol. They are designed to show the main characteristics of each class of aircraft, so that the user can find his way immediately to the right chapter after catching a fleeting glimpse of, say, a delta shape in the sky. In some cases one symbol has had to stand for two classes of aircraft. It would have been difficult to suggest high or low wings with simple plan-views, just as the addition of something to indicate fixed or retractable undercarriage would have made those symbols unnecessarily complicated. One symbol has therefore been used for both high and low-wing twin-propeller aircraft, while all three classes of single propeller designs are represented by a single plan view.

Jet, swept wing, fuselage engine(s)

Jet, swept wing, flank/root engines

Jet, swept wing, underwing engines

Jet, swept wing, rear engines

Jet, straight wing, rear engines

Jet, delta wing

Jet, variable geometry

Jet, straight wing, fuselage/wing engine(s)

Twin propellers

Four propellers

Single propeller

Amphibians

Biplanes

Twin booms

Helicopter, single rotor, light

Helicopter, single rotor, medium/heavy

Helicopter, twin rotors

9

A relatively simple aircraft like the British
Aerospace Hawk trainer can look very
different when fully equipped for ground
attack. This example is carrying bombs
under the wings and has a centreline 30mm
cannon pack.

When landing, with undercarriage and flaps down, an
aircraft can look very different from its "cleaned-up" cruising
configuration. In this view of the VC10 even the big, high-set
tailplane is largely masked by the wing.

THE BASICS OF RECOGNITION

The initial approach to aircraft recognition is daunting, confronting the student with a mass of shapes, hundreds of odd names, curious designations, incomprehensible specifications and strange descriptive terms.

It is essential for any student to work in stages, gradually acquiring knowledge and storing it. Like people's faces and figures, every aircraft and helicopter has its own characteristics. It may have one engine and straight wings; four engines and swept wings; a fat fuselage; a triangular wing; a tailplane on top of the fin; or, in the case of a helicopter, one or two rotors.

The permutations are endless, but ultimately all powered flying machines can be sorted out into categories for detailed study. This book is divided into categories based on wing shape and engine layout in the case of fixed-wing aircraft, and size and number of rotors for helicopters.

The basic structure of an aircraft has to be studied from the outset. Every powered flying machine (other than helicopters) has some wing form, a fuselage and a tail structure, the last-mentioned having either a horizontal stabiliser and a fin, or a fin alone (as in the case of some delta-wing designs such as the Mirage and Concorde). Every wing, fuselage and tail structure differs in some respects from another, as do the engine installations and air intakes, be they for gas turbines or piston engines. It is the combination of these features with individual characteristics that makes up an aircraft's total shape. Knowledge of such shapes is the essence of recognition.

The same theory applies to helicopters, except that wings appear only occasionally in stub form, tail structures consist of rear rotors and some miniature tails, and the main rotor(s) dominate the shape.

The best way for the beginner to use this book is to look first at totally different types, say the Hawk trainer and the Boeing 747 airliner, or the Jaguar ground-attack aircraft and Chinook twin-rotor helicopter. In the first case, a single-engined two-seat trainer with the engine in the fuselage just cannot resemble a giant 385-seater with four jets slung under the wings. In the second case, the swept-wing Jaguar hardly compares with the Chinook, with its squat, boxlike fuselage and twin overhead rotors.

This process should be continued at random, selecting from the different sub-sections of the book. At the same time, the annotated drawings on pages 18-25 should be consulted to find out what the various parts of flying machines are and, in the case of flying controls, what they do. For an understanding of aviation terminology the glossary of terms and abbreviations at the end of this book can be used.

The second stage is for the reader to look at two of the aircraft in each sub-section which are similar in general layout but very different in detail characteristics. Take, for instance, the Corsair II and the Lightning in Section 1. The two wing shapes immediately strike the eye: that of the Corsair is broad in chord and moderately swept back, while the Lightning's resembles a triangle with two triangular notches cut out at the roots. The Corsair fuselage is dumpy, with a distinctive "pimple" above the nose intake. The Lightning, on the other hand, has a circular intake with a pointed centrebody. Unlike the Corsair, with its simple engine and exhaust arrangement, the Lightning has two engines mounted one above the other in the fuselage and exhausting through twin afterburning jetpipes. Finally, the fin of the Corsair tapers to what looks like a curved top, while the Lightning's fin is much broader and cut sharply across the top.

After several excursions through the pages to see how shapes differ markedly or are superficially similar, the student should select his basic first 30 aircraft. If he is a member of a military or paramilitary force, he can choose the friendly and unfriendly types which he is most likely to encounter.

A mixed first 30 could consist of the following:

Military	Civil
Mirage	Airbus A300
Corsair II	Boeing 737
Bear	Boeing 747
Phantom	McDonnell Douglas DC-8
F-15	McDonnell Douglas DC-9
F-5	McDonnell Douglas DC-10
Jaguar	BAe One-Eleven
Firebar	Lockheed TriStar
Tornado	Tu-134
Viggen	Comanche
Foxbat	Codling
Starfighter	F.27 Friendship
Fishbed	BAe 748
B-52	Piper Cherokee
Backfire	Beech Mentor

For helicopters an initial eight could be:

Military	Civil
Westland Lynx	Mi-24 Hind
Ka-25 Hormone	Aérospatiale Alouette
Boeing Chinook	Hughes 500
Sikorsky S-61	MBB BO105

The student who wants to devise his own programme could well make his first selection from the types which fly from the nearest civil or military airfield, or both. After the first 30, a further 30 can be chosen, and so on. After the student has mastered his first 30 aircraft, he will be able to apply his self-acquired training to any types of his choice.

The Tupolev Tu-16 Badger is one of a small class of large aircraft with engines in the wing roots. One variant carries underwing-mounted Kelt missiles, which at long range can look like additional engines.

A standard Soviet ground-attack fighter, the all-swept Sukhoi Su-7 Fitter appears here with undercarriage and flaps lowered.

Throughout, the recognition of an aircraft must involve a total impression of the shape, but with certain distinctive elements borne in mind. When any aircraft appears it must be watched right across the sky so that it can be viewed from every angle.

In the air, the head-on view of an F-15 fighter looks very different to a side or plan view, possibly leading to confusion with the Soviet Foxbat. Aircraft viewed from the rear, going away, also often provide problems, as with the Mirage and Viggen. Particularly difficult are the head-on and retreating views of the transports with twin and triple rear-engine layouts, not least the Soviet Crusty and Careless airliners. The Soviet Badger and Bear bombers are easily confused at a distance, when the difference in size cannot be estimated.

Helicopters require special study as, at a distance and in poor weather, their shapes tend to be ill-defined. In certain cases very detailed knowledge of outlines is needed to differentiate between types. Examples of similar outlines are the German MBB BO105 and the Hughes 500D helicopters.

The only way to progress in aircraft recognition is to "look and learn"as frequently as possible. This means not only scanning the skies but examining every photograph or drawing in newspapers and magazines and watching for aircraft on television. A scrapbook of picture cuttings and notes is an excellent way of improving the art.

A typical light helicopter, the Aérospatiale Alouette III has a single main rotor, unfaired engine and a fixed tricycle undercarriage.

External stores radically alter the outlines of combat aircraft. This Panavia Tornado is shown (top) "clean" and (above) with a variety of wing and fuselage-mounted weapons.

When an unknown aircraft flies over, or an uncaptioned photograph appears in a journal, note its main features and consult the appropriate section in this book. The more "mental images" of different types that can be stored away, the easier recognition becomes.

Changing outline

Having learned the flying exterior of an aircraft, the effects of external items that may be attached to it require attention. Modern military aircraft carry a great variety of external "stores": missiles, rocket pods, bombs, reconnaissance pods, externally mounted guns, electronic jamming pods and auxiliary fuel tanks, to mention a few. As an example of the resulting outline change, the podded fuel tanks under the wings of a Hercules transport can, at a distance, give the

Heavy transport types can also accommodate a variety of outline-changing underwing loads. This Lockheed DC-130 Hercules is carrying a pair of Teledyne Ryan drones and two long-range fuel tanks.

impression of six engines instead of four. Radomes and other bumps or bulges on an aircraft also change the shape when viewed from different angles.

Variable-geometry or swing-wing aircraft present problems, as moving the wings from straight to fully swept changes the outline continuously.

Finally, an aircraft preparing to land can appear completely different from its normal cruising self. For instance, a Boeing 747 cruising across the sky is not the same as a 747 on the approach to an airfield with its multi-wheel undercarriage down and massive flaps extended.

To appreciate all the changing aspects of aircraft in the air, it is essential to keep watching with the eyes or, preferably, with binoculars. When there is cloud, watch where the aircraft enters and judge where it may reappear.

Viewed from above
For the military pilot, aircraft flying below or positioned on the ground are very important. The pilot's view can be very different from that of the ground observer. It takes a sharp eye to recognise a fleeting shape parked near a hangar, in a revetment, or with its nose sticking out of a shelter. Special study is needed to separate shapes on the ground from their surroundings, and camouflage makes this even more difficult.

In the air, it is easier to recognise aircraft seen from below. From above, aircraft blend with the terrain, particularly when they are camouflaged, or have their outlines broken up by reflected light.

Contrails
At high altitude condensation of the water vapour in the exhaust gas of an aero-engine produces a "contrail", a tell-tale stream of white vapour across the sky. On a clear day it is often possible to recognise the aircraft at the head of the trail, but usually binoculars are essential. When there is patchy cloud the point of entry of the contrail should be noted to find the direction of exit. Large multi-engined aircraft make several trails which usually blend into one. With a lot of experience it is possible to differentiate between certain types, but great care is needed.

Sound
Sound is very often the first indication that an aircraft or helicopter is approaching. Weather effects and the varied abilities of human ears can however make sound very misleading. It may appear to come from completely the wrong quarter, causing the observer to miss the approaching aircraft altogether. With fast aircraft, the subject may be well ahead of its noise. Sound is nevertheless important and certain basic facts can be gleaned from it. It is usually possible to differentiate between a piston engine and a jet; a turboprop is distinctive, while the beat of a helicopter rotor sounds different from the noise of a fixed-wing aircraft.

It is important to both watch *and* listen in order to associate sound with a particular type. A great deal of practice is needed before making snap judgements on sound alone, and even then there is a higher chance of error.

TEACHING RECOGNITION

Teaching aircraft recognition, whether in the services or a club, is an exacting task calling for method, efficiency and, above all, background knowledge of the subject. The ace spotter who can recognise anything does not necessarily make a good instructor, as he may be too far removed from the novice's problems.

An instructor must be able to make the subject live and to translate flat pictures and silhouettes into 3D images which will remain imprinted on the pupil's mind; hence the need for background knowledge. The tools of the instructor's trade are silhouettes, black-and-white or colour photographs and slides, filmstrips, the slide projector, the episcope and the overhead projector. Sometimes a film can provide excellent material, though a particular view cannot be shown again as quickly as with the other devices. A blackboard on which instructor and students can put quick sketches is extremely useful.

Models are also good tools, both to make and look at. Putting a plastic kit together will leave a lasting impression of the subject's shape and characteristics. Models may also be used in conjunction with the easy-to-make "shadowgraph", a diagram of which is shown here. The "flash trainer" is also an effective aid, though not always easy to obtain. The essence of the flash trainer is a shutter which flashes the image onto the screen for a brief period. With a little ingenuity it is possible to adapt an old camera shutter for use with either an episcope or a slide projector.

In approaching recognition training, it is essential to plan ahead and not swamp the pupils with an excess of information. An initial test will decide the standard of the class, while discussion will reveal the level of understanding of terms and nomenclature. A large sketch of the basic elements of fixed-wing aircraft and helicopters is a must for absolute beginners.

As mentioned earlier, contrasting types should be illustrated first to give the pupil some "feel"; thereafter types should be taught in groups. The make-up of the groups will depend on the priorities and interests of the class: whether they are servicemen or civilians, for instance.

Biscuit-tin shadowgraph projector and screen.

Each aircraft should be the subject of a lesson on its own, with a mixture of silhouettes and photographs or slides. When instruction has been given in a dozen types, there should be a full revision session and a test. As the pupils become more proficient, so the tests should be varied and made more difficult.

The instructor must ensure that he does not overload the class, which will cause confusion, and also that he does not bore them. Boredom has been the enemy of good recognition training since aircraft were first used in war.

As time goes on, it will become apparent that certain types are more difficult to recognise, largely because they can be confused in outline with others of similar shape. Every effort should be made to show pictures and silhouettes of these difficult aircraft at frequent intervals until the points of difference are clearly understood. Care should however be taken to see that the pupils do not get into the bad habit of recognising the photograph rather than the aircraft itself.

The instructor can use a variety of methods to hold the students' interest. If an aviation incident, military or civil, has been headlined in the newspapers or shown on television recently, a short illustrated talk on the type or types involved should be given while the subject is fresh in the pupils' minds.

If possible, the classroom walls should be decorated with aircraft illustrations, preferably large ones, which can be changed or added to at intervals. If this is not possible, sections of hardboard covered with suitable pictures and captions should be taken along to the meetings. One such board can be used for an "aircraft of the week" to which the class can give special attention.

"Sillographs", which form good training and test material, can be made very simply by inking in photographs with a black felt pen or a brush and black ink or paint. The proficiency test at the end of this book is presented in sillograph form. Cartoons are also of assistance, as the exaggeration stresses key points of outline. To achieve greater variety, photographs from journals can be cut into pieces showing a fin, nose, engine nacelle or part of a wing, for example.

A scrapbook can be kept handy and added to by both instructor and class. Prizes can be given for success in recognition tests. Finally, properly organised visits to airfields and attendance at air displays will make recognition training come alive.

A typical modern combat aircraft: McDonnell Douglas AV-8B Harrier II

1 Nose cone
2 ARBS sensor aperture
3 Hughes Angle Rate Bombing System (ARBS) receiver
4 ARN-128 all-weather landing system receiver
5 Upper IFF aerial
6 ARBS signal processor
7 Nose pitch-control valve
8 Pitch trim unit
9 Lower IFF aerial
10 Pitot tube
11 Artificial feel system spring struts
12 Front pressure bulkhead
13 Yaw vane
14 Ram-air intake (cockpit fresh air)
15 One-piece wrap-around windscreen
16 Instrument panel shroud
17 De-misting air duct
18 Rudder pedals
19 Cockpit floor level
20 Underfloor avionics bay
21 Air-data computer
22 ASN-130 inertial navigation system
23 Low-voltage formation lighting strips
24 Control system linkages
25 Nosewheel doors
26 Port console panel
27 Main fuel cock
28 Engine throttle lever
29 Nozzle-angle control lever
30 Cockpit-section composite construction
31 Ejection seat
32 Canopy frame
33 Head-up display (HUD)
34 Cockpit canopy cover
35 Starboard canopy cover
36 Miniature detonating cord (MDC) canopy-breaker
37 Sliding canopy rail
38 Ejection-seat headrest
39 Ejection-seat launch rails
40 Cockpit rear pressure bulkhead
41 Nosewheel bay
42 Boundary-layer bleed-air duct
43 Cockpit air-conditioning plant
44 Nosewheel hydraulic retraction jack
45 Nose undercarriage leg pivot fixing
46 Port air intake
47 Landing/taxiing lamp
48 Nosewheel forks
49 Nosewheel

50 Two-row intake blow-in doors
51 Intake centre fairing
52 Air-conditioning system heat-exchanger
53 Engine compressor face
54 Bleed-air spill ducts
55 Air-conditioning intake scoops
56 Starboard leading-edge root extension (LERX)
57 Engine equipment bay access doors
58 Upper formation lighting strips
59 Engine auxiliary equipment compartment
60 Alternators
61 Rolls-Royce Pegasus (F402-RR-404A) turbofan engine
62 Oil tank
63 Forward fuel tank
64 Flush air intake
65 Engine bay venting air controls
66 Hydraulic ground servicing bay
67 Crossdam fence (forward-retracting)
68 Ventral cushion-augmentation strakes, port and starboard (fitted in place of gun packs)
69 Zero-scarf forward nozzle fairing
70 Rotary nozzle bearing
71 Port leading-edge root extension (LERX)
72 Reaction-control system bleed-air ducting
73 Auxiliary power unit/gas turbine starter
74 APU intake
75 APU exhaust duct
76 Centre wing spar
77 Centre wing integral fuel tank
78 Starboard wing reaction-control air duct
79 Inboard pylon
80 Fixed leading-edges fences
81 Supercritical wing section
82 Drop tank
83 Intermediate wing pylon
84 Starboard wing integral fuel tank, total internal system capacity 7,500lb (3,402kg)
85 AIM-9L Sidewinder air-to-air missile
86 Missile launch rail
87 Outboard pylon
88 Radar-warning antenna
89 Starboard navigation light
90 Roll-control air valves
91 Starboard formation light
92 Fuel jettison

93 Starboard aileron
94 Fuel jettison valve
95 Aileron/air valve interconnection
96 Aileron hydraulic jack
97 Outrigger wheel fairing
98 Starboard outrigger wheel, retracted position
99 Torque scissor links
100 Hydraulic retraction jack
101 Starboard positive-circulation slotted flap
102 Flap vane
103 Fuel system piping
104 Centre wing fairing panels
105 Centre wing construction
106 Water/methanol tank
107 Engine rear divider duct
108 Rear nozzle bearing
109 Centre fuselage fuel tank
110 Inboard leading-edge fence
111 Hydraulic reservoir
112 Nozzle fairing
113 Twin mainwheels
114 Rear (hot stream) exhaust nozzle
115 Titanium fuselage heatshield
116 Flap hydraulic jack
117 Wing spar/fuselage attachment joint
118 Fuel filler cap
119 Rear fuselage fuel tank
120 Aft fuselage avionics bay
121 Fuselage frame construction
122 Ram-air intake
123 Avionics cooling-air ducts
124 Avionics air-conditioning plant
125 Rudder hydraulic actuator
126 Fin construction
127 Formation lighting strip
128 Fin leading-edge ribs
129 Starboard tailplane
130 Graphite/epoxy tailplane skin panels
131 Temperature probe
132 Fin-tip communications aerial
133 Radar beacon antenna
134 Rudder honeycomb construction
135 Rudder
136 Rudder tab
137 Yaw-control air valves
138 Tail boom
139 Tail pitch-control air valve
140 Radar-warning tailcone
141 Port tailplane
142 Tailplane composite construction
143 Fin attachment joint
144 Tailplane sealing plate
145 Tail bumper
146 Ventral fin
147 Lower communications aerial

148 Tailplane hydraulic jack
149 Rear fuselage main frame
150 Reaction-control system air ducting
151 Fuselage frame-and-stringer construction
152 Lower formation lighting strip
153 Avionics-bay access door
154 Airbrake hydraulic jack
155 Ventral airbrake
156 Port slotted flap composite construction
157 Honeycomb flap-vane construction
158 Outrigger wheel fairing
159 Port aileron
160 Aileron composite construction
161 Outer wing panel construction
162 Fuel jettison
163 Port formation light
164 Roll-control air valve
165 ACR-67 radar-warning signal processor
166 Port navigation light
167 Radar-warning antenna
168 AIM-9L Sidewinder air-to-air missile
169 Missile launch rail
170 Outboard pylon
171 Drop tank, capacity 300 US gal (1,136 lit)
172 Port intermediate pylon
173 Port outrigger wheel
174 Aileron hydraulic actuator
175 Outrigger leg strut
176 Hydraulic retraction jack
177 Leading-edge bleed-air ducting
178 Graphite epoxy composite wing construction
179 Outboard leading-edge fence
180 Pylon fixing hardpoint
181 Port inner pylon
182 Triple-ejector bomb rack
183 Mk 82 HE bombs
184 Bomb fuse controls
185 Starboard ventral gun pack
186 Port ventral gun pack
187 Ammunition tank, 100 rounds
188 Ammunition feed chute
189 Cartridge-case collector box
190 25mm cannon
191 Gun pack cushion-augmentation strake
192 Gun attachment link
193 Muzzle fairing
194 Gun gas vents
195 Crossdam fence
196 Crossdam fence hydraulic jack

A typical airliner: Fokker F.28 Mk 4000 Fellowship

1 Radome
2 Weather-radar scanner
3 Front pressure bulkhead
4 Radar equipment mounting
5 Windscreen wipers
6 Windscreen frame
7 Instrument panel shroud
8 Back of instrument panel
9 Rudder pedals
10 Ram-air intake
11 Cockpit roof control panel
12 Overhead window
13 Co-pilot's seat
14 Pilot's seat
15 Control column
16 Pilot's side console
17 Air-conditioning plant
18 Nosewheel doors
19 Nose undercarriage leg
20 Twin nosewheels
21 Cockpit roof construction
22 Radio and electronics rack
23 Radio-rack cooling duct
24 Galley
25 Stewardess's seat
26 Curtained doorway to passenger cabin
27 Handrail
28 Entrance vestibule
29 Entry stairway
30 VHF aerial
31 Main passenger door
32 Upper VHF aerial
33 Air-conditioning duct
34 Forward-cabin passenger seating
35 Seat rails
36 Freight and baggage-hold door
37 ADF loop aerials
38 Fuselage frame-and-stringer construction
39 Soundproofing panels
40 Underfloor freight and baggage hold
41 Window panels

42 Cabin floor construction
43 Hot-air duct
44 Wing centre-section front spar
45 HF aerial fixing
46 Leading-edge fence
47 Starboard wing integral fuel tank
48 Fuel filler
49 Starboard navigation light
50 Static-discharge wicks
51 Starboard aileron
52 Aileron tab
53 Flap-mechanism fairings
54 Starboard outer flaps
55 Outboard spoilers (open)
56 Starboard inboard flaps
57 Inboard spoilers (open)
58 Centre-section main fuselage frames
59 Air distribution duct
60 Wing centre-section construction
61 Emergency escape windows
62 Pressurised cover of mainwheel well
63 Port mainwheel well
64 Cabin-window trim panels
65 Rear-cabin seating
66 Passenger overhead service panels
67 Overhead luggage rack
68 Cabin rear bulkhead
69 Starboard engine cowling
70 Toilet
71 Washbasin
72 Air intake to APU
73 Fin-root fairing
74 Fuselage sloping frames
75 De-icing air duct
76 HF aerials
77 Fin leading-edge de-icing
78 Fin construction
79 Tailplane hydraulic jacks
80 Tailplane de-icing air duct
81 Anti-collision light
82 Starboard tailplane

83 Starboard elevator
84 Tailplane pivot fairing
85 Elevator hinge controls
86 Tailcone fairing
87 Tail navigation light
88 Port elevator
89 Tailplane construction
90 Leading-edge de-icing
91 Tailplane pivot
92 Rudder
93 Rudder hydraulic jack
94 Port airbrake (open)
95 Airbrake jack housing
96 Rear fuselage construction
97 Hydraulic accumulators
98 Exhaust silencer nozzle
99 Engine pylon fairing
100 Bleed-air ducting
101 Rolls-Royce Mk 555-15 Spey Junior engine
102 Engine mountings
103 Engine cowlings
104 Auxiliary power unit (APU)
105 Engine mounting beam
106 Air intake
107 Five-abreast passenger seating
108 Underfloor air duct
109 Trailing-edge wing-root fairing
110 Inboard flap-track fairing
111 Port inboard spoilers
112 Port flaps
113 Flap mechanism fairings
114 Port outboard spoilers
115 Flap construction
116 Aileron tab
117 Port aileron
118 Static-discharge wicks
119 Port wingtip
120 Port navigation light
121 Outer-wing rib construction
122 Leading-edge de-icing air ducts
123 Leading-edge construction
124 Lattice ribs
125 Wing integral fuel tanks

126 Twin mainwheels
127 Main undercarriage leg
128 Leading-edge fence
129 Undercarriage retraction-jack fixing
130 Wing-panel bolted joint
131 Corrugated inner wing skin
132 Wing spar-attachment frame
133 Leading-edge de-icing air duct

A typical military helicopter: Westland Sea King HAS5

1 Fixed-tailplane construction
2 Static dischargers
3 Tail navigation light
4 Anti-collision light
5 Tail rotor gearbox
6 Six-bladed tail rotor
7 Blade pitch-change mechanism
8 Tail rotor drive shaft
9 Tail pylon construction
10 Glassfibre trailing-edge panel
11 Intermediate-shaft gearbox
12 Shaft coupling
13 Folding tail pylon hinges
14 Transponder aerial
15 Rotor blade cross-section
16 Blade tracking weights
17 Blade balance weights
18 D-section aluminium spar
19 Tail rotor control gear
20 Tailcone frame-and-stringer construction
21 Tail rotor transmission shaft
22 Dorsal spine fairing
23 UHF aerial
24 Shaft bearings
25 Tie-down ring
26 Fuselage/tailcone production joint
27 Maintenance walkway
28 Fuel jettison pipe
29 Non-retracting tailwheel
30 Tailwheel levered-suspension leg strut
31 Tailwheel castoring leg fixing
32 Mk 46 torpedo
33 Torpedo propellers
34 Parachute launch pack
35 Mk 11 depth charge
36 Weapon pylon shackles
37 Weapon-release unit (4)
38 Cabin flooring
39 Smoke marker container
40 Door latch
41 Cabin rear bulkhead

42 Radar-scanner support mounting
43 MEL Sea Searcher radar scanner
44 HF aerial cable
45 Cabin wall soundproofing panels
46 Rescue hoist/winch
47 Winch floodlight
48 Transponder transmitter/receiver
49 Radar transmitter/receiver
50 Data-processing station (Marconi LAPADS)
51 Crew emergency exit window
52 Sonobuoy launch tube
53 Swivelling seat mounting
54 Pressure refuelling connection
55 Plessey Type 195 dipping sonar
56 Emergency flotation bag (shown inflated)
57 Flotation bag inflation bottles
58 Bilge pump access covers
59 Underfloor fuel tanks, total fuel capacity 704 Imp gal (3,200 lit) in five cells
60 Fuselage main longeron
61 Sonobuoy stowage racks
62 Winch operating control lever
63 Sliding freight door
64 Freight door rail
65 Data display panels
66 Sonar operator's seat
67 Port radar observer's seat
68 Sonar/radar instrumentation racks
69 Gearbox mounting support structure
70 Hydraulic system connectors
71 Oil cooler
72 Oil cooler air outlet
73 Rotor-head tail fairing
74 Engine fire-extinguisher bottles
75 Handhold
76 Oil cooler fan
77 Gearbox-driven accessory units
78 Rotor-head hydraulic control jack (3)

79 Main gearbox
80 Swashplate mechanism
81 Blade pitch-control rods
82 Blade attachment joints
83 Master (non-folding) rotor blade
84 Nos 2-5 rotor blades folded position
85 Rotor-head fairing
86 Hydraulic oil reservoir
87 Blade-folding hinge joints
88 Rotor-head mechanism
89 Cooling-air louvres
90 Engine exhaust duct
91 Cabin roof construction
92 Folding step/handhold
93 Tie-down ring
94 Main undercarriage strut mounting
95 Kick-in steps
96 Undercarriage energy-absorbing side strut
97 Main undercarriage housing sponson
98 Starboard navigation light
99 Main undercarriage leg strut
100 Retraction strut
101 Twin mainwheels
102 Stub wing/walkway
103 Folding step
104 Forward underfloor fuel tanks
105 Cabin air ducting
106 Dipping sonar housing
107 Sonar winch cable drum
108 Winch "pit-head"gear
109 Tape recorder
110 Engine mounting deck
111 Rolls-Royce Gnome H.1400-1 turboshaft engine
112 Engine bay firewall
113 Port engine nacelle
114 Engine oil tank
115 Port engine air intake
116 Engine starter housing
117 Starboard engine air intake

118 Engine mounting strut
119 Intake foreign-object deflector
120 Pitot tube
121 Control rod linkages
122 Heating/ventilation system air intake
123 Fuel control computers
124 Cabin heater/blower
125 Boat-hull chine longeron
126 Electrical equipment bay
127 Cockpit floor level
128 Fire-extinguisher
129 Sliding side window panel
130 Pilot's seat
131 Cockpit bulkhead
132 Radio rack
133 Port entry doorway
134 Rotor brake lever
135 Overhead switch panels
136 Engine control cables
137 Entry door upper segment (open)
138 Pitot tube
139 Cockpit eyebrow windows
140 Windscreen panels
141 Windscreen wipers
142 Air-temperature probe
143 Co-pilot's seat
144 Instrument panel shroud
145 Centre control console
146 Cyclic-pitch control column
147 Back of instrument panel
148 Yaw-control rudder pedals
149 Downward-vision window
150 Radio and electronics equipment
151 Anti-collision light
152 Homing aerials
153 Retractable landing/taxiing lamps
154 Vertical landing lamps
155 Bow compartment hinged access door
156 Battery compartment
157 Fresh-air intakes
158 VHF aerial

A typical general-aviation aircraft: Piper T-1040

1 Starboard navigation light
2 Wing leading-edge de-icer boot
3 Main wing spar
4 Starboard aileron
5 Aileron trim tab (starboard only)
6 Aileron control linkage
7 Access panels
8 Starboard Fowler-type flap
9 Starboard nacelle baggage locker
10 Locker door
11 Nacelle systems access panels
12 Starboard main landing gear actuating cylinder
13 Wing inner section
14 Intercooler assembly (right)
15 Starboard hydraulic gear
16 Auxiliary air intakes
17 Engine bleed air
18 Louvres
19 Exhausts
20 Hartzell three-blade fully reversing propeller
21 Propeller de-icer boots
22 Spinner
23 Intake de-icer boot
24 Starboard engine air intake
25 Nose cone
26 Weather radar
27 Forward electronics pack
28 Nose frames
29 Nose compartment door
30 Door latch
31 Nose baggage compartment
32 Nosewheel
33 Axle fork
34 Electronics packs
35 Access hatch
36 Nosewheel bay
37 Bulkheads
38 De-icer installation
39 Power-pack assembly
40 Hydraulic system power
41 Instrument panel shroud

42 Windscreen
43 Windscreen wiper (port screen only)
44 Dual control columns
45 Instrument display
46 Rudder pedal assembly
47 Control column linkage
48 Control runs
49 Cross-ventilation window panels
50 Pilots' seats
51 Pilots' (optional) forward entry door
52 Fixed starboard window
53 Flight-deck curtain
54 Nine-passenger cabin accommodation
55 Curtained cabin windows
56 Aft window (starboard)
57 Tailfin root fillet
58 Forward spar attachment
59 Starboard tailplane de-icer boot
60 Starboard tailplane
61 Elevator balance
62 Starboard elevator
63 Elevator hinge
64 Tailfin de-icer boot
65 Tailfin structure
66 Rudder post
67 Tail navigation light
68 Rudder balance
69 Rudder structure
70 Rudder trim tab
71 Elevator trim tab
72 Port elevator structure
73 Elevator balance
74 Port tailplane de-icer boot
75 Tailplane structure
76 Tailplane spar/elevator hinge
77 Port tailplane attachment
78 Fuselage aft frames
79 Pneumatics
80 Rear fuselage structure
81 Rear fuselage baggage hold
82 Baggage loading door section

83 Passenger entry door upper section
84 Door jacks
85 Fuselage aft step
86 Integral entry steps (door lower section)
87 De-icer ejector assembly
88 Cabin windows
89 Pressure regulator and valve
90 Port mainwheel door actuating cylinder
91 Wing main spar attachment
92 Pneumatic pressure switch
93 Wing-root fillet
94 Engine ice-protection harness connector
95 Hartzell three-blade fully reversing propeller
96 Exhausts
97 Propeller de-icer boots
98 Spinner
99 Propeller hub
100 Counterweights
101 Port engine air intake
102 Intake de-icer boot
103 Pratt & Whitney PT6A-11 turboprop engine
104 Auxiliary intake
105 Engine bearer
106 Bearer supports
107 Port wing inner tanks
108 Port mainwheel well
109 Wing inboard structure
110 Wing-root fairing
111 Flap inboard section
112 Nacelle frames
113 Locker door
114 Port nacelle baggage locker
115 Port Fowler-type flap
116 Port wing outer tanks
117 Main spar
118 Port mainwheel
119 Mainwheel door
120 Port wing leading-edge de-icer boot

121 Wing structure
122 Aileron control linkage
123 Port aileron
124 Wing ribs
125 Port wingtip
126 Port navigation light

GAS-TURBINE ENGINES

TURBOJET

TURBOFAN

TURBOPROP

TURBOSHAFT

A basic understanding of the four major classes of gas-turbine engine is an important part of aircraft-recognition training. For instance, one of the principal differences between such broadly similar types as the C-141 Starlifter and C-5A Galaxy is the fact that the former is powered by small-diameter turbofans while the latter has high-bypass-ratio turbofans, with their distinctive outsize front fans.

Gas turbines basically consist of an air compressor at the front, combustion chambers for burning the compressed air and a turbine at the back which is driven by the hot gases. In these drawings the hot-air flow is indicated by shading. The turbojet is a reaction engine which obtains its power by thrusting backwards a large weight of air. The turbofan is also a reaction engine but it differs from the turbojet in having part of the compressed air bypassed round the hot section of the engine, finally merging with the hot-air stream at the back. The turboprop has an extra turbine which drives the propeller in front. The turboshaft engine is virtually a turboprop without a propeller, the extra turbine being coupled to a shaft to drive a helicopter rotor.

AIRCRAFT DESIGNATIONS

The letters and numbers used to designate aircraft can be very confusing for the student. Apart from learning shapes, he has to say exactly what they are or his visual knowledge is useless. A name is always the easiest thing to remember, but in a number of cases names are not allocated or the type will appear initially with a designation before being named later. Examples of the latter are the Panavia Tornado, which began life as the MRCA (Multi-Role Combat Aircraft), and the Lockheed L-1011, which was subsequently named TriStar.

Many nations use company design numbers and/or a name, with sub-variants simply given as mark numbers. It is necessary in many cases to know the mark numbers, as the aircraft can look very different. For instance, Britain's Nimrod AEW3 will differ significantly from the Nimrod MR2.

On the civil side there are many types which are un-named and bear only design numbers, such as the Boeing 707, 727 and 747, and McDonnell Douglas DC-8, DC-9 and DC-10. Airliners also tend to acquire suffix letters or numbers to denote different variants: 747SP, 707-320C and BAe One-Eleven 500, for example.

There are four countries for which special designation systems exist: the United States, the Soviet Union, the United Kingdom and Canada.

UNITED STATES MILITARY

The US military system appears at first to be very complicated but is in fact quite logical. It is based on the use of letters and numbers.

All United States service aircraft are assigned designations which describe the machine's basic mission, its place in the sequence of aircraft designed for that function, and its place in the sequence of variants of the type. The designations are broken down as follows:

Status prefix letters

For aircraft fulfilling other than their intended purpose: **G** Permanently grounded; **J** Special test, temporary; **N** Special test, permanent; **X** Experimental; **Y** Prototype; **Z** Obsolete.

Modified mission letters

For aircraft modified from their original roles or with an additional restricted capability: **A** Attack; **C** Transport; **D** Director (control aircraft for unpiloted vehicles); **E** Special electronics installation; **H** Search and rescue; **K** Tanker; **L** Cold weather; **M** Missile carrier; **O** Observation; **Q** Drone (pilotless aircraft); **R** Reconnaissance; **S** Anti-submarine; **T** Trainer; **U** Utility; **V** Staff duties; **W** Weather.

Basic mission letters

Primary function of aircraft: **A** Attack; **B** Bomber; **C** Transport/cargo; **E** Special electronics installation; **F** Fighter; **FB** Fighter-bomber; **H** Helicopter; **K** Tanker; **O** Observation; **P** Patrol; **R** Reconnaissance; **S** Anti-submarine; **SR** Strategic reconnaissance; **T** Trainer; **U** Utility; **V** Vtol (vertical take-off and landing) or Stol (short take-off and landing); **X** Research.

Design numbers

Basic identification of aircraft within its class. For example, the F-4 is the fourth in the modern sequence of fighters.

Series letters

Designation of each new variant of the same type in alphabetical order. Other administrative letters can follow as necessary.

The YUH-4B is a typical example:

Y . Status prefix letter (prototype)
U Modified mission letter (utility)
H Basic mission letter (helicopter)
4 Design number (fourth type of helicopter)
B Series letter (second version of UH-4)

Although not essential for recognition purposes, it is worth recording the US designation system for rockets and guided missiles to avoid confusion with aircraft. Designations are broken down as follows:

Status prefix letters

For rockets and missiles fulfilling other than their intended or ultimate purpose: **J** Special test, temporary; **N** Special test, permanent; **X** Experimental; **Y** Prototype; **Z** Planning.

Launch environment letters

Indicating mode of rocket or guided-missile launch: **A** Air; **B** Multiple; **C** Coffin; **F** Individual; **G** Runway; **H** Silo-stored; **L** Silo-launched; **M** Mobile; **P** Soft pad; **R** Ship; **S** Underwater.

Mission letters

Function or purpose of rockets and guided missiles: **D** Decoy; **E** Special electronics installation; **G** Surface attack; **I** Intercept, aerial; **Q** Drone; **T** Training; **V** Underwater attack; **W** Weather.

Vehicle letters

Designations of class of guided missile, probe or rocket: **M** Guided missile/drone; **N** Probe; **R** Rocket.

A typical example is the YAIM-7F:

Y Status prefix letter (prototype)
A Launch environment letter (air-launched)
I Mission letter (intercept)
M Vehicle letter (guided missile)
7 Design number (seventh missile)
F Series letter (sixth version of AIM-7)

While other nations have basic type names, in the United States such descriptions are known as "popular names" when attached to a general designation. The following is the current list of aircraft and missiles so described:

Popular name	Designation	Service
Academe	TC-4C	Navy
Aero Commander	U-4/U-9	AF
Albatross	HU-16E	Navy/CG
Apache	AH-64	Army
Aquila	XMQM-105	Army
Asroc	RUR-5A	Navy
Atlas	GCM-16	AF
Aztec	U-11A	Navy
Beaver	U-6A	Army/Navy
Bird Dog	O-1	Army
Black Hawk	UH-60A	Army
Bomarc	CQM-10B	AF
Bronco	OV-10	Navy/AF
Buckeye	T-2	Navy
Bulldog	AGM-83A	Navy

Popular name	Designation	Service	Popular name	Designation	Service
Bullpup	AGM-12	Navy	Gulfstream II	VC-11A	CG
Canberra	B-57	AF	Harm	AGM-88A	Navy
Cardinal	MQM-61A	Army	Harpoon	AGM-84A	Navy
Caribou	C-7A	AF	Harrier	AV-8A	Marines
Cayuse	OH-6A	Army	Harrier II	AV-8B	Marines
Cheyenne	AH-56A	Army	Hawk	MIM-23	Army/Navy
Chinook	CH-47	Army	Hawkeye	E-2	Navy
Choctaw	CH-34	AF/Army	Hellfire	YAGM-114A	Army
Cobra	AH-1G	Army	Hercules	C-130	AF/Navy/CG
Cochise	T-42A	Army	Honest John	MGR-1	Army
Condor	AGM-53	Navy	Hornet	F-18/A-18	Navy/Marines
Constellation	C-121A	AF	Hound Dog	AGM-28B	AF
Corsair II	A-7	Navy	Hueycobra	AH-1G	Army
Cougar	F-9	Navy	Huron	U-25	AF
Crusader	F-8	Navy	Huskie	HH-43F	AF
Delta Dagger	F-102A	AF	Intruder	A-6	Navy
Delta Dart	F-106	AF	Iroquois	UH-1	Army
Destroyer	RB-66	AF	JetStar	C-140	AF
Dolphin	HH-65A	CG	Jolly Green Giant	HH-3E	AF
Eagle	F-15A	AF	Kiowa	OH-58	Army/Navy
Extender	KC-10A	AF	Lance	XMGM-52B	Army
Falcon	AIM-4	AF	Liftmaster	C-118	AF/Navy
Fighting Falcon	F-16A	AF	Maverick	AGM-65	AF/Navy
Firebee	BQM-34	AF/Army/Navy	Mentor	T-34	AF/Navy
Flying Classroom	T-29	AF	Mescalero	T-41	Army/AF
Focus I	AGM-87A	Navy	Minuteman	LGM-30	AF
Freedom Fighter	F-5A/B	AF	Mohawk	OV-1	Army
Galaxy	C-5A	AF	Mojave	CH-37	AF/Navy
Genie	AIR-2	AF	Neptune	P-2	Navy
Greyhound	C-2	Navy	Nightingale	C-9A/C	AF
Guardian	HU-25A	CG	Nike Ajax	MIM-3	Army

Popular name	Designation	Service	Popular name	Designation	Service
Nike Hercules	MIM-14A	Army	Sergeant	MGM-29A	Army
Nike Zeus	XLIM-49A	Army	Shillelagh	MGM-51	Army
Orion	P-3	Navy	Shooting Star	T-33A	AF/Navy
Osage	TH-55A	Army	Shrike	AGM-45	Navy/AF
Otter	U-1	Army/Navy	Sidewinder	AIM-9	Navy/AF
Pelican	HH-3F	CG	Sioux	H-13	Army
Pershing	XMGM-31A	Army	Skyhawk	A-4	Navy
Phantom II	F-4	Navy/AF	Skymaster	C-54	AF/Navy
Phoenix	AIM-54A	Navy	Skyraider	A-1	Navy/AF
Polaris	UGM-27	Navy	Skytrain	C-47/C-117	AF/Navy
Provider	C-123	AF	Skytrain II	C-9B	Navy
Prowler	EA-6B	Navy	Skywarrior	A-3	Navy
Quail	ADM-20C	AF	Sparrow	AIM-7	Navy/AF
Raven	H-23	Army	SRAM	AGM-69A	AF
Redeye	XMIM-43	Army/Navy	Standard	RIM-66/67	Navy
Redhead Road Runner	MGM-42	Army	Standard ARM	AGM-7/8	Navy/AF
Regulus	RGM-15A	Navy	Starfighter	F-104	AF
Sabre	QF-86H	Navy	Starlifter	C-141	AF
Sabreliner	T-39	AF/Navy	Stinger	XFIM-92A	Army
Samaritan	C-131	AF	Stratofortress	B-52	AF
Sea Cobra	AH-1J	Navy	Stratofreighter	KC-97L	AF
Sea Guard	HH-52A	CG	Stratojet	EB-47E	Navy
Seahawk	SH-60B	Navy	Stratolifter	C-135	AF
Sea King	H-3	Navy/CG	Stratoliner	C-137	AF
Sea Knight	H-46	Navy	Stratotanker	KC-135	AF
Sea Ranger	TH-57A	Navy	Streaker	MQM-107A	Army
Sea Sparrow	AIM-7	Navy	Subroc	UUM-44A	Navy
Seasprite	H-2	Navy	Super Constellation	C-121	AF
Sea Stallion	CH-53A	Navy	Super Stallion	CH-53E	Army
Seminole	U-8	Army	Super Genie	AIR-2B	AF
Sentry	E-3A	AF	Super Jolly	C/HH-53B/C	AF

Popular name	Designation	Service
Super Sabre	F-100	AF
Talon	T-38	AF
Talos	RIM-8	Navy
Tarhe	CH-54A	Army
Tartar	RIM-24	Navy
Terrier	RIM-2	Navy
Thunderchief	F-105	AF
Thunderbolt II	A-10	AF
Tiger II	F-5E	AF
Tigershark	F-5G	—
Titan	LGM-25C	AF
Tomahawk	YBGM-109	Navy
Thor	PGM-17	AF
Tomcat	F-14A	Navy
Tracer	E-1B	Navy
Tracker	S-2	Navy
Trader	C-1A	Navy
Trident	UGM-96A	Navy
Trojan	T-28	AF/Navy
Typhon	RIM-55A	Navy
US Roland	XMIM-115	Army
Ute	U-21	Army
Vigilante	RA-5C	Navy
Viking	S-3A	Navy
Viper	XFGR-17A	Army
Voodoo	F-101	AF
Warning Star	EC-121K	Navy
Weapon Alpha	RUR-4A	Navy
Zap	XAGR-14A	Navy

SOVIET UNION MILITARY AND CIVIL

In the Soviet Union there are a number of design bureaux from which all Soviet aircraft emanate. Security is such in the Soviet Union that many new designations, particularly military, are suspect and only a certain proportion can be confirmed. For this reason the North Atlantic Treaty Organisation countries have evolved a code-name system for Soviet aircraft and this has been widely adopted elsewhere.

The known current Soviet design bureaux are:

An	Antonov
Be	Beriev
Il	Ilyushin
Ka	Kamov
Mi	Mil
MiG	Mikoyan (originally with Gurevich)
Mya	Myasishchev
Su	Sukhoi
Tu	Tupolev
Yak	Yakovlev

Code names are allotted by Nato on the basis of function:

B	Bomber
C	Cargo/transport
F	Fighter/ground attack
H	Helicopter
M	Trainer, flying boat and maritime reconaissance.

The code names, together with Soviet designations where known for current types, are as follows:

Code name	Designation	Description
Backfire	Tu-26	Variable-geometry bomber
Badger	Tu-16	Twinjet bomber
Beagle	Il-28	Twinjet bomber
Bear	Tu-95	Turboprop bomber
Bison	M-4	Four-jet bomber
Blinder	Tu-22	Rear-jet bomber
Brewer	Yak-28	Strike/attack
Cab	Li-2	Soviet-built DC-3
Camber	Il-86	Wide-bodied jet transport
Camel	Tu-104	Twinjet transport
Careless	Tu-154	Rear trijet transport
Camp	An-8	Twin-turboprop transport
Candid	Il-76	Four-jet transport
Cash	An-28	Turboprop version of Clod
Cat	An-10	Four-turboprop transport
Charger	Tu-144	Supersonic airliner
Clank	An-30	Survey version of Coke
Classic	Il-62	Rear four-jet airliner
Cleat	Tu-114	Turboprop transport version of Bear
Cline	An-32	Overwing turboprop version of Curl
Clobber	Yak-42	Enlarged version of Codling
Clod	An-14	Light piston twin
Coach	Il-12	Piston twin
Coaler	An-72	Stol replacement for Curl
Cock	An-22	Four-turboprop heavy transport
Codling	Yak-40	Trijet light transport
Coke	An-24	Twin-turboprop transport
Colt	An-2	Biplane
Cookpot	Tu-124	Smaller Camel

Code name	Designation	Description
Coot	Il-18	Four-turboprop airliner
Crate	Il-14	Developed Coach
Creek	Yak-12	Light aircraft
Crusty	Tu-134	Rear twinjet version of Cookpot
Cub	An-12	Four-turboprop transport
Cuff	Be-30	Light Stol transport
Curl	An-26	Rear-door variant of Coke
Fagot	MiG-15	First swept-wing Soviet fighter in service
Farmer	MiG-19	Supersonic fighter
Fencer	Su-24	V-g bomber, same class as US F-111
Fiddler	Tu-28P	Swept-wing all-weather fighter
Firebar	Yak-28P	All-weather version of Brewer
Fishbed	MiG-21	Multi-variant delta fighter
Fishpot-B/C	Su-9/11	All-weather delta fighter; Su-11 lengthened
Fitter-A	Su-7B	Swept-wing ground attack fighter
Fitter-C/D	Su-17/20/22	V-g fighter
Flagon	Su-15	Supersonic delta fighter
Flipper	—	Experimental fighter
Flogger	MiG-23/27	V-g fighter/bomber; various versions
Forger	Yak-36	Supersonic Vtol carrier fighter
Foxbat	MiG-25	Supersonic interceptor
Foxhound	—	Development of Foxbat
Freehand	—	Experimental Vtol aircraft
Fresco	MiG-17	Fighter; development of Fagot
Halo	Mi-26	Heavy helicopter
Hare	Mi-1	Light helicopter
Harke	Mi-10	Crane variant of Hook
Haze	Mi-14	Naval variant of Hip

Code name	Designation	Description
Hen	Ka-15	Light helicopter
Helix	Ka-32(?)	Development of Hormone
Hind	Mi-24	Attack helicopter
Hip	Mi-8	Military/civil helicopter
Hog	Ka-18	Development of Hen
Homer	Mi-12	World's largest helicopter
Hoodlum	Ka-26	General-purpose helicopter
Hook	Mi-6	Heavy military/civil helicopter
Hoplite	Mi-2	Small turbine helicopter
Hormone	Ka-25	Naval helicopter
Hound	Mi-4	Military/civil helicopter
Madge	Be-6	Flying boat
Maestro	Yak-27U	Trainer version of Firebar/Brewer
Maiden	Su-11U	Two-seater variant of Fishpot
Mail	Be-12	Turboprop maritime amphibian
Magnum	Yak-30	Aerobatic jet aircraft
Mandrake	—	High-altitude reconnaissance aircraft
Mangrove	Yak-27	Reconnaissance
Mantis	Yak-32	Jet trainer
Mascot	Il-28U	Trainer variant of Beagle
Max	Yak-18	Club trainer and sporting aircraft
May	Il-38	Maritime reconnaissance version of Coot
Midget	MiG-15UTI	Trainer variant of Fagot
Mongol	MiG-21U	MiG-21 trainer
Moose	Yak-18	Trainer
Moss	Tu-126	Airborne early warning aircraft
Moujik	Su-7U	Trainer variant of Fitter-A
Mule	Po-2	Utility biplane

CANADA MILITARY

The Canadian system of military designations is similar to that of the United States. All designations are prefixed with the letter "C", denoting Canadian version. After this comes one of six role letters: **C** Transport; **F** Fighter; **H** Helicopter; **P** Maritime patrol; **SR** Search and rescue; **T** Trainer.

The actual type number follows after a hyphen. The following is a list of types in service with the Canadian Forces.

Canadian designation	Canadian Forces name
CF-5	CF-5
CF-18	Hornet
CF-100	CF-100
CF-101	Voodoo
CF-104	Starfighter
CP-107	Argus
CC-108	Caribou
CC-109	Cosmopolitan (Convair 640)
CH-112	Nomad (Hiller)
CH-113	Labrador (Vertol 107)
CH-113A	Voyageur (Vertol 107)
CT-114	Tutor
CC-115	Buffalo
CC-117	Falcon
CH-118	Iroquois
CP-121	Tracker
CRS-123	Otter
CH-124	Sea King
CT-129	Dakota
CC-130	Hercules
CC-132	DHC-7 (Dash 7)

Canadian designation	Canadian Forces name
CT-133	Silver Star (T-33)
CT-134	Musketeer
CH-135	Twin-Huey (Iroquois)
CH-136	Kiowa (JetRanger)
CC-137	Boeing 707
CC-138	Twin Otter
CP-140	Aurora (Orion)
CH-147	Chinook

UNITED KINGDOM MILITARY

The British service system of aircraft designations is the reverse of that employed in the United States in that the type name is the primary reference and role letters and mark number follow.

Role letters used by the three services are:

AEW	Airborne Early Warning
AH	Army Helicopter
AL	Army Liaison
AS	Anti-submarine
B	Bomber
B(I)	Bomber/Interdictor
B(K)	Bomber (Tanker)
B(PR)	Bomber (Photo-reconnaissance)
C	Transport
CC	Transport and Communications
D	Drone or unmanned aircraft
E	Electronic
F	Fighter
FGA	Fighter Ground Attack
FG	Fighter Ground Attack
FGR	Fighter Ground Attack Reconnaissance
FR	Fighter Reconnaissance
FRS	Fighter Reconnaissance Strike
GR	Ground Attack Reconnaissance
HAR	Helicopter, Air Rescue
HAS	Helicopter, Anti-submarine
HC	Helicopter, Cargo
HT	Helicopter, Training

HU	Helicopter, Utility
K	Tanker
MR	Maritime Reconnaissance
R	Reconnaissance
O	Observation
PR	Photographic Reconnaissance
R	Reconnaissance
S	Strike
T	Trainer
TT	Target Towing
W	Weather

Typical examples are Scout AH1 (Army Helicopter Mk 1), Harrier GR3 (Ground Attack Reconnaissance Mk 3) and Nimrod AEW3 (Airborne Early Warning Mk 3).

Aircraft and helicopter designations current in use are as follows:

Designation	Operator	Notes
Alouette		
AH2	Army	French Alouette II
Andover		
C1	RAF	Freighter
CC2	RAF	Passenger
E3	MoD (PE)	Flight checking
BAe 125		
CC1	RAF/RN	BAe 125-400
CC2	RAF	BAe 125-600
Basset		
CC1	MoD (PE)	Only three in use

Designation	Operator	Notes
Beaver		
AL1	Army	DHC-2 built in Canada
Buccaneer		
S2A	RAF	No Martel missiles
S2B	RAF	Martel-carrier
S2C	RAF	} Ex-RN aircraft
S2D	RAF	
S50	SAAF	S2 export to South Africa
Bulldog		
T1	RAF	Primary trainer
Canberra		
B2	RAF & RN	Some still in use
PR3	MoD	One only
T4	RAF & RN	B2 trainer
B6	RAF	One only
PR7	RAF	Improved PR3
B(I)8	MoD	One only
PR9	RAF	In service
D10	MoD	Unmanned target
T11	Sweden	AI trainer
D14	MoD	Version of D10
B15	RAF	B6 sold abroad
E15	RAF	Flight checking
B16	MoD	Modified B15
T17	RAF	Special B2
TT18	RAF/RN	Target-tug conversion
T19	RAF	T11 conversion
B20	RAAF	Australian-built B2
T21	RAAF	B20 trainer version

Designation	Operator	Notes
T22	RN	With Buccaneer nose radar
B52	Ethiopia	As B2
T54	India	As T4
B(I)56	Peru	As B6
PR57	India	As PR7
B(I)58	India	As B(I)8
B62	Argentina	As B2
T64	Argentina	As T4
B66	India	As B15/B16
PR67	India	PR7 conversion
T67	India	PR67 conversion
B(I)68	India	B(I)8 conversion
B72	Peru	B2 conversion
T74	Peru	T4 conversion
B(I)78	Peru	B(I)8 conversion
B82	Venezuela	B2 conversion
B(I)82	Venezuela	B2 conversion
PR83	Venezuela	PR3 conversion
T84	Venezuela	T4 conversion
B(I)88	Venezuela	B(I)8 conversion
Chinook		
HC1	RAF	US CH-47
Chipmunk		
Mks 1-9	Canada	
T10	RAF/Army	British-built trainer
Mks 21-23	Civil	
Commando		
Mk 1	Egypt	} Troop transport adapted
Mk 2	Saudia Arabia	from Sea King

Designation	Operator	Notes
Dakota		
C3	MoD	One only
Devon		
C2	RAF	Service Dove
Dominie		
T1	RAF	BAe 125 military trainer
Gazelle		
AH1	Army & RM	Gazelle B
HT2	RN	Gazelle C
HT3	RAF	Gazelle D
Gnat		
T1	MoD (PE)	Trainer
Harrier		
GR3	RAF	Pegasus 103 engine
T4	RAF	Two-seater, Pegasus 103
GR5	RAF	AV-8B Harrier II
Mk 50	US Marines	AV-8A
Mk 52	British Aerospace	T-4, company-owned
Mk 54	US Marines	T4
Mk 55	Spanish Navy	Known as Matador/AV-8S
Harvard		
T2B	MoD	Three only
Hawk		
T1	RAF	Trainer
T2	RAF	Trainer
Mk 51	Finland	Trainer
Mk 52	BAe	Demonstrator

Designation	Operator	Notes
Hercules		
C1	RAF	C-130K transport
W2	RAF	Meteorological conversion
C3	RAF	Stretched fuselage
Heron		
C4	RN	Light transport
Hunter		
F6	RAF	Few
F6A	RAF	F6 to FGA9 standard
T7	RAF	Two-seat trainer
T7A	MoD (PE)	T7 modified
T8	RN	T7 for Navy
T8M	RN	Sea Harrier radar trainer
FGA9	RAF	F6 with increased weapon load
GA11	RN	Naval
Mk 12	MoD (PE)	Fly-by-wire experimental
F50	RSAF	Sweden, F4
F51	RDAF	Export to Denmark
F52	Peru	Export
T53	RDAF	T7, Denmark
FGA56	India	F6 for ground attack
FGA57	Kuwait	FGA9
F58	Switzerland	F6
FGA59	Iraq	FGA9
T62	Peru	One only, F4
T66	India	T7 with modified armament
T66B	Jordan	
T66C	Lebanon	
T67	Kuwait	Two-seat version of FGA57

Designation	Operator	Notes
T69	Iraq	Two-seat version of FGA59
T70	Lebanon	T7
FGA71	Chile	FGA9
T72	Chile	T7
FGA73	Jordan	FGA9
FGA74	Singapore	FGA9
FR74A	Singapore	PR version of FGA9
T75	Singapore	T7
FGA76	Abu Dhabi	FGA9
FR76A	Abu Dhabi	PR version of FGA9
T77	Abu Dhabi	T7
FGA78	Qatar	FGA9
T79	Qatar	T7
Jaguar		
GR1	RAF	Strike
T2	RAF	Two-seat trainer
Jet Provost		
T3	RAF	Trainer
T3A	RAF	Modified avionics
T5	RAF	Pressurised
T5A	RAF	Modified avionics
T51–55	Various	Export versions
Jetstream		
T1	RAF	Twin trainer
T2	RAF/RN	Modified
Lightning		
F3	RAF	Interceptor
T5	RAF	Two-seat trainer
F6	RAF	Final production version

Designation	Operator	Notes
F52	⎫	
F53	⎬ Saudia Arabia	Interim issue of F2s, F3 export and T5 export
F55	⎭	
Lynx		
AH1	Army & RM	WG13
HAS2	RN	ASW equipment
HAS3	RN	Update
HAS4	French Navy	
Mk 80	Denmark	
Mk 81	Netherlands	
Mk 83	Saudi Arabia	
Mk 84	Qatar	
Mk 85	United Arab Emirates	
Mk 86	Norway	
Mk 87	Argentina	
Mk 88	West Germany	
Meteor		
T7	RAF/MoD	Few
NF11	MoD (PE)	One only
D16	MoD (PE)	Three only
Nimrod		
MR1	RAF	Maritime reconnaissance
R1	RAF	Three for special EW work
MR2	RAF	Modified MR1
AEW3	RAF	Airborne early warning
Pembroke		
C1	RAF	Transport

Designation	Operator	Notes
C(PR)1	RAF	C1 photographic
C51–55	Various nations	Export C1
Phantom		
FG1	RAF	McDonnell Douglas F-4K
FGR2	RAF	McDonnell Douglas F-4M
Puma		
HC1	RAF	As French SA.330
Scout		
AH1	Army	As Wasp
Sea Devon		
C20	RN	Naval Devon
Sea Harrier		
FRS1	RN	Naval Harrier, nose radar
Sea Heron		
C2	RN	Transport
Sea King		
HAS1	RN	Similar to Sikorsky SH-3D
HAS2	RN	Improved HAS1
HAR3	RAF	Rescue
Mk 41	West Germany	
Mk 42	India	
Mk 43	Norway	
Mk 45	Pakistan Navy	
Mk 48	Belgium	
Mk 50	Australia	
Sea Prince		
C1	RN	Forerunner of Pembroke

Designation	Operator	Notes	Designation	Operator	Notes
T1	RN	Flying classroom	T55	Several	Export trainer
C2	RN	C1 with modified tailplane	VC10		
Sea Vixen			C1	RAF	Long-range transport
FAW2	MoD (PE)	Few	K2	RAF	Converted Standard VC10
D3	MoD (PE)	Unmanned target version	K3	RAF	Converted Super VC10
Shackleton			Victor		
AEW2	RAF	Early-warning conversion of MR2	K2	RAF	Tanker
MR2	RAF	Two only	Wasp		
MR3	SAAF	Maritime reconnaissance	HAS1	RN	Naval Scout AH1
Sioux			Wessex		
AH1	Army & RM	Bell 47G-3B-1 helicopter	HAS1	RN	UK-built S-58
Strikemaster			HC2	RAF	Single exhaust stub
Mk 80	Saudi Arabia		HAS3	RN	Re-engined HAS1, has dorsal hump
Mk 81	South Yemen				
Mk 82	Muscat & Oman		HCC4	RAF	Queen's Flight
Mk 83	Kuwait	Similar to armoured Jet Provost 5	HU5	RN & RM	Commando-carrier version
			Mk 31	RAN	HAS1 for Australia
Mk 84	Singapore		Mk 52	Iraq	
Mk 87	Kenya		Mk 53	Ghana	
Mk 88	New Zealand		Mk 54	Brunei	
Mk 89	Ecuador		Mk 60	Civil	Passenger
Tornado			Whirlwind		
GR1	RAF	Interdiction/strike version	HAR10	RAF	Whirlwind Series 3, with Gnome engines
F2	RAF	Air-defence variant			
Vampire					
T33	RAAF	Trainer Vampire, Australia			
T34	RAN	Navalised T11, Australia			
T35	RAAF	T33 with increased range, Australia			

AIRCRAFT REGISTRATIONS

Registration markings are a useful aid to recognition if they can be seen. This is the list of national civil prefixes:

AP	Pakistan	(F)	Vanuatu	OH	Finland
A2	Botswana	G	United Kingdom	OK	Czechoslovakia
A6	United Arab Emirates	HA	Hungary	OO	Belgium
A7	Qatar	HB	Liechtenstein	OY	Denmark
A40	Oman	HB	Switzerland	P	Korea, Democratic
B	China	HC	Ecuador		People's Republic of
C	Canada	HH	Haiti	PH	Netherlands, Kingdom of the
CC	Chile	HI	Dominican Republic	PJ	Netherlands Antilles
CCCP	Union of Soviet	HK	Colombia	PK	Indonesia
	Socialist Republics	HL	Korea, Republic of	PP, PT	Brazil
CN	Morocco	(HMAY),		PZ	Surinam
CP	Bolivia	(6HMAY)	Mongolia	P2	Papua New Guinea
(CR-C)	Cape Verde Republic	HP	Panama	RDPL	Lao, People's
CR, CS	Portugal	HR	Honduras		Democratic Republic of
CU	Cuba	HS	Thailand	RP	Philippines
CX	Uruguay	HZ	Saudi Arabia	SE	Sweden
C2	Nauru	H4	Solomon Islands	SP	Poland
C5	The Gambia	(H4)	Vanuatu	ST	Sudan
C6	Bahamas	I	Italy	SU	Egypt
C9	Mozambique	JA	Japan	SX	Greece
D	Germany, Federal	JY	Jordan	S2	Bangladesh
	Republic of	J2	Djibouti	S7	Seychelles
DM	Germany, Democratic	J5	Guine-Bissau	S9	Sao Tome and Principe
	Republic of	J6	St Lucia	TC	Turkey
DO	Fiji	LN	Norway	TF	Iceland
D2	Angola	LO, LV	Argentina	TG	Guatemala
D6	Comoro, Republic of	LX	Luxembourg	TI	Costa Rica
EC	Spain	LZ	Bulgaria	TJ	Cameroun
EI, EJ	Ireland, Republic of	(MONGOL)	Mongolia	TL	Central African Republic
EL	Liberia	N	United States of	TN	Congo, People's Republic of the
EP	Iran		America and outlying	TR	Gabon
ET	Ethiopia		territories	TS	Tunisia
F	France, French	OB	Peru	TT	Chad
	overseas departments	OD	Lebanon	TU	Ivory Coast
	and territories	OE	Austria	TY	Benin

TZ	Mali	XU	Democratic Kampuchea	5N	Nigeria
T3	Kiribati		(Cambodia)	5R	Malagasy Republic
VH	Australia	XV	Vietnam		(Madagascar)
(VN)	Vietnam	XY, XZ	Burma	5T	Mauritania
VP, VQ, VR	United Kingdom	YA	Afghanistan	5U	Niger
	colonies and	YI	Iraq	5V	Togo
	protectorates	YK	Syria	5W	Western Samoa
VP-F	Falkland Islands	YN	Nicaragua	5X	Uganda
(VP-H)	Belize	YR	Romania	5Y	Kenya
VP-LAA to		YS	El Salvador	6O	Somalia
VP-LJZ	Antigua/Barbuda	YU	Yugoslavia	6V, 6W	Senegal
VP-LKA to		YV	Venezuela	6Y	Jamaica
VP-LLZ	St Kitts/Nevis/Anguilla	ZA	Albania	7O	Yemen, Democratic
VP-LMA to		ZK, ZL, ZM	New Zealand		People's Republic of the
VP-LUZ	Montserrat	ZP	Paraguay	7P	Lesotho
VP-LVA to		ZS, ZT, ZU	South Africa	7Q-Y	Malawi
VP-LZZ	Virgin Islands	(ZS)	Transkei	7T	Algeria
VP-V	St Vincent and	(ZS)	Namibia (South-West	8P	Barbados
	Grenadines		Africa)	8Q	Maldives
(VP-W, VP-Y)	Zimbabwe	(ZS)	Boputhatswana	8R	Guyana
VQ-G	Grenada	3A	Monaco	9G	Ghana
VQ-H	St Helena	3B	Mauritius	9H	Malta
VQ-L	St Lucia	3C	Equatorial Guinea	9J	Zambia
VQ-T	Turks and Caicos	3D	Swaziland	9K	Kuwait
	Islands	3X	Guinea, Republic of	9L	Sierra Leone
VR-B	Bermuda	4R	Sri Lanka	9M	Malaysia
VR-C	Cayman Islands	4W	Yemen, Arab Republic	9N	Nepal
VR-G	Gibraltar		of the	9O	Zaire
VR-H	Hong Kong	4X	Israel	9U	Burundi
VR-U	Brunei	5A	Libya	9V	Singapore
VT	India	5B	Cyprus	9XR	Rwanda
XA, XB, XC	Mexico	5H	Tanzania, United	9Y	Trinidad and Tobago
XT	Upper Volta		Republic of	—	Tonga Friendly Islands

Notes:
Registration marks shown in brackets denote either those countries which have become independent during the last few years but have not yet notified ICAO of a new nationality mark, or the use of unofficial marks. Into the latter category come (MONGOL), (HMAY), (6HMAY) and (VN). No marks have been allocated or are being used by Tonga.

41

This important class of aircraft is wholly military, embracing fighters, fighter-bombers, strike/attack types and trainers. Single and twin-engined aircraft have not been separated as, at a distance, it is difficult to differentiate on this basis and mistakes can be made unless overall shapes are known.

The first point to be looked for is the location of the intake or intakes: in the nose, on the sides of the fuselage or in the wing roots. Nose intakes, as on the F-100 and Fitter, generally supply air to one engine. The exception is the Lightning, on which the intake feeds two engines, one above the other, in a deep fuselage. Fuselage or flank intakes are the most common, with the actual shape either rounded (Harrier) or rectangular (Phantom). Wing-root intakes usually take the form of a triangular slot (Hunter).

Wing shapes vary greatly, from long-chord and squared-off, as on the Phantom, to slimmer and curve-tipped (the Hunter). The angle of sweep is important, as in some cases it can make for confusion with variable-geometry aircraft.

Dassault-Breguet/Dornier Alpha Jet

General Dynamics F-16 Fighting Falcon

Tailplane positions vary and alter outlines significantly. The Buccaneer has its tailplane on top of the fin, while the Phantom has a low-set tailplane with marked anhedral, a major recognition point.

Trainer variants present a different aspect side-on, while nose shapes often change with different types of avionic equipment. Two particular examples are the Jaguar and the Phantom.

When there is obvious confusion between aircraft, attention must go to details such as slight changes in wing shape, nose differences, position and span of tailplane, cockpit shape and armament variations.

Long-lived military types invariably undergo a continuous process of modification and evolution of new marks. For instance, both Harrier and Jaguar have undergone nose

Sepecat Jaguar

roughly the same wing shape in planform, and shoulder wing with anhedral plus dihedral tailplane in the head-on view.

Two unusual-looking aircraft are the Voodoo and the Thunderchief. The Voodoo has short-span swept wings with big root fairings, engine exhausts under the rear fuselage and a high-set tailplane with dihedral. In planform the Thunderchief has a very long nose like that of the Voodoo, but the triangular-shaped intakes are quite distinctive.

Stubby swept wings and twin fins are the main similarities between the Soviet Foxbat and the American F-15 Eagle. Main differences lie in wingtip and wing trailing-edge shape, intakes in the head-on view, and fin shape from the side.

Dassault Mirage F.1

changes resulting from the addition of laser equipment. These types, plus the Buccaneer, have also sprouted radar warning fairings on the tail.

The Sea Harrier has a raised cockpit, which is also a feature of the AV-8B Harrier II. The latter has two additional wing pylons which, when carrying stores, alter the shape when the aircraft is viewed from beneath.

At a distance the Soviet Forger shipborne aircraft seems conventional apart from a short-span wing. It is only on close examination that the aft rotating nozzles, for vertical thrust, are apparent.

The Crusader and the Corsair II have a remarkable similarity of layout, with nose intake and radome above,

Fuji T1 Hatsutaka *Confusion:* Sabre

Power: 1 × Orpheus or 1 × J3 turbojet *Span:* 34ft 5in (10.5m) *Length:* 39ft 9in (12.12m)

The first aircraft to be designed and built in Japan after the Second World War, the T1 Hatsutaka two-seat military trainer entered service with the Japan Air Self-Defence Force at the end of the 1950s. Bearing a superficial resemblance to the American Sabre, the T1 was initially powered by a British Orpheus engine (T1A), while later versions had the Japanese-built J3 turbojet (T1B and T1C). One machine gun is carried in the nose, and air-to-air missiles, rockets or bombs under the wings. External fuel totals 200 Imp gal (910lit) in two underwing tanks. Maximum speed of the T1A at 20,000ft (6,100m) is 575 mph (925km/hr). Some 40 T1As and 22 T1Bs were built for the Japan Air Self-Defence Force. *Country of origin:* Japan. *Picture:* T1A.

Power: 1 × J47 turbojet   *Span:* 39ft 1in (11.91m)   *Length* (F-86F): 37ft 6in (11.43m)

The best interceptor of its day, the F-86 outfought the MiG-15s used by the Communists in the Korean War. The type has seen service with 25 nations and 9,502 were built. Main versions are the F-86A, F-86D, F-86E, F-86F, F-86K and TF-86F. Of these, three differ in general outline, the F-86D/K having a large radome in the nose above the intake and the TF-86F having a longer fuselage with two seats in tandem. The US Navy adapted the Sabre for carrier use as the FJ-4. Sabres remain in service with many air forces, carrying a variety of air-to-air and ground-attack weapons. *Country of origin:* USA. *Main silhouette:* F-86F; *upper side view:* F-86D. *Picture:* F-86F.

North American F-100 Super Sabre

Confusion: Super Mystère B.2, Sabre

Power: 1 × J57 reheated turbojet   *Span:* 38ft 9in (11.81m)   *Length:* 54ft 3in (16.54m)

First fighter with genuine supersonic level speed to enter service, the F-100 Super Sabre is still used by Turkey and Taiwan. Versions include the F-100A, C, D and F. A reconnaissance variant is designated RF-100, and the TF-100 is a two-seat trainer. An outstanding design, the Super Sabre can operate at high and low altitudes. Armament of the F-100F comprises four 20mm cannon and 6,000lb (2,720kg) of external weapons on eight wing pylons. *Country of origin:* USA. *Main silhouette:* F-100D; *lower side view:* F-100F. *Picture:* F-100F.

Power: 1 × Orpheus turbojet   *Span:* 28ft 1in (8.56m)   *Length:* 33ft 9in (10.3m)

Originally a Fiat design, the G.91 won a Nato light fighter-bomber design contest in the 1950s and was adopted by the Italian and Western German air forces. Italian Air Force G.91s and G.91Rs have two underwing pylons, while the German G.91R3s and R4s have four. Internal armament is either four machine guns or two 30mm cannon. Maximum speed is 675 mph (1,086km/hr). The two-seat advanced trainer version is the G.91T (*upper side-view silhouette*). The G.91 is also used by Portugal and Angola. *Country of origin:* Italy. *Picture:* G.91R.

Fiat G.91Y

Confusion: G.91, Hunter, Etendard

Power: 2 × J85 reheated turbojets   *Span:* 29ft 6½in (9.01m)   *Length:* 38ft 3½in (11.67m)

A fighter-bomber and reconnaissance aircraft, the G.91Y was a direct development of the G.91, with twin J85 turbojets replacing the single Orpheus. After a first flight in 1966, a total of 55 G.91Ys were built for the Italian Air Force. Armament comprises two fuselage-mounted 30mm cannon and four underwing pylons for rockets, bombs or guided missiles. Maximum speed at sea level is 690 mph (1,110km/hr). Cameras are mounted in the nose. *Country of origin:* Italy.

Power: 1 × Atar turbojet   *Span:* 34ft 6in (10.50m)   *Length:* 46ft 1in (14.04m)

The Super Mystère B.2 was the first European production aircraft capable of supersonic speed in straight-and-level flight. Some 180 of these fighter-bombers were built in the late 1950s. France has phased the type out but it remains in service in the Honduras. Armament comprises two 30mm cannon, rocket pods and bombs. Performance figures include a maximum level speed at 36,000ft (11,000m) of 743 mph (1,195km/hr); rate of climb at 19,840lb (9,000kg) of 17,500ft/min (5,340m/min); service ceiling of 55,775ft (17,000m); and range of 600 miles (965km). The Super Mystère B.2s operated by the Honduras were acquired from Israel and have been fitted with J52 engines in place of the original Atar 101s. *Country of origin:* France.

Mikoyan-Gurevich MiG-15 Fagot

Confusion: Sabre, Fresco, Farmer

Power: 1 × RD-45 turbojet   *Span:* 33ft (10.08m)   *Length:* 32ft 11in (10.04m)

The Soviet MiG-15 swept-wing fighter, Nato code-named Fagot, caused a world sensation when it first appeared over the Korean War battlefields in 1950. Very large numbers of Fagots were built for use by many air forces. Some are still employed for ground attack. Built-in armament consists of one 37mm and two 23mm cannon, while bombs, rockets and other stores can be carried under the wings. The MiG-15UTI two-seat advanced trainer, code-named Midget, was supplied throughout the Warsaw Pact and to 17 other countries. Like the Fagot, the Midget is powered by a pirated development of the Rolls-Royce Nene. The trainer carries a cannon or a machine gun in the fuselage. The Midget is shown in the upper side view. *Country of origin:* USSR. *Picture and main silhouette:* MiG-15.

Mikoyan-Gurevich MiG-17 Fresco

Power: 1 × VK-1F reheated turbojet   *Span:* 31ft 7in (9.63m)   *Length:* 36ft 5in (11.09m)

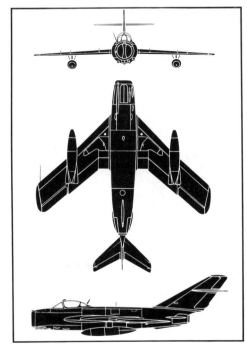

Though outwardly the MiG-17 Fresco bears a close similarity to the MiG-15 Fagot, the wing and tailplane were in fact redesigned and the rear fuselage was lengthened. Later versions (Fresco-C and D) incorporated an afterburner. Frescos are widely used in the fighter-bomber role by air forces round the world. Armament consists of underwing bombs and rocket pods plus three 23mm fuselage cannon on some variants and Alkali radar-homing missiles on others. Fresco-D and E carry centrebody nose radars in addition to radar gunsights in the upper engine-intake lip. *Country of origin:* USSR. *Picture and silhouette:* Fresco-C.

Mikoyan MiG-19 Farmer

Confusion: **Fresco, Super Sabre**

Power: **2 × Mikulin or 2 × Tumansky reheated turbojets**   *Span:* **29ft 6in (9m)**   *Length:* **42ft 11in (13.09m)**

The Soviet Union's first production supersonic fighter, the MiG-19 Farmer has been widely used and remains in service in China, Cuba, Egypt, Albania, Vietnam and Pakistan. Standard variants are Farmer-B (MiG-19PF and MiG-19PM with air-to-air missiles) and Farmer-C (MiG-19SF) with Tumansky engines. Rocket projectiles and bombs can be fitted on underwing pylons for ground attack. Farmer has been built in China as the J-6 and some 2,000 are believed to be in service there. Normal gun armament is three 30mm cannon. *Country of origin:* USSR. *Silhouette:* **Farmer-C.** *Picture:* **Farmer-B.**

Power: 1 × Lyulka reheated turbojet   *Span:* **29ft 3in (8.9m)**   *Length:* **57ft (17.37m)**

First flown in the mid-1950s, the Fitter-A fighter/ground attack aircraft is in service throughout the Warsaw Pact countries and in India and Egypt. Capable of Mach 1.6, Fitter carries two 30mm cannon, rockets and bombs. External loads are carried under both fuselage and wings. Some Fitters are equipped with rocket-assisted take-off gear to improve short-field performance. The two-seat trainer version, with pilot and pupil in tandem under an extended cockpit, is the Su-7U, code-named Moujik (upper side view). Performance figures include a maximum level speed at 36,000ft (11,000m) of 1,055 mph (1,700km/hr); service ceiling of 49,700ft (15,150m); and combat radius of 200–300 miles (320–480km). *Country of origin:* USSR.

BAC Lightning *Confusion:* Fitter

Power: 2 × Avon reheated turbojets   *Span:* 34ft 10in (10.61m)   *Length:* 55ft 3in (16.84m)

The Lightning was the RAF's first Mach 2 interceptor, entering service in its original (F1) form in 1960. In the mid-1960s the more powerful F3 entered service. A broader, square-tipped vertical tail distinguishes the F3 from earlier models. This was closely followed by the F6, the mainstay of the RAF interceptor force until the Phantom entered service. Two squadrons of Lightnings remain with the RAF and the type is in service in Saudi Arabia. *Country of origin:* UK. *Main silhouette:* F6; *upper side view:* T5. *Picture:* Lightning F6.

Finally phased out of production in 1979, the Phantom is probably the most numerous aircraft in Western air force inventories (over 5,000 built). Designed as an attack fighter for the US Navy, it was soon adopted by the USAF, serving in the interceptor, close support, reconnaissance (RF-4) and ECM roles. A licence-built version (F-4EJ) is in service in Japan, and Spey-engined models in the UK (F-4K/M), while certain early models in the US have been converted into pilotless target aircraft (QF-4B). A wide variety of stores can be carried, including Gatling guns, Sparrow and Sidewinder air-to-air missiles, bombs, rockets, and ECM and recce pods. There are a variety of nose shapes, depending on equipment carried. *Country of origin:* USA. *Silhouette and picture:* F-4F.

Sepecat Jaguar

Confusion: T-2/F-1, Phantom

Power: 2 × Adour reheated turbofans   *Span:* 27ft 10in (8.49m)   *Length:* 50ft 11in (15.52m)

The result of a collaborative agreement signed by the British and French governments in 1965, the Jaguar strike fighter/trainer is in large-scale service with the RAF and the Armée de l'Air. Twenty-two have been sold to Oman, 12 to Ecuador and 40 to India. Single and two-seat versions have been built. Export versions have uprated engines and provision for the carriage of overwing air-to-air missiles in addition to twin 30mm cannon and underwing bombs, rockets and drop tanks. RAF designations for Jaguar are GR1 and T2. *Country of origin:* UK/France. *Silhouette and picture:* GR1.

Power: 2 × **Adour reheated turbofans**   *Span:* **25ft 10in (7.8m)**   *Length:* **58ft 7in (17.85m)**

Bearing a marked resemblance to the Sepecat Jaguar, which preceded it by some two years, the T-2 was selected for development as a two-seat supersonic trainer for the Japan Air Self-Defence Force in 1967. Eighty-one T-2 advanced and T-2A combat trainers have been ordered, plus 70 of a single-seat, close-support fighter variant designated F-1. F-1 carries bombs, rockets, a 20mm cannon and air-to-air missiles and has a nose radome. Powered by licence-built Rolls-Royce Adour engines similar in output to those fitted in the basic Jaguar, the T-2 is marginally faster and lighter than its European counterpart. *Country of origin:* **Japan.** *Silhouette:* F-1. *Picture:* T-2.

Dassault-Breguet Mirage F.1 *Confusion:* Crusader, Corsair II

Power: 1 × Atar reheated turbojet   *Span:* 27ft 7in (8.4m)   *Length:* 49ft 2in (15m)

The swept-wing Mach 2 F.1 is a single-seat multi-purpose fighter/attack aircraft, over 620 examples of which have been ordered. The F.1A and F.1E perform the ground attack role, the F.1B and F.1D are two-seat trainers, the F.1C is an interceptor and the F.1R is for reconnaissance. The F.1C-200 of the Armée de l'Air is equipped for air-to-air refuelling. A variety of air-to-air and air-to-ground missiles and other weapon loads can be carried in addition to two 30mm cannon. First flown in December 1966, the F.1 is being built in France. South Africa holds production rights. *Country of origin:* France. *Silhouette and picture:* F.1C.

Power: 1 × turbojet + 2 × liftjets   *Span:* 24ft 7in (7.50m)   *Length:* 52ft 6in (16m)

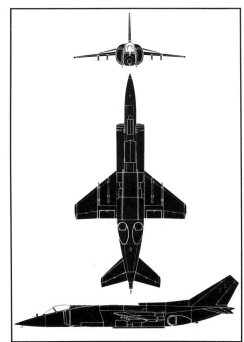

First seen aboard the aircraft carrier *Kiev* in 1976, the naval Yak-36 Forger is the first Soviet Vtol aircraft to enter service. It is intended for use in the interceptor/attack/reconnaissance roles and in its present form is just supersonic in straight-and-level flight. The powerplant layout is unusual, consisting of a single main turbojet exhausting through vectoring nozzles at the rear plus two lift engines mounted just behind the cockpit. The outer wing sections fold upwards for movement on the deck lift and hangar stowage. Armament, carried on inner wing pylons, includes guns, bombs, rockets and air-to-air missiles. A two-seat tandem trainer version is known as Forger-B. *Country of origin:* USSR. *Silhouette and picture:* Forger-A.

BAe Harrier *Confusion:* Hunter, Forger, Etendard

Power: 1 × **Pegasus vectored-thrust turbofan**   *Span:* **25ft 3in (7.70m)**   *Length* **(GR3): 45ft 8in (13.91m)**

Of all the fixed-wing, vertical take-off aircraft to be conceived in the West in the late 1950s/early 1960s, the Harrier, derived from the P.1127, which first flew in 1960, is the only one to gain operational status. It is in large-scale service as a strike reconnaissance fighter with the RAF (GR3) and the US Marine Corps (AV-8A), serving as a close support and tactical reconnaissance aircraft. The Spanish navy also operates a small number (designated Matador). Both the RAF and USMC have adopted a two-seat trainer version of the aircraft with elongated fuselage (RAF T2/USMC TAV-8A). Harrier carries two 30mm Aden guns, bombs, rockets and Sidewinder air-to-air missiles. RAF Harriers have been modified with a longer nose housing a laser rangefinder. *Country of origin:* **UK**. *Main silhouette and picture:* GR3; *upper side view:* T2.

Power: **1 × Pegasus vectored-thrust turbofan**   *Span:* **25ft 3in (7.7m)**   *Length:* **47ft 7in (14.5m)**

Derived from the basic Harrier close-support aircraft, the Sea Harrier has been modified for operations in a maritime environment, 34 having been ordered by the Royal Navy for operation from shipborne platforms, including *Invincible*-class anti-submarine carriers. Principal visible differences between Sea Harrier and its land-based counterpart are a redesigned, raised cockpit and the replacement of the laser nose with a pointed radome housing the Blue Fox radar for airborne intercept and ship detection roles. Armament includes 30mm Aden guns, bombs, rockets and AIM-9L air-to-air missiles. Later the turbojet-powered Sea Eagle air-to-surface missile will be fitted. *Country of origin:* **UK.** *Silhouette and picture:* **Sea Harrier FRS1.**

McDonnell Douglas AV-8B/BAe Harrier GR5

Confusion: Harrier GR3, Sea Harrier, Forger

Power: 1 × Pegasus vectored-thrust turbofan   *Span:* 30ft 4in (9.24m)   *Length:* 46ft 4in (14.12m)

With raised cockpit, composite-material wing with leading-edge root extensions, fuselage underside strakes and six wing weapons/fuel pylons, the AV-8B Harrier II is a second-generation V/Stol aircraft based on the Harrier formula. Jointly produced by McDonnell Douglas and BAe, the AV-8B is expected to run to 354 examples for the US Marines plus 60 GR5s for the RAF. Production lines are being set up in both the USA and the UK. Compared with the existing AV-8A/Harrier GR3, the AV-8B/GR5 will have radius of action raised to 692 miles (1,114km) and, for shorter sorties, a maximum external store load of 9,200lb (4,173kg). Weapons include two 30mm cannon or a 25mm Gatling gun, bombs, cluster bombs and Maverick and Sidewinder missiles. In-service dates are 1985 for the US Marines and 1986 for the RAF. *Country of origin:* USA/UK. *Silhouette and picture:* AV-8B.

Power: 2 × Larzac turbofans   *Span:* 29ft 11in (9.11m)   *Length:* 40ft 3in (12.29m)

A joint venture by France and Germany, the Alpha Jet is a two-seater to be used as an advanced trainer by the French (Alpha Jet E) and as a light attack aircraft (Alpha Jet A) by the West Germans. First flown in 1973, the Alpha Jet has been ordered by France, West Germany and eight other countries, the order book totalling 476 examples. Alpha Jet can carry a 30mm or 27mm gun pod under the fuselage, while the light attack version has four wing pylons suitable for the carriage of a variety of weapons. *Country of origin:* France/West Germany. *Silhouette:* Alpha Jet A. *Picture:* Alpha Jet E.

Soko Orao/CNIAR IAR-93

Confusion: Jaguar, Alpha Jet, Harrier

Power: **2 × Viper turbojets**   *Span:* **24ft 7in (7.5m)**   *Length:* **42ft 8in (13m)**

Flown for the first time in 1974, this ground-attack fighter is a joint development by the Jugoslav and Romanian industries. The overall programme is known as "Yurom", while the type is designated Orao in Jugoslavia and IAR-93 in Romania. Western suppliers provide a number of key systems, notably the engines (Rolls-Royce) and undercarriage (Messier-Hispano). Some 400 examples of the subsonic Orao, which has a maximum weapon load of approximately 4,500lb (2,000kg), are expected to be produced for the Jugoslav and Romanian air forces. Each country has also flown single prototypes of a two-seat dual-control operational trainer, and this version is now in production.

Power: 1 × **J57** reheated turbojet   *Span:* **35ft 8in (10.87m)**   *Length:* **54ft 6in (16.61m)**

A supersonic carrierborne fighter and reconnaissance aircraft, the Crusader first entered service in 1957 and remains in small numbers with US Navy reserve units, the French Navy and the Philippines. Four 20mm cannon are mounted in the fuselage, and there are four positions for air-to-air missiles, air-to-surface missiles or bombs. Two underwing weapon/fuel tank pylons can also be fitted. The wing has variable incidence for low-speed flight. Versions in use are the F-8H, K, J and L interceptors and the RF-8G reconnaissance aircraft. Performance figures include a maximum level speed of 1,200 mph (1,930km/hr) at 36,000ft (11,000m); service ceiling of 38,400ft (11,700m); and combat radius of 440 miles (708km). *Country of origin:* USA. *Silhouette and picture:* F-8E(FN).

Vought A-7 Corsair II

Confusion: Crusader

Power: 1 × TF41 turbofan   *Span:* 38ft 8in (11.79m)   *Length:* 46ft 1in (14.05m)

Capable of carrying a massive weapon load, the single-seat subsonic Corsair II is a standard attack aircraft in both the USAF and USN. Initially powered by American engines, the A-7 was later fitted with the Allison licence-built version of the Rolls-Royce Spey. The USAF version is the A-7D, the USN version the A-7E and the two-seat trainer is designated TA-7C. The type has been exported to Greece and Portugal. Up to 15,000lb (6,804kg) of bombs, rockets, air-to-surface and air-to-air missiles and gun pods can be carried. A 20mm cannon is mounted in the fuselage. *Country of origin:* USA. *Silhouette:* A-7E. *Picture:* A-7D.

Dassault-Breguet Etendard IVM

Power: 1 × Atar turbojet   *Span:* 31ft 6in (9.6m)   *Length:* 47ft 3in (14.4m)

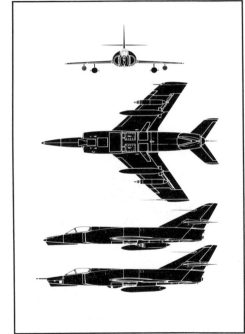

Originally introduced aboard French aircraft carriers in 1962, the Etendard IVM is a single-seat strike fighter. Ninety Etendards were built, of which 21 were designated IVP and equipped with cameras in the nose and gun bay. The IVP is shown in the lower side view. All the IVPs and some IVMs are fitted with flight-refuelling probes. Armament of the IVM includes two 30mm cannon, Nord 5103 air-to-surface and Sidewinder air-to-air missiles, bombs and rockets. The Etendard is just supersonic. *Country of origin:* France. *Picture:* Etendard IVM.

Dassault-Breguet Super Etendard

Confusion: Etendard, Hunter, G-91Y

Power: 1 × Atar turbojet   *Span:* **31ft 6in (9.60m)**   *Length:* **46ft 11½in (14.31m)**

The successor to the Etendard IVM, the Super Etendard is a transonic single-seat strike fighter designed for operation from French aircraft carriers. The engine has increased thrust, a modern navigation/attack system is fitted and an Agave radar is housed in the nose. The wing has also been modified. The first three Etendards were converted from IVMs and production deliveries began in 1978. A total of 71 are to be acquired by the French Navy, plus 14 for the Argentinian Navy. As on the IVM, the gun armament consists of twin 30mm cannon. A variety of weapons, including Exocet anti-ship missiles, can be carried on four underwing and one fuselage pylon. *Country of origin:* France.

Power: 2 × J79 reheated turbojets   *Span:* 53ft (16.15m)   *Length:* 75ft 10in (83.11m)

Originally produced as a nuclear/conventional-armed aircraft, the Vigilante proved to be an outstanding design. Capable of just over Mach 2 at altitude, the earlier versions of the type formed the nuclear strike force for the US fleet. The variant still in service is the RA-5C, used for reconnaissance. Cameras, sideways-looking radar and other sensors are fitted in the fuselage, while four long-range fuel tanks can be mounted under the wings. Special electronic countermeasures equipment is fitted to some Vigilantes. *Country of origin:* **USA.** *Silhouette and picture:* RA-5C.

Tupolev Tu-28P Fiddler *Confusion:* Vigilante

Power: 2 × Lyulka reheated turbojets   *Span:* 65ft (19.8m)   *Length:* 90ft (27.43m)

A long-range interceptor of massive size, the Tu-28P, code-named Fiddler, carries two crew, a large radar and up to four air-to-air missiles. As on many Soviet types, the main undercarriage retracts into blisters on the wing trailing edge. Although production is believed to have ceased in the late 1960s, Fiddler remains in Soviet Air Force service in specialist roles. Maximum speed is Mach 1.75 and range 3,100 miles (4,989km). *Country of origin:* USSR

Power: 2 × J52 turbojets   *Span:* 53ft (16.15m)   *Length* (A-6E): 54ft 7in (16.64m), (EA-6B): 59ft 5in (18.11m)

A highly versatile carrierborne aircraft, the Intruder was designed in the late 1950s as a two-seat, low-level, long-range attack bomber for the US Navy, being broadly equivalent to the Royal Navy's contemporary Buccaneer. In addition to its all-weather bombing rôle (A6A/B/E), the Intruder evolved during the Vietnam War as a tanker (KA-6D) and electronic warfare aircraft, the EA-6A/B Prowler (upper side view). The last-mentioned differ from other models in having a large electronics pod mounted on the fin, while the EA-6B has accommodation for two additional EW operators in an extended nose. *Country of origin:* USA. *Main silhouette:* A-6E. *Picture:* A-6A.

Siai-Marchetti S.211

Confusion: Hawk, Ajeet

Power: 1 × JT15D turbofan   *Span:* 26ft 3in (8m)   *Length:* 30ft 5in (9.27m)

A low-cost lightweight jet basic trainer, the S.211 has been developed as a private venture in Italy. The crew are seated in tandem and the four underwing hardpoints can carry bombs or rocket projectiles for weapon training. Maximum speed of the S.211 is 449 mph (723km/hr) while maximum cruising range, with external tanks, is 1,673 miles (2,693km). The prototype S.211 flew in April 1981 and deliveries were scheduled to begin during 1982. *Country of origin:* Italy.

Power: 1 × Adour turbofan *Span:* 30ft 10in (9.40m) *Length* (over probe): 39ft 2in (11.96m)

First flown in 1974, the Hawk T1 trainer was ordered by the RAF and entered service in 1976. The RAF's 175 Hawks are replacing all of its advanced trainers, including the Jet Provost, Gnat and Hunter T7. The standard version carries a 30mm Aden gun pack and two wing pylons for 1,000lb (450kg) bombs, though the weapon load can be increased by adding outboard wing pylons and removing the gun pack. Ninety RAF Hawks will carry two Sidewinder missiles each for interception duties over the UK. Export orders have been placed by Finland, Indonesia, Zimbabwe and Kenya, and the type is to be used as a trainer by the US Navy. *Country of origin:* UK.

Hindustan Aeronautics HF-24 Marut

Confusion: Hunter, Gnat

Power: 2 × Orpheus turbojets   *Span:* 29ft 6in (9m)   *Length:* 52ft (15.87m)

Developed indigenously for the Indian Air Force as a ground-attack fighter, the Marut (Wind Spirit) was designed for Mach 2 operation by a German, Dr Kurt Tank of Focke-Wulf fame. Lack of funds for acquisition or development of suitable afterburning engines has kept performance down to the transonic regime, however, and production of the basic Mk 1 version was maintained at a low rate during the 1960s and 1970s. A tandem two-seat trainer version (Mk 1T) has also been adopted by the IAF. Built-in armament comprises 4 × 30mm Aden cannon, supplemented by 4,000lb (1,800kg) of underwing stores. The Marut equips a total of three IAF units. Weights include 13,658lb (6,200kg) empty, 19,734lb (8,960kg) loaded clean, and 24,085lb (10,935kg) maximum. Ceiling is 60,000ft (18,300m) and maximum speed 673 mph (1,083km/hr) at 40,000ft (12,200m) (Mach 1.02). *Country of origin:* India. *Silhouette:* Mk 1T. *Picture:* Mk 1.

Power: 1 × Orpheus turbojet   *Span:* 22ft 2in   *Length* (Ajeet): 29ft 9in (9.06m)

Designed originally by the Folland company as an ultra-lightweight interceptor, the Gnat Mk 1 was adopted in that role by India and Finland and as a two-seat trainer by the RAF. Two hundred Gnat Mk 1 fighters were built at Bangalore by Hindustan Aeronautics. The current production model is the Gnat Mk 2 Ajeet ground-attack fighter, with more power and systems improvements. The Ajeet is also built in two-seat trainer form. Ajeet carries two 30mm cannon plus underwing bombs or rockets. The Indian Air Force is to receive up to a hundred Ajeets, and production deliveries of the two-seat trainer began in 1981. Performance figures for the Gnat/Ajeet include maximum speeds of 695 mph (1,118km/hr) at 20,000ft (6,100m) and 647 mph (1,040km/hr) at 36,000ft (11,000m); ceiling of 50,000ft (15,250m); and combat radius of 500 miles (805km). RAF Gnats have been replaced by the Hawk. *Country of origin:* India/UK. *Main silhouette:* Ajeet, *lower side view:* Ajeet trainer. *Picture:* Ajeet.

Hawker Siddeley Hunter

Confusion: Ajeet, Hawk, Marut, Etendard

Power: 1 × Avon turbojet *Span:* 33ft 8in (10.26m) *Length:* 45ft 10in (13.98m)

Undoubtedly the most successful and most numerous of post-war British fighter designs, with around 2,000 produced, the Hunter has been largely phased out of service by Western air forces, except in Switzerland and the UK. Many remain in service in the Middle and Far East, Africa, India and South America, however. The RAF still uses Hunters in a variety of roles, including advanced training with the two-seat T7. Hunters carry two internally mounted 30mm guns plus underwing rockets, bombs and fuel tanks. Two Hunter T7s have been converted into advanced trainers for the Sea Harrier, carrying the Blue Fox radar in the nose. *Country of origin:* UK. *Main silhouette:* FGA9; *upper side view:* T7. *Picture:* FGA9.

Hawker Siddeley Buccaneer

Power: **2 × Spey** turbojets   *Span:* **44ft** (13.4m)   *Length:* **63ft 5in** (19.33m)

Originally built as a Royal Navy low-level, two-seat carrierborne strike/attack aircraft, the Buccaneer was later adopted by the RAF as a land-based type for the same purpose. First production aircraft (S1) had the Gyron Junior engine, but subsequent variants (S2) are powered by the Rolls-Royce Spey. The RAF is now the sole UK Buccaneer operator and the type will remain in service, in the maritime role, after the introduction of Tornado. The South African Air Force has one squadron. Armament is carried internally and on four wing pylons. Bullpup, Sea Eagle or Martel missiles can be carried. Buccaneer performance is characterised by outstanding stability at low level and high speed. *Country of origin:* UK. *Silhouette and picture:* S2.

Saab 105 *Confusion:* Buccaneer

Power: 2 × Aubisque or 2 × J85 turbojets   *Span:* 31ft 2in (9.5m)   *Length:* 34ft 5in (10.5m)

Produced in the 1960s as a standard basic trainer for the Royal Swedish Air Force, the two-seat 105 is unusual in having a shoulder wing and T-tail. Four versions have been built: the Sk60A for training, Sk60B for weapons training/light attack, Sk60C for reconnaissance (all with Turboméca Aubisque engines), and the 105XT exported to Austria with General Electric J85 engines. The Sk60C (upper side view) has a longer nose than other variants. One hundred and ninety 105s were completed. *Country of origin:* Sweden. *Main silhouette and picture:* Sk60A.

Power: 2 × J57 turbojets   *Span:* 39ft 8in (12.09m)   *Length* (F-101B): 67ft 5in (20.55m)

Now to be found only in North America, serving with the US National Guard and the Canadian air-defence squadrons, the supersonic Voodoo was first supplied in the late 1950s. Current versions are the F-101B two-seat fighter, RF-101C photographic reconnaissance aircraft, and the F-101F with dual controls. Armament consists of Falcon and Genie air-to-air missiles and four 20mm cannon in the fuselage. In all 807 Voodoos were built and the type has had a remarkably long life. Voodoo performance figures include a maximum speed at 40,000ft of 1,220 mph (1,963km/hr) and a sea-level rate of climb of 14,000ft/min (4,270m/min). *Country of origin:* USA. *Main silhouette:* RF-101C; *top side view:* F-101B; *middle side view:* RF-101A. *Picture:* CF-101F.

Power: 1 × **J65 turbojet**   *Span:* **33ft 6in (10.21m)**   *Length:* **47ft 6in (14.48m)**

Produced in the 1950s, the single-seat RF-84F Thunderflash was the tactical reconnaissance version of the F-84F Thunderstreak fighter, which has a nose intake. On the Thunderflash the nose contains cameras. The Greek Air Force operates 18 Thunderflashes and 12 Thunderstreaks, the latter being used for training. Twin long-range fuel tanks can be carried under the wings. The F-84F/RF-84F have maximum speeds of over 650 mph (1,040km/hr). *Country of origin:* USA. *Silhouette and picture:* RF-84F.

Power: 1 × J75 reheated turbojet   *Span:* **34ft 11in (10.65m)**   *Length:* **64ft 3in (19.58m)**

Successor to the F-84F Thunderstreak of the mid-1950s, the Thunderchief long-range supersonic fighter-bomber entered service late in that decade. Some 150 F-105Bs and F-105Ds still serve in the US National Air Guard. Very heavy armament is carried: 14,000lb (6,350kg) of bombs internally and under the wings, and a multi-barrel 20mm cannon. F-105F and G versions have two seats in tandem. Over 800 operational Thunderchiefs were built for service with the USAF. *Country of origin:* USA. *Main silhouette:* F-105D; *upper side view:* F-105F. *Picture:* F-105D.

McDonnell Douglas F-15 Eagle

Confusion: Tomcat, Foxbat

Power: 2 × F100 reheated turbojets   *Span:* 42ft 9in (13.04m)   *Length:* 63ft 9in (19.44m)

A sophisticated single-seat, all-weather air-superiority fighter, the F-15 Eagle has a performance in excess of Mach 2 at altitude. In addition to a rotary cannon in the fuselage, the F-15 can carry four Sparrow and four Sidewinder air-to-air missiles. Operating in the USA and Europe with the USAF, the F-15 has also been sold to Israel, Japan and Saudi Arabia. First production aircraft flew in 1974 and nearly 1,000 have been ordered. With its twin fins and rudders and near-delta planform, the F-15 is very distinctive. The tandem two-seat version is designated TF-15. *Country of origin:* USA. *Silhouette and picture:* F-15.

Mikoyan MiG-25 Foxbat

Power: 2 × Tumansky reheated turbojets   *Span:* 41ft (12.5m)   *Length:* 70ft (21.33m)

A very-high-performance, high-altitude interceptor, the Foxbat is capable of speeds of between Mach 2.5 and 3.0. Because of its very high speed and 80,000ft (24,400m) operational ceiling Foxbat presents a problem to any air-defence system. Foxbat-A is an interceptor with a large nose radar and four underwing air-to-air missiles. Foxbat-B is a reconnaissance version with cameras in the nose, Foxbat-C (MiG-25U) is a two-seat trainer and Foxbat-D carries a modified radar. *Country of origin:* USSR. *Silhouette:* Foxbat-A. *Picture:* Foxbat-B.

There are only a handful of aircraft with swept wings and turbine engines mounted in the fuselage flanks or the wing roots. The Comet, now out of service, was the first type to have four engines buried in the wings. The Nimrod is a direct development of the Comet, with a much deeper fuselage but the same wing shape. The maritime reconnaissance Nimrod has a rod-like tail extension housing a magnetic anomaly detector for submarine search.

The airborne early warning (AEW) version of Nimrod is distinguished by its very large radomes at nose and tail. The Victor, now used for in-flight refuelling by the RAF, is easily recognised by its combination of crescent-shaped wings and large tailplane mounted on top of the fin.

Tupolev Tu-16 Badger

British Aerospace Victor

The Soviet Badger and Bison bombers, with root-mounted engines, are easily confused. Points to look for are size, four engines versus two, wingtip tanks on Bison and fin shapes.

Camel and Cookpot are very similar, the main differences being fuselage length and wing span.

BAe Nimrod AEW3

Power: 4 × Spey turbofans   *Span:* 115ft 1in (35.08m)   *Length:* 137ft 9in (41.97m)

Airborne early warning is achieved by putting a high-power surveillance radar into an aircraft, making it mobile and able to "see" over long distances. It is vital to look down on low-level bombers, which cannot be detected early enough by ground installations. The RAF aircraft for this role is the Nimrod AEW3, modified from the maritime reconnaissance Nimrod. Main point of difference is the fitting of large bulbous radomes in nose and tail, the former being particularly prominent. Eleven MR Nimrods are to be converted to AEW standard. Ordered in March 1977 in preference to the Boeing E-3A Sentry (see Jet, swept wing, underwing engines), the Nimrod AEW3 will replace the RAF's present airborne early-warning force of Shackleton AEW2s (see Four propellers). The Nimrod force will be integrated with the new UK ground-based air-defence system. *Country of origin:* UK.

BAe Nimrod MR

Confusion: Nimrod AEW3

Power: **4 × Spey turbofans**   *Span:* **114ft 10in (35m)**   *Length:* **126ft 9in (38.63m)**

Developed from the basic Comet airframe, the Nimrod MR1 is the RAF's standard long-range maritime reconnaissance aircraft. Capable of up to 12hr endurance and a maximum speed of 575 mph (926km/hr), the Nimrod is one of the most advanced anti-submarine aircraft in the West. The RAF Nimrod fleet is currently having its avionics and communications equipment completely updated to Mk 2 standard. Three Nimrod R1s are used for electronic surveillance. The R1 has a cut-off fuselage tail extension. Armament of the maritime reconnaissance variants includes bombs, mines, depth charges and torpedoes in the weapons bay. *Country of origin:* **UK.** *Silhouette and picture:* **MR1.**

Power: 4 × Conway turbofans   *Span:* 120ft (36.58m)   *Length:* 114ft 11in (35m)

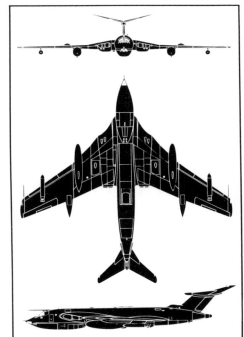

One of the three V-bombers which formed the British nuclear deterrent force of the 1950s and 1960s, the Victor was unusual in having a crescent-shaped wing leading edge and high-set tailplane. The B1 had Sapphire engines and the B2 Rolls-Royce Conways. The Victors in RAF service are all K2 tankers. Three aircraft can be refuelled simultaneously through hoses trailed from the belly and pods under the wings. *Country of origin:* UK. *Silhouette and picture:* K2.

Tupolev Tu-104 Camel *Confusion:* Cookpot, Badger

Power: 2 × Mikulin turbojets   *Span:* 113ft 4in (34.54m)   *Length:* 131ft 5in (40m)

The first pure-jet transport produced by the Soviet Union, the Tu-104 Camel was derived from the airframe of the Badger bomber. Early versions carried 50 passengers, while later variants were stretched to take successively 70 and 100 passengers. The fully stretched Camel with engines of increased power is known as the Tu-104B. Maximum cruising speed is 560 mph (900km/hr) and range 1,300 miles (2,100km). Production totalled approximately 50 Tu-104s, 100 Tu-104As and 100 Tu-104Bs. Maximum take-off weight is 167,550lb (76,000kg) and maximum payload 26,455lb (12,000kg), of which 8,820lb (4,000kg) can be carried in two underfloor holds. *Country of origin:* USSR. *Silhouette:* Tu-104B. *Picture:* Tu-104.

Power: **2 × Soloviev turbofans**   *Span:* **83ft 9in (25.55m)**   *Length:* **100ft 4in (30.58m)**

Closely resembling the Tu-104 Camel, the Tu-124 is in fact smaller and has less range. When it entered service in 1962 Cookpot was the first airliner in the world with turbofan engines. Seating 56 passengers, Cookpot operates over sectors up to 760 miles (1,220km) at an economical cruising speed of 497 mph (800km/hr). Cookpot was exported in small numbers and a VIP version was also produced. *Country of origin:* USSR.

Tupolev Tu-16 Badger

Confusion: Bison, Cookpot

Power: 2 × Mikulin turbojets   *Span:* 108ft (32.93m)   *Length:* 114ft 2in (34.8m)

First put into service in the mid-1950s as a bomber, the 596 mph (960km/hr) Tu-16 Badger remains in use with Soviet maritime squadrons. Used for overwater surveillance and electronic intelligence–gathering, the Badger-D has a long nose radome and three underfuselage blisters. Badger-E and F have glazed noses, the E mounting only two blisters and having a belly camera, and F having an electronic equipment pod under each wing. Badger-C carries Kelt air-to-surface missiles under the wings. Badgers use air-to-air refuelling and some act as tankers. There are twin tail guns. Maximum range with the maximum bomb load of 19,800lb (9,000kg) is 3,000 miles (4,800km), increasing to 3,975 miles (6,400km) with 6,600lb (3,000kg) at 480 mph (770km/hr). Normal take-off weight is 150,000lb (68,000kg). *Country of origin:* USSR. *Silhouette:* Badger-C. *Picture:* Badger-D.

Myasishchev M-4 Bison

Power: 4 × Soloviev turbofans   *Span:* 170ft (51.82m)   *Length:* 162ft (49.38m)

Originally designed as the rival to the Boeing B-52 strategic bomber, the M-4, code-named Bison, first flew in 1953 and entered service with the Soviet Air Force in 1955. Initial versions were powered by four Mikulin turbojets but later machines were fitted with Soloviev turbofans. As ballistic missiles took over the task of nuclear delivery, the Bison was converted to the B and C standards for the long-range maritime reconnaissance role. There are three positions for twin 23mm cannon and a probe for in-flight refuelling is fitted. A number of radar and electronic warfare sets are carried, and a special feature is the bicycle undercarriage with two sets of mainwheels under the fuselage and outrigger wheels at the wingtips. Maximum speed is 625 mph (1,060km/hr) and endurance is about 15hr. *Country of origin:* USSR. *Silhouette:* Bison-A. *Picture:* Bison-B.

The majority of aircraft in this class are transports, but there are also a significant number of military types such as the Brewer series, the B-52 and the S-3A Viking.

Underwing podded engines are either mounted on pylons clear of the wing, as on the Skywarrior and Boeing 747, or close up to the wing, as on the Boeing 737.

The Kawasaki C-1A is unusual in being a rear-loading, twin-podded transport with a T-tail. It resembles a smaller version of one of the bigger military transports such as the C-141 Starlifter.

The three-engined DC-10 and TriStar airliners are included in this section because, when the fin is not clearly visible, they can appear to be large underwing-engined twins like the Airbus A300. One noticeable difference between the DC-10 and TriStar is the mounting of the centre engine.

Confusion among the underwing-engined transports has been compounded by the appearance of the Boeing 757 and 767 and Airbus A310.

Boeing 737

There is a close similarity between the Boeing 707 and the DC-8, the differences being mainly in the nose shape, pod spacing and wing chord. There is little such difficulty with the DC-8 Super 60s, which have highly distinctive stretched fuselages.

Based on a 707 airframe, the Boeing E-3A Sentry (Awacs) is distinguished by its large over-fuselage radome. But there

Boeing 707-320C

McDonnell Douglas DC-10

is a possibility of confusion between the basic 707 and the Il-86 Camber, and the width of the fuselage of the latter is the point to note.

Additional fuselage length and width mark the wide-body Boeing 747, and engine spacing is also a significant feature.

Boeing's B-52 heavy bomber is noteworthy for its long, slim fuselage and plank-like wings. It has eight engines paired in four pods, but the addition of underwing guided weapons and auxiliary fuel tanks can at long range make the type look as if it has six engine pods.

The heavy medium/long-range military transports with four underwing engines are very similar. All have T-tails, upward-canted rear-fuselage undersides with loading doors, and main undercarriages retracting into fuselage bulges. The BAe 146 airliner is similar but smaller. Fuselage shape and cross-section plus engine spacing are the points to look for.

One odd-man-out among the twinjets with wing-mounted engines is the VFW 614, which has turbofan pods located

Airbus Industrie A300

above instead of below the wing. This is the only aircraft with such an arrangement.

Finally, two turboprop aircraft, the Bear and the Moss, have been included in this section. Both have swept wings and tailplane and, at a distance, are more likely to be confused with swept-wing jets than with straight-wing propeller-driven types.

Lockheed S-3A Viking

Confusion: Skywarrior, C-1A

Power: 2 × TF34 turbofans　　*Span:* 68ft 8in (20.93m)　　*Length:* 53ft 4in (16.26m)

A highly sophisticated carrierborne anti-submarine aircraft, the S-3A Viking went into US Navy service in 1974 as a replacement for the Grumman Tracker. With its podded turbofans and top speed of 507 mph (816km/hr), the S-3A can fly to a search area very rapidly. The fuselage weapons bay carries torpedoes, depth charges or mines, while weapons or fuel tanks can be carried on wing pylons. Four crew members are carried. A carrier on-board delivery (COD) version is designated US-3A. The prototype of the US-3A, produced by modifying a development S-3A, first flew in 1976 and underwent sea trials aboard the USS *Kitty Hawk* in 1978. *Country of origin:* USA. *Silhouette:* S-3A. *Picture:* US-3A.

Kawasaki C-1A

Power: 2 × JT8D turbofans   *Span:* 100ft 4in (30.6m)   *Length:* 95ft 2in (29m)

A medium-range tactical transport, the C-1A equips the Japan Air Self-Defence Force. Up to 60 troops or vehicles/freight, loaded via the rear doors and ramp, can be carried. Twenty-four C-1As were delivered, in addition to two prototypes and two pre-production models. Maximum speed is 489 mph (787km/hr), and range with full payload 865 miles (1,295km). At reduced payload (4,850lb, 2,200kg) and with maximum fuel, range increases to 2,084 miles (3,353km). Maximum sea-level rate of climb at normal take-off weight (85,320lb, 38,700kg) is 3,500ft/min (1,065m/min). Service ceiling is 38,000ft (11,580m). *Country of origin:* Japan.

Yakovlev Yak-28P Firebar

Confusion: Flashlight, Brewer

Power: 2 × Tumansky reheated turbojets   *Span:* 41ft (12.5m)   *Length:* 72ft (21.95m)

Developed from the Flashlight/Mangrove series, the Yak-28P Firebar is an all-weather interceptor with low-supersonic performance. Firebar has a long, pointed nose radome, two seats in tandem and two or four underwing air-to-air missiles. The Firebar first flew in 1960, was built in large numbers and remains in standard service with the Eastern Bloc. Like the rest of the family, the Firebar has a bicycle undercarriage with outrigger wheels near the wingtips. At high altitude the Firebar has a radius of action of 550 miles (885km). *Country of origin:* USSR.

Power: 2 × Tumansky reheated turbojets   *Span:* 41ft (12.05m)   *Length:* 70ft (21.34m)

Like Firebar, the Brewer is a derivative of the basic Flashlight airframe. A redesigned and higher-powered successor to the Flashlight, the Brewer has a glazed nose similar to that of an interim reconnaissance variant, the Yak-27R Mangrove, which differs little externally. Brewer is a multi-purpose tactical bomber (Brewer-A, B and C), reconnaissance (D) and electronic countermeasures (E) aircraft. A key task of Brewers now in Soviet service is electronic warfare, for which a variety of sensors are housed in fuselage blisters. The trainer version is the Yak-28U, code-named Maestro, which has an additional cockpit forward of the main position and no glazing on the nose. *Country of origin:* USSR. *Silhouette and picture:* Brewer-C.

Douglas A-3 Skywarrior   *Confusion:* Viking, C-1A

Power: 2 × J57 turbojets   *Span:* 72ft 6in (22.10m)   *Length:* 76ft 4in (23.27m)

Introduced in the 1950s and originally used as a standard US Navy bomber, the Skywarrior now performs the electronic countermeasures and tanker roles. The ECM version, with a variety of fuselage bulges housing special equipment, is known as the EKA-3B. The airborne tanker is designated KA-3B. Skywarrior production totalled 280 machines. The original armament of two 20mm cannon in the tail has been deleted from the present versions, which are conversions of earlier bomber/reconnaissance aircraft. *Country of origin:* USA. *Silhouette and picture:* EKA-3B.

Power: 2 × JT8D turbofans   *Span:* 93ft (28.35m)   *Length:* 100ft (30.48m)

A very successful short/medium-haul transport, this type first entered service with Lufthansa in 1967 as the 115-seat 737-100. Seating was subsequently increased to 130 in the 737-200, a variant which has sold in large numbers round the world (over 1,000 at the time of going to press). Nineteen 737s designated T-43A were delivered to the USAF as navigation trainers. The 737-200 can fly 2,370 miles (3,815km) with maximum payload. Maximum cruising speed is 576 mph (927km/hr). Now under development is the 737-300 with stretched fuselage and CFM56 turbofans. This version is scheduled to make its first flight in 1984. *Country of origin:* USA. *Silhouette and picture:* 737-200.

Airbus Industrie A300

Confusion: DC-10, TriStar, A310, 757, 767

Power: 2 × CF6 or 2 × JT9D turbofans   *Span:* 147ft 1in (44.84m)   *Length:* 175ft 11in (53.62m)

First flown in 1972, the 330-seat wide-body A300 is built by a European consortium of companies: Aérospatiale, Deutsche Airbus, British Aerospace, Casa and Fokker-VFW. The B2 and B4 are current versions, the latter having more fuel and leading-edge flaps. The A300 is intended for medium-range routes and can fly 2,530 miles (4,074km) with full payload and reserves. Maximum cruising speed is 578 mph (930km/hr). New versions of the A300 are the B2-200 and B4-400 with A310 rear fuselage, two more seat rows and improved engines. These variants will be in service in 1984. *Country of origin:* France/Germany/Netherlands/Spain/UK, plus other associated countries. *Silhouette:* A300B2. *Picture:* A300B4.

Power: 2 × CF6 or JT9D turbofans   *Span:* 144ft (43.9m)   *Length:* 153ft (46.6m)

A combination of a shortened-fuselage A300 and a new advanced-technology wing has produced the Airbus A310, a direct rival to the Boeing 767. Like the 767, the A310 is offered with two different powerplants. By January 1982 88 A310s had been ordered and options on a further 90 were held. First flown in April 1982, the type is scheduled to go into service in spring 1983, with Lufthansa and Swissair the first two users. With maximum payload the A310 can fly 2,540 miles (4,090km) at a speed of 514 mph (828km/hr). Convertible passenger/freight and all-freight versions are on offer. *Country of origin:* France/Germany/Netherlands/Spain/UK, plus other associated countries.

Boeing 767

Confusion: 757, A300, A310, TriStar, DC-10

Power: 2 × JT9D or CF6 turbofans   *Span:* 156ft 4in (47.65m)   *Length:* 159ft 2in (48.5m)

First flown in September 1981, the Boeing 767 is a medium-haul wide-body airliner seating a maximum of 255 passengers. The 767 and the Airbus A310 are direct competitors and they closely resemble each other in external shape. First delivery of the 767 was made in August 1982, with the production rate due to build up to eight per month in 1984. By spring 1982 firm orders totalled 173, plus 38 options. Like its sister aircraft the 757, the 767 is offered with a choice of powerplants. Companies in Italy and Japan are building elements of the 767. With its full payload the 767 has a range of 2,554 miles (4,110km) and cruising speed is 528 mph (850km/hr). *Country of origin:* USA.

Power: 2 × RB.211 or 2 × PW2037 turbofans   *Span:* 124ft 6in (37.95m)   *Length:* 155ft 3in (47.32m)

Reversing the trend towards wide-body twin-aisle transports, the slim-body twin-fan single-aisle Boeing 757 airliner first flew in February 1982, with deliveries to airlines beginning ten months later. Firm orders for the short/medium-haul 757 total 121, with some airlines selecting Rolls-Royce and others Pratt & Whitney powerplants. In mixed-class international layout the 757 seats 204 passengers, cruises at 528 mph (850km/hr) and has a maximum range of over 2,476 miles (3,984km). The 757 and the wide-body 767 form a new family of Boeing airliners which will be used in large numbers round the world. *Country of origin:* USA.

Lockheed L-1011 TriStar

Confusion: DC-10, A300, A310, 767

Power: 3 × RB.211 turbofans   *Span:* 155ft 4in (47.35m)   *Length* (except -500): 177ft 8in (54.17m)

Produced to meet the same wide-body requirement as the McDonnell Douglas DC-10, the Lockheed TriStar was the first aircraft to be equipped with the Rolls-Royce RB.211 big-fan engine. The various versions are the 1011-1, 1011-100, 1011-200, 1011-250 and the 1011-500; the last-named has a 13ft 6in (4.11m) reduction in fuselage length. Capacity varies up to 400 passengers in all-economy. Cruising speed is Mach 0.84 and maximum range, achieved by the -500, is 6,100 miles (9,815km). Lockheed has now decided to close the TriStar production line, probably in 1984. *Country of origin:* USA. *Silhouette:* L-1011-500. *Picture:* L-1011-1.

Power: 3 × CF6 or 3 × JT9D turbofans   *Span* (30/40): 165ft 4in (50.41m)   *Length* (30/40): 182ft (55.5m)

Over 330 DC-10 wide-body airliners have been sold and further stretched developments of the type are expected. The Series 10 was the initial version, followed by the Series 30 and 40, both with 10ft (3.05m) more wingspan. The Series 10 and 30 have CF6 engines and the Series 40 the JT9D. Convertible cargo versions are in service and the USAF has ordered the type for use as an airborne tanker/cargo aircraft designated KC-10. Like the TriStar, which it resembles, the DC-10 first flew in 1970. Maximum seating is for 380 and maximum range is 7,197 miles (11,580km). *Country of origin:* USA. *Silhouette:* DC-10-30. *Picture:* KC-10A.

Convair 880/990 *Confusion:* 707, DC-8

Power: 4 × CJ805 turbojets/turbofans   *Span:* 120ft (36.58m)   *Length* (990): 139ft 2in (42.43m)

Designed as a rival to the Boeing 707 and Douglas DC-8 over medium ranges, the Convair 880 and 990 were built in relatively small numbers. In an attempt to improve performance over the initial 880 version, the 990 Coronado was fitted with turbofans instead of turbojets and two "Kuchemann carrot" fairings were mounted on each wing trailing edge. The 990 has a maximum cruising speed of 625 mph (1,000km/hr), can carry up to 106 passengers and has a range of 3,800 miles (6,115km). *Country of origin:* USA. *Silhouette and picture:* Convair 990.

Power: 4 × JT3D turbofans   *Span:* 142ft 5in (43.41m)   *Length:* 150ft 6in (45.87m)

Along with the Boeing 707 and the Comet, the DC-8 pioneered the airline jet age, and 294 of the Series 10–50 were built. First flown in 1958, the DC-8 went into service in 1959, some fitted with Rolls-Royce Conway engines. The Series 50 can carry up to 173 passengers for 5,720 miles (9,205km). Known as the Jet Trader, a freight and freight/passenger version was introduced into airline service in 1962. *Country of origin:* USA. *Silhouette:* DC-8-50. *Picture:* DC-8-53.

McDonnell Douglas DC-8 Super Sixty *Confusion: 707*

Power: 4 × JT3D turbofans   *Span* (Super 63): 148ft 5in (45.23m)   *Length* (Super 63):187ft 5in (57.12m)

The process of "stretching" jet transports is nowhere more evident than in the DC-8, the ultimate variant of which, the Series 63, has grown by more than 30ft (9.14m) compared with earlier versions. The Super 62, with more wingspan than the Series 50, is the shortest version of this range. The Super 61 has the Series 50 wing and a 20ft (6.08m) fuselage extension, while the Super 63 has the longest fuselage and the bigger wing. All versions are used for passengers or freight. The Super 63 can carry up to 259 passengers. In all, 262 Super Sixties were built, divided up as follows: 78 Super 61, 10 Super 61F/CF, 51 Super 61, 16 Super 62F/CF, 47 Super 63 and 60 Super 63F/CF. The Super Sixties offer a unique combination of payload and range. *Country of origin:* USA. *Silhouette:* Super 63. *Picture:* Super 61.

Power: 4 × JT3D or 4 × Conway turbofans   *Span:* 145ft 9in (44.2m)   *Length:* 152ft 11in (46.61m)

The most successful of the first generation of medium/long-range jet airliners, the 707 first flew in prototype form in 1954. Initial versions seated up to 181 passengers , while the smaller 720 seated 153. Later versions such as the -320 and -420 carry up to 195 passengers and there are variants for cargo and mixed passenger/cargo. The 707 has a maximum cruising speed of 605 mph (973km/hr) and can fly 6,240 miles (10,040km) with maximum fuel. The airborne tanker version is designated KC-135 and has a refuelling boom under the tail. Some 940 707/720s have been produced. *Country of origin:* USA. *Silhouette:* 707-320. *Picture:* 707-320C.

Boeing E-3A Sentry

Confusion: DC-8, 707, Moss

Power: 4 × TF33 turbofans   *Span:* 145ft 9in (44.42m)   *Length:* 152ft 11in (46.61m)

A radar station in the sky, the E-3A Sentry is also known as Awacs (Airborne Warning and Control System). The aircraft is basically a 707 transport fitted with a very large circular radome above the fuselage and a complete air-defence operations centre in the cabin. The 17-man crew track numerous hostile targets and direct fighters onto them. The Sentry is in production for the US Air Force and a European Nato order has been placed. The first development aircraft, flown in 1972, was known as the EC-137. The first E-3A was delivered to the USAF's Tinker Air Force Base in 1977. The USAF is to acquire a total of 34 and Nato is planning to operate an 18-aircraft force. *Country of origin:* USA. *Silhouette and picture:* E-3A.

Power: 4 × Kuznetsov turbofans   *Span:* 157ft 8in (48.06m)   *Length:* 195ft 4in (59.54m)

The Soviet Union's first wide-bodied jet, the Il-86, Nato code-named Camber, was first reported in 1972, subsequently underwent extensive redesign, and finally emerged in December 1976. Seating up to 350 passengers, the Il-86 is intended for use over sectors of 1,460 miles (2,350km) at a speed of around 560 mph (900–950km/hr). The high specific fuel consumption of the Kuznetsov turbofans led to approaches to the West for licences to build the RB.211 and the CF6 turbofans in the Soviet Union, but no agreement was forthcoming. The Il-86 entered service with Aeroflot in 1980. Major subcontract work on the Il-86 is carried out in Poland. A longer-range version is under development. *Country of origin:* USSR.

Boeing 747 *Confusion:* 707, DC-8

Power: 4 × JT9D, CF6 or RB.211 turbofans   *Span:* 195ft 8in (59.64m)   *Length:* 231ft 4in (70.51m)

The largest airliner in the world, the Boeing 747 was the first of the wide-bodied "jumbo jets". It can seat up to 490 passengers in economy class and cruise at 589 mph (948km/hr) over sectors of up to 7,080 miles (11,395km). Initial version was the -100, followed by the -200 with more fuel. Passenger/cargo and all-cargo 747s are known as the -200C and -200F respectively. A short-range variant is designated 747SR. The short-fuselage 747SP (Special Performance) carries 360 passengers for up to 9,570 miles (15,400km). Latest version is the 747 Extended Upper Deck (EUD), with the upper front fuselage extended aft to accommodate 37 more passengers. *Country of origin:* USA. *Main silhouette:* 747-200B; *lower side view:* 747EUD. *Picture* 747-200B.

Boeing B-52 Stratofortress

Power: 8 × J57 turbojets or 8 × TF33 turbofans   *Span:* 185ft (56.42m)   *Length:* 157ft 7in (48.03m)

In service since 1957, the B-52 still forms the backbone of the USAF's Strategic Air Command. Its life is to be extended to allow it to carry air-launched cruise missiles. Main versions in service are the B-52G and B-52H, the former with J57 and the latter with TF33 engines. With a crew of six and full weapon load, the B-52 can carry 60,000lb (27,215kg) of internal weapons, plus missiles or other equipment on wing pylons. Outboard external fuel tanks can be fitted. The aircraft carries a wide variety of ECM systems. A multi-barrel radar-controlled 20mm Gatling gun is carried in the tail. Some 173 B-52Gs are to be modified to carry 12 Boeing Air Launched Cruise Missiles each. *Country of origin:* USA. *Silhouette and picture:* B-52H.

Lockheed C-141B Starlifter

Confusion: Galaxy, Candid, BAe 146

Power: 4 × TF33 turbofans   *Span:* 160ft (48.74m)   *Length:* 168ft 4in

The USAF's first pure-jet strategic freighter, the Starlifter entered service in 1964. Altogether 285 Starlifters were built and they are in use in many parts of the world with Military Airlift Command. Up to 59,800lb of cargo, or vehicles, equipment, guns and missiles can be carried. Range with maximum payload of 89,096lb (44,450kg) is 2,650 miles (4,264km). The Starlifter is loaded through rear under-fuselage doors. All Starlifters in the USAF have now been rebuilt to C-141B standard, with longer fuselage. *Country of origin:* USA. *Silhouette and picture:* C-141B.

Power: **4 × D-30 turbofans**   *Span:* **165ft 8in (50.50m)**   *Length:* **152ft 10in (46.59m)**

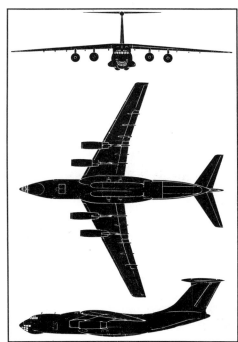

The Soviet answer to the Lockheed Starlifter, the Il-76 first flew in 1971. A massive strategic transport, the Candid is designed to operate from short, rough airfields. Maximum payload is 88,185lb (40,000kg) and cruising speed 528 mph (850km/hr). Tanks, guns and a variety of other vehicles and equipment can be loaded through rear doors. The Il-76 is in use with both the Soviet Air Force and Aeroflot, and has been exported. *Country of origin:* USSR.

Lockheed C-5 Galaxy

Confusion: Starlifter, 747, Candid, BAe 146

Power: 4 × TF39 turbofans   *Span:* 222ft 8in (67.88m)   *Length:* 247ft 10in (75.54m)

The world's largest military transport, the Galaxy can carry up to 345 troops on two decks, or 265,000lb (120,200kg) of freight for 2,950 miles (4,745km). First flown in 1968, the Galaxy went into service as the C-5A in 1970. The 77 aircraft in service form four squadrons in Military Airlift Command. Cruising at 537 mph (864km/hr), the Galaxy has a maximum-fuel range of 6,500 miles (10,460km). All Galaxies are to be retrofitted with a new, stronger wing. *Country of origin:* USA.

Power: 4 × ALF502 turbofans   *Span:* 86ft 5in (26.34m)   *Length* (Series 100): 85ft 10in (26.16m)

Unusual as a civil transport combining four jets, high wing and T-tail, the BAe 146 is a short-field, short-haul feederliner first flown in September 1981. Two versions are being developed: the Series 100 with 71/93 seats, and the Series 200 with length increased to 93ft 8in (28.55m) and seating 82/109. Mixed passenger/freight versions are on offer and the 146 has been projected for military transport, airborne early warning and maritime reconnaissance roles. The Series 200 cruises at 436 mph (702km/hr) over ranges of up to 1,704 miles (2,743km). The order book so far covers eleven Series 200 (plus twelve options) and two Series 100. *Country of origin:* UK. *Main silhouette:* 146 Series 200; *lower side view:* 146 Series 100. *Picture:* Series 100.

Tupolev Tu-20 Bear

Confusion: Stratofortress

Power: 4 × Kuznetsov turboprops   *Span:* 159ft (48.5m)   *Length:* 155ft 10in (47.50m)

Originally employed by the Soviet Air Force as a long-range strategic bomber (Bear-A and B), the Bear is now used for maritime and electronic warfare work by the Soviet Navy. The 530 mph (805km/hr) Bear is very unusual in having swept wings combined with turboprop engines driving contra-rotating propellers. Bear-C has a nose radome and rear-fuselage radomes, Bear-E has a smaller nose radome and under-fuselage cameras, and Bear-F has larger wing trailing-edge fairings. Standard armament is two 23mm cannon in the tail. Performance figures for Bear-A include a maximum level speed at 41,000ft (12,500m) of about 500 mph (805km/hr); maximum range of 7,800 miles (12,555km); and maximum take-off weight of 340,000lb (154,220kg). Up to 25,000lb (11,340kg) of weapons can be carried in an internal bay. About 50 Bears serve with the Soviet Navy. *Country of origin:* USSR. *Main silhouette:* Bear-B; *middle side view:* Bear-C; *lower side view and picture:* Bear-D.

Power: 4 × Kuznetsov turboprops *Span:* 168ft (51.2m) *Length:* 188ft (57.3m)

Adapted from the Tu-114 Cleat airliner (which has the wings and tail of Bear), the Moss is an airborne early warning and control aircraft in the same operational class as the Sentry and Nimrod AEW. The Moss carries a massive radar scanner of 37.5ft (11.4m) diameter above the rear fuselage. The cabin operations room houses radar operators and control staff. The aircraft is equipped for in-flight refuelling. Moss is designed to work with advanced interceptors. Having located incoming low-level strike aircraft, Moss would pass their height and speed to fighters armed with "snap-down" missiles capable of being fired from a height of 20,000ft (6,100m) or more. It could also warn Soviet strike aircraft if they were about to come under attack. About 12 Tu-126s are in service with the Soviet Air Force. *Country of origin:* USSR.

119

VFW 614 *Confusion:* ——

Power: 2 × M45H turbofans   *Span:* 70ft (21.5m)   *Length:* 67ft 7in (20.6m)

A short-haul inter-city transport, the VFW 614 failed to attract major airline orders. The first prototype flew in 1971, with production deliveries beginning in 1975. The programme was cancelled early in 1978. The 614 was a joint venture by German, Dutch and Belgian manufacturers. The type is unusual in having its podded engines mounted over the wings instead of underneath. The 614 cruises over sectors of up to 1,250 miles (2,010km) with 40 passengers. Some 614s remain in German military service. *Country of origin:* Germany/Netherlands.

Rear-engined jets with swept wings are among the most difficult for the recognition student to sort out. The observer is faced with a collection of types which at first glance appear to be near-identical. At long range the problem gets worse, with the lack of scale effect making it possible to confuse small rear-engined executive jets and much larger transports. There is a further complication when there are three engines at the rear; the third engine is often invisible from below, and the observer has to decide first whether the aircraft is a twin or a trijet.

The best approach is to try to sort out wing shapes and the position of the engines in relation to the wing. For instance, the Gulfstream II's engine nacelles are mounted high on the fuselage and in the plan view they appear to merge into the trailing edge.

Aérospatiale Corvette

The Fellowship is shorter in length than the BAe One-Eleven or the DC-9, and has shorter-span wings with prominent flap guides on the trailing edge. The Caravelle has its tailplane set well down the fin, while the Fellowship, BAe One-Eleven, DC-9 and Gulfstream II all have T-tails. Nose shapes are also worthy of study.

The Tu-22 Blinder is very unusual for a military aircraft in having its twin engines mounted on top of the rear fuselage. The undercarriage, as on other Tupolev designs, retracts into underwing fairings which should not be confused with similar installations on civil transports such as Crusty and Careless.

Wing shape is important in distinguising the Trident and 727. The later, stretched versions of the DC-9 look completely different because of their extreme fuselage length. In plan view this brings the stretched DC-9s into recognition competition with the 727.

Wing and tailplane planform are the main points to look for when comparing the Soviet Classic and British VC10 airliners, both of which have four rear-mounted engines. The only other type with four rear engines is the Lockheed JetStar executive aircraft, but the differences of size, wing shape, tailplane position and wing auxiliary fuel tanks readily mark this design out from the much larger Classic and VC10.

Close examination of wing shapes, nose shapes and wing and tailplane outlines is needed to differentiate executive jets such as the BAe 125, Sabreliner, Challenger and Falcon 20. The Falcon 50 is unique in this class in having a third engine.

Its forward-swept wings make the MBB Hansa very easy to recognise under most conditions.

Gulfstream American Gulfstream II/III

Confusion: One-Eleven, Fellowship, Falcon

Power: 2 × Spey turbofans   *Span:* 68ft 10in (20.98m)   *Length:* 79ft 11in (24.36m)

The Gulfstream II is one of the largest purpose-built executive transports, offering luxury accommodation for 19 passengers. The aircraft cruises at 495 mph (976km/hr) and range with maximum fuel is an impressive 4,275 miles (6,880km). One Gulfstream II is operated by the US Coast Guard under the designation VC-11A. The Gulfstream II first flew in 1966. Wingtip tanks can be fitted. The first of a new version, the Gulfstream III with lengthened fuselage and Whitcomb winglets, first flew on December 2, 1979, and is now in production. *Country of origin:* USA. *Silhouette:* Gulfstream III. *Picture:* Gulfstream II.

Power: 2 × TFE731 turbofans Span: 53ft 3in (16.3m) Length: 55ft 6in (16.9m)

The Citation III bears little resemblance to its straight-wing predecessors, described in the next section. With a high-aspect-ratio swept wing and T-tail, the Citation III is an executive transport seating six to thirteen passengers. Maximum cruising speed is 540 mph (869km/hr) and range with six passengers is 2,858 miles (4,600km). The prototype Citation III first flew in May 1979 and production deliveries were due to begin in December 1982. Production rate is scheduled to rise to 10 per month by spring 1985. *Country of origin:* USA.

Aérospatiale Caravelle

Confusion: One-Eleven, DC-9

Power: 2 × Avon or 2 × JT8D turbojets   *Span* (Caravelle 12): 112ft 6in (34.30m)   *Length:* 118ft 10in (36.24m)

Designed originally by Sud-Est, the Caravelle was the first pure-jet short-haul airliner to go into service. Caravelles I, IA, III, VI-N and VI-R had Rolls-Royce Avon engines while the Series 10R, 11R, Super B and 12 have the Pratt & Whitney JT8D. Early versions accommodated 64–80 passengers, while the Super B and Series 12 carry 104 and 139 respectively. Maximum cruising speed of the Caravelle 12 is 512 mph (8,25km/hr) and range is 2,150 miles (3,465km). The Caravelle is still in general use and a total of 279 were built, excluding prototypes. *Country of origin:* France. *Main silhouette:* Caravelle 11R; *top and bottom side views:* Caravelle 6R and 12 respectively. *Picture:* Caravelle 10B.

Power: 2 × Spey turbofans   *Span* (Series 500): 93ft 6in (28.50m)   *Length:* 107ft (32.61m)

A successful short-haul transport, the One-Eleven first flew in 1963, remains in production and is being built under licence in Romania. Some 227 One-Elevens have been ordered and the type has been developed through the Series 200, 300, 400, 475 and 500. The short-fuselage versions carry up to 89 passengers, while the long-fuselage Series 500 can accommodate up to 119. Maximum cruising speed is 541 mph (871km/hr), and range up to 1,865 miles (3,000km). The Series 475 is intended for operations from very short airfields. *Country of origin:* UK. *Main silhouette:* Series 500; *upper side view:* 400. *Picture:* 500.

Fokker F.28 Fellowship *Confusion:* One-Eleven, Gulfstream II, Trident, Crusty

Power: 2 × Spey turbofans   *Span* (Mk 6000): 82ft 3in (25.07m)   *Length* (Mk 6000): 87ft 9in (26.76m)

The Fellowship twin-engined short-haul transport first flew in 1967 and has sold steadily, with over 190 ordered so far. The different versions are: Mk 1000, short fuselage, up to 65 seats; Mk 2000, longer fuselage, 79 seats; Mk 3000, like 4000 but with short fuselage, 65 passengers; Mk 4000, long fuselage, 85 passengers; Mk 5000, wings of Mk 6000 with 65-seat cabin; Mk 6000, long-span wings and long fuselage with up to 85 seats. Fellowships have also been sold for cargo and VIP use. A distinctive feature of the F.28 is the large twin-shell airbrake in the tail. Cruising speed is 416 mph (670km/hr). *Country of origin:* **Netherlands**. *Silhouette and picture:* Mk 4000.

Confusion: Crusty, One-Eleven, Gulfstream II, Fellowship   **McDonnell Douglas DC-9**

Power: 2 × JT8D turbofans   *Span* (Series 40): 93ft 5in (28.47m)   *Length* (Series 40): 125ft 7in (38.28m)

First flown in 1965, the DC-9 was steadily developed and stretched to meet a demand for more seats. Initially, as the DC-9 Series 10, the aircraft carried up to 90 passengers; the long-fuselage Series 30 then appeared, with extended wings and capacity for up to 119. Extended wings and short fuselage resulted in the Series 20, while further fuselage stretches produced the Series 40 (125 passengers) and Series 50 (139 passengers). Military variants are designated C-9A Nightingale and VC-9C by the USAF and C-9B Skytrain II by the USN. Around 1,000 DC-9s have been ordered. The Series 40 cruises at 510 mph (821km/hr) and has a range of up to 1,070 miles (1,723km). *Country of origin:* USA. *Main silhouette:* DC-9-50; *upper side view:* DC-9-10. *Picture:* DC-9-30

McDonnell Douglas DC-9 Super 80   *Confusion:* DC-9 Series 40/50

Power: 2 × JT8D turbofans   *Span:* 107ft 10in (32.85m)   *Length:* 147ft 10in (45.08m)

Probably the ultimate in stretching, the DC-9 Super 80 is 43ft 5in (13.26m) longer than the original DC-9 Series 10, and passenger capacity has gone up from 90 to 172. The wing's span has been extended, its tips altered and its root changed in shape. The tailplane has been increased in area. The JT8D-209 engine has a new front fan and gives not only more power but is much quieter. Deliveries of the Super 80 began in 1980 and in mid-1982 the order book totalled 112. The Super 80 cruises at 522 mph (840km/hr) and has a maximum range of 3,280 miles (5,280km). *Country of origin:* USA.

Power: 2 × reheated turbojets   *Span:* 91ft (27.74m)   *Length:* 133ft (40.50m)

A most unusual military design, the Blinder bomber has two large turbojets mounted above the rear fuselage, a sharply swept wing, and main undercarriage housed in wing fairings. First flown around 1960, the Blinder is capable of Mach 1.5 at altitude. In basic form, as Blinder-A, the type was used as a reconnaissance bomber, while the B carried a Kitchen missile under the fuselage. The maritime reconnaissance Blinder-C is also equipped with a variety of electronic intelligence equipment. A trainer version, Blinder-D, has an additional raised cockpit. A flight refuelling probe is carried in the nose. A long-range interceptor variant of Blinder has been reported. *Country of origin:* USSR. *Silhouette:* Blinder-C. *Picture:* Blinder-B.

Tupolev Tu-134 Crusty

Confusion: Trident, One-Eleven, DC-9, 727

Power: 2 × Soloviev turbofans   *Span* (Tu-134): 95ft 2in (29m)   *Length:* 112ft 8in (34.35m)

Designed as a successor to the Tu-124 Cookpot, the Tu-134, Nato code-named Crusty, followed the contemporary Western trend of rear-mounted turbofans and T-tails. The Tu-124-type main undercarriage, housed in wing fairings, was retained. First flown in 1962, the 72-seat type went into service with Aeroflot in 1967. A stretched version, the 80-seat Tu-134A, entered service in 1970. Some Tu-134As have the glazed nose replaced with a streamlined radome. The Tu-134 has a maximum cruising speed of 540 mph (870km/hr) and a range of 1,490 miles (2,400km). Other performance figures include a maximum rate of climb at sea level and 97,000lb (44,000kg) take-off weight of 2,913ft/min (888m/min), and a service ceiling of 39,370ft (12,000m) at an all-up weight of 92,600lb (42,000kg). Maximum payload is 16,975lb (7,700kg) and maximum take-off weight 98,105lb (44,500kg). Over 200 Tu-134/134As have been built and a number are in use with Warsaw Pact airlines. *Country of origin:* **USSR**. *Silhouette and picture:* Tu-134A.

Power: 3 × Kuznetsov turbofans   *Span:* 123ft 2in (37.55m)   *Length:* 157ft 2in (47.9m)

The Tu-154, code-named Careless, was designed as the Soviet counterpart to the Boeing 727 and the Trident, but with the added ability to operate from short, rough runways. The trijet, T-tail Careless retains the characteristic Tupolev main undercarriage housed in wing fairings. First flown in 1968, the Careless entered service with Aeroflot in 1972 and has been exported to other Eastern European countries and to Egypt. The latest version is the Tu-154B-2 with improved avionics and seating for 154–180 passengers. Cruising speed is 560 mph (900km/hr). *Country of origin:* USSR.

BAe Trident *Confusion:* 727, DC-8, One-Eleven, Careless

Power: 3 × Spey turbofans   *Span* (2E/3B): 98ft (29.87m)   *Length* (3B): 131ft 2in (39.98m)

The Trident was built for the then British European Airways in the early 1960s. The original 1 and 1E versions were followed by the 2E with more range, and the 3B with a longer fuselage. The 3B carries up to 180 passengers compared with 132 on the 2E. The Trident, of which a total of 117 were sold, pioneered the use of Autoland for all-weather operations. China bought a large fleet of Trident 2Es and 3Bs. The Trident can cruise at up to 600 mph (965km/hr), and the 2E has a range of 2,464 miles (3,965km). Trident production has now finished. *Country of origin:* UK. *Silhouette:* 2E. *Picture:* 3B.

Power: 3 × JT8D turbofans   *Span* (-200): 108ft (32.92m)   *Length* (-200): 153ft 2in (46.69m)

The most widely sold of all Western jet airliners, the Boeing 727 has amassed orders totalling more than 1,825 at the time of writing. The only rear-engined aircraft in the Boeing family, the 727 first flew in 1963. The 727-100 seats up to 131 passengers and can be converted to carry cargo. The stretched -200, seating up to 189 passengers, became available in the mid-1960s. This was followed by the Advanced 727-200 with greater all-up weight and more fuel and range. The -200 has range of 2,645 miles (4,260km) and an economical cruising speed of 570 mph (917km/hr). *Country of origin:* USA. *Main silhouette:* -200; *upper side view:* -100. *Picture:* -200.

BAe VC10/Super VC10 *Confusion:* Classic

Power: 4 × Conway turbofans *Span:* 146ft 2in (44.55m) *Length* (Super VC10): 171ft 8in (52.32m)

The VC10 was designed to meet a British Overseas Airways Corporation requirement for a long-range airliner with good hot-and-high airfield performance. The type has proved very robust and reliable in service. The VC10 first flew in 1962, followed by the larger, longer-fuselage Super VC10 in 1964. The Super VC10 can carry 174 economy passengers, has a maximum range of 7,128 miles (11,470km) and cruises at 550 mph (886km/hr). The VC10 is used by the RAF as a standard passenger/freight transport and a batch is being converted as three-point in-flight refuelling tankers. These aircraft are expected to work principally with the RAF's Air Defence Variant (ADV) Tornados, permitting them to patrol far to the north of Britain. A total of 54 VC10/Super VC10s were built. *Country of origin:* UK. *Main silhouette:* Super VC10; *upper side view:* VC10. *Picture:* VC10 C1.

134

Power: 4 × Kuznetsov or 4 × Soloviev turbofans   *Span:* 141ft 9in (43.2m)   *Length:* 174ft 3in (53.12m)

The Soviet Union's first commercial four-engined long-range jet transport, the Il-62, code-named Classic, first flew in 1963 and went into service with Aeroflot in 1967. Classic and the VC10 are the only rear-engined four-jet airliners to be built. Classic normally seats 186 passengers. The basic aircraft is powered by Kuznetsov engines, while the Il-62M, introduced in 1974, has Soloviev turbofans. The Il-62M has more power, more fuel and better payload range figures. The aircraft cruises at up to 560 mph (900km/hr) and in Il-62M form has a maximum range of 6,400 miles (10,300km). A high-density variant, the Il-62M-200, can seat up to 198 passengers. Range with maximum payload (50,700lb, 23,000kg) and reserves is 4,960 miles (8,000km). A further derivative is the Il-62MK with strengthened wings. *Country of origin:* USSR. *Silhouette and picture:* Il-62M.

Yakovlev Yak-42 Clobber *Confusion:* Codling

Power: 3 × Lotarev turbofans   *Span:* 114ft 6in (34.90m)   *Length:* 119ft 4in (36.38m)

Following on from the straight-wing Yak-40 Codling, the Yakovlev bureau designed the larger swept-wing Yak-42, code-named Clobber, which first flew in 1975 and went into service with Aeroflot in 1980. The Clobber is replacing the Tu-134 Crusty and it is expected that up to 2,000 of the type may ultimately be built. The cabin seats up to 120 passengers and the range of the aircraft is 1,243 miles (2,000km), cruising at 466 mph (750km/hr). Clobber is being offered for export in straight passenger form and as a combined passenger/cargo aircraft. In an effort to improve the type's prospects in the export market, the Yakovlev bureau worked closely with Western airworthiness authorities. *Country of origin:* USSR.

Power: 2 × Viper turbojets or 2 × TFE731 turbofans   *Span:* 47ft (14.33m)   *Length* (Series 700): 50ft 8in (15.46m)

Over 530 BAe 125 twinjet business aircraft have been sold worldwide since the type first flew in 1962. Main versions are the Series 400, 600 and 700. The 600 has a longer fuselage than earlier variants and seats up to 14 passengers. All 125s up to and including the Series 600 are powered by Rolls-Royce Viper engines. The latest 125 on the line, the Series 700, has Garrett AiResearch turbofans and a longer, more pointed nose. The 125-700 cruises at 464 mph (747km/hr) and has a range of 2,683 miles (4,318km). The Viper-powered 125s used in the RAF are called the Dominie T1 as trainers and CC1 and CC2 as communications aircraft. *Country of origin:* UK. *Silhouette and picture:* Series 700.

Rockwell Sabreliner *Confusion:* BAe 125, Falcon, Corvette

Power: 2 × JT12A turbojets or 2 × CF700 or TFE731 turbofans *Span* (Series 65): 50ft 5in (15.37m) *Length* (Series 65): 46ft 11in (14.30m)

Originally supplied in quantity to the USAF and US Navy as the T-39 and CT-39, the Sabreliner was developed into the Series 40 and 60 executive transports. The former carries nine passengers and the latter ten in a lengthened fuselage, both powered by JT12A engines. The 75A is powered by CF700 turbofans and has various refinements, including a wider-span tailplane. Over 500 Sabreliners have been delivered and the version now on the production line is the Sabreliner 65, with TFE731 engines and a redesigned wing. Eight passengers can be carried. *Country of origin:* USA. *Silhouette:* Series 75A. *Picture:* Series 65.

Power: 2 × JT15D turbofans   *Span:* 43ft 5in (13.23m)   *Length:* 48ft 4in (14.73m)

Made in component form in Japan, the Diamond 1 twin-engined executive aircraft is assembled and flown at San Angelo, Texas. First flown in August 1978, the Diamond 1 began to be delivered in January 1982 against an order book of over 120. The aircraft seats 6–8 passengers, cruises at 466 mph (750km/hr) and has a maximum range of 1,484 miles (2,389km). Various versions of the Diamond 1 are at the project stage, including one with a fuselage stretch and additional capacity. *Country of origin:* Japan/USA.

Dassault-Breguet Falcon 10

Confusion: Falcon 20, BAe 125, Corvette

Power: 2 × TFE731 turbofans   *Span:* 42ft 11in (13.08m)   *Length:* 45ft 5in (13.85m)

Essentially a scaled-down version of the Mystère 20/Falcon 20, the Falcon 10 seats seven in its A form and nine in the B. The B also has a fourth window on each side. Both wing and fin shape differ from those of the Falcon 20. Falcon 10 can also be used for military training, communications and ambulance work. The prototype flew in December 1970 and deliveries began in 1973. Orders total over 220. Max cruising speed 586 mph (915km/hr), range 2,209 miles (3,555km). *Country of origin:* **France.** *Silhouette and picture:* **Falcon 10A.**

Power: 2 × CF700 turbofans or 2 × ATF3-6 turbofans   *Span:* 53ft 6in (16.30m)   *Length:* 56ft 3in (17.15m)

Dassault and Aérospatiale combined to build the successful Mystère 20/Falcon 20 8/10-seat executive aircraft. First flown in 1963, the aircraft is also used as an air force transport, freighter (with large side door) and trainer. Several hundred have been built and the type is in use in many places round the world. The Falcon name was adopted originally for aircraft sold in the USA. Main versions are the 20F and 20G, the latter having Garrett AiResearch ATF3-6 engines in place of GE CF700s. Latest version is the Falcon 200 maritime surveillance aircraft, known in the French Navy as the Gardian and in the US Coast Guard as the HU-25A Guardian. This variant has large side windows for observation. *Country of origin:* **France.** *Silhouette and picture:* 20F.

Dassault-Breguet Falcon 50

Confusion: Clobber, Falcon 10, Falcon 20

Power: 3 × TFE731 turbofans   *Span:* 61ft 10in (18.86m)   *Length:* 60ft 6in (18.43m)

Seeking more range for executive and other duties, Dassault designed a three-engined development of the Falcon series with new wings but retaining the front and centre-fuselage sections of the Falcon 20. The resulting Falcon 50 seats 8–10 passengers and has a large fuselage fuel tank. Initial deliveries were made in 1979, following a first flight in 1976. Maximum cruising speed is 540 mph (870km/hr) and range with four passengers is 3,450 miles (5,560km). The order book totals over 150. *Country of origin:* France.

Power: 2 × JT15D turbofans   *Span:* 42ft 2in (12.87m)   *Length:* 45ft 4in (13.83m)

Produced only in small numbers, the Corvette is a 6/14-passenger executive/air taxi/freighter aircraft first flown as the SN 600 in the summer of 1970. Maximum cruising speed is 472 mph (760km/hr) and range 967 miles (1,555km). Fuel tanks are fitted to the wingtips. A crew of two is carried. By mid-1978 Aérospatiale had sold or leased 36 Corvettes, of which ten were being operated by third-level carriers. Production was terminated after completion of the 40th example. Performance figures include an economical cruising speed of 352 mph (566km/hr) at 39,000ft (11,900m); maximum rate of climb at sea level of 2,700ft/min (823m/min); and service ceiling of 41,000ft (12,500m). *Country of origin:* France.

Lockheed JetStar   *Confusion:* BAe 125, Falcon 10, Falcon 20, Corvette, Challenger

Power: 4 × JT12 or 4 × TFE731 turbofans   *Span:* 54ft 5in (16.16m)   *Length:* 60ft 5in (18.42m)

Derived from the original twin-Orpheus JetStar I, the JetStar II is powered by four TFE731 turbofans. The JetStar II seats up to ten and cruises at 508 mph (817km/hr). Differences from earlier versions include a new engine nacelle shape, shortened long-range tanks on the wings, and the addition of a small air intake in the base of the fin. Production is complete. *Country of origin:* USA. *Silhouette and picture:* JetStar II.

Power: 2 × ALF502 or 2 × CF34 turbofans *Span:* 61ft 10in (18.83m) *Length:* 68ft 5in (20.82m)

Designed for use as an executive jet, commuter airliner and express cargo aircraft, the Canadair CL-600 Challenger first flew in August 1978. It has a roomy cabin seating up to 28 passengers and has a cruising speed of 463 mph (745km/hr). A later version is the CL-601, which is a development of the basic airframe using GE CF34 engines. Orders for the two variants total 138. *Country of origin:* **Canada**. *Silhouette and picture:* CL-600.

MBB HFB 320 Hansa *Confusion:* Learjet 35/36

Power: 2 × CJ610 turbojets   *Span:* 47ft 6in (14.49m)   *Length:* 54ft 6in (16.61m)

Remarkable in having forward-swept wings, the HFB 320 Hansa business jet and light transport first flew in 1964. In executive form the Hansa carries 7/9 passengers and two crew, while up to 12 passengers can be accommodated in a high-density layout. Fifty Hansas were built, including eight for the German Air Force. Production of the type is complete. The Hansa cruises at 513 mph (825km/hr) and has a range of 1,472 miles (2,370km). Quick-change facilities allow the Hansa to be readily switched from one role to the other. Maximum payload of the passenger version is 3,913lb (1,775kg). Maximum rate of climb at sea level and an all-up weight of 16,530lb (7,500kg) is 4,250ft/min (1,295m/min). *Country of origin:* West Germany.

There are only seven aircraft in this class, all but one of which are light transport or executive types. The exception is the Thunderbolt II, a heavily armed ground-attack aircraft.

While the Citation and Codling look very alike from below, from any other viewpoint the T-tail and third engine of the Codling are immediately apparent. Again, when the Learjet 23 and the Piaggio PD-808 are compared, the T-tail of the former is a significant point of difference. The engines are also set much closer to the fuselage on the 808, and the Italian type has the broader fuselage. Length is the key when comparing the earlier Learjets with the Learjet 35.

The Westwind/Jet Commander has close-mounted engines in the head-on view and the undercarriage is unusual in that it retracts outwards into the wings. Unlike the Learjet family and the PD-808, the Westwind/Jet Commander has its engines well clear of the wing trailing edge in plan view.

Yakovlev Yak-40 Codling

The Thunderbolt II is unique among combat aircraft, with its rear engines, twin fins and forward-retracting undercarriage. The massive underwing armament that it carries does however tend to blur the outline of the wing, particularly at a distance.

Cessna Citation II

Fairchild A-10 Thunderbolt II

Cessna Citation I/II

Confusion: PD-808, Westwind

Power: 2 × JT15D turbofans   *Span* (Citation I): 47ft 1in (14.35m)   *Length:* 43ft 6in (13.26m)

Initially known as the Fanjet 500, the Cessna Citation seven/eight-seat twin-turbofan executive transport first flew in 1969. The original production version, the Citation 500, was superseded by the Citation I with longer-span wings and uprated turbofans. The Citation II has increased span, a longer fuselage and accommodation for up to 10 passengers. Citation II cruises at 420 mph (675km/hr) and has a range of 1,986 miles (3,167km). Several hundred Citations have been built. A swept-wing development, the Citation III, is dealt with in the previous section. *Country of origin:* USA. *Main silhouette:* Citation 500; *upper side view:* Citation II. *Picture:* Citation I.

Power: 2 × Viper turbojets   *Span:* 37ft 6in (11.43m)   *Length:* 42ft 2in (12.85m)

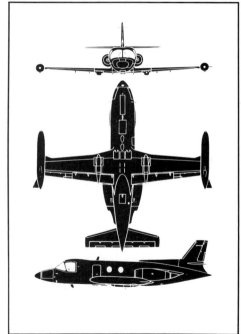

A light jet utility/executive aircraft, the PD-808 was first flown in 1964 and ordered by the Italian Defence Ministry. A maximum of ten passengers can be seated in the cabin, cruising speed is 449 mph (722km/hr) and range is 1,270 miles (2,045km). The Italian Air Force uses the PD-808 as a transport, VIP aircraft, navigation trainer and ECM aircraft. All versions carry one or two flight crew; the VIP transport carries six passengers and the electronic countermeasures version is operated by two pilots and three equipment specialists. The designation PD recalls the two companies which launched the project, Piaggio and Douglas. *Country of origin:* Italy.

Gates Learjet 23/24/25 *Confusion:* Learjet 35/36

Power: 2 × CJ610 turbojets   *Span:* 35ft 7in (10.84m)   *Length* (25D): 47ft 7in (14.50m)

Flown for the first time in 1963, the Gates Learjet series of executive transports has been steadily developed and built in large numbers. With six seats and two crew, the Learjet 24 cruises at 481 mph (774km/hr). The tailplane/fin bullet of earlier versions was deleted from the Model 24. The Learjet 25 is 4ft 2in (1.27m) longer and seats two extra passengers. A belly camera installation has been fitted to some aircraft. *Country of origin:* USA. *Silhouette:* Learjet 24D. *Picture:* Learjet 24.

Power: 2 × TFE731 turbofans   *Span:* 39ft 6in (12m)   *Length:* 48ft 8in (14.82m)

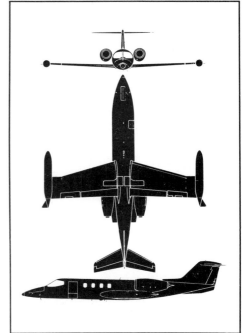

A new series of enlarged Learjet executive aircraft was introduced in 1973. Both wingspan and length have been increased, there are five starboard windows instead of four, and the engine nacelles are more bulbous. The wingtips have short rectangular extensions on which the fuel tanks are mounted. Like the Learjet 25, the 35/36 seats eight passengers. Currently in production are the 35A and six-seat, longer-range 36A, being built at a rate of seven a month. *Country of origin:* USA. *Silhouette and picture:* Learjet 35.

Gates Learjet 28/55 Longhorn

Confusion: Learjet 35/36, Citation

Power: 2 × TFE731 turbofans   *Span* (55): 43ft 9in (13.35m)   *Length* (55): 47ft 8in (14.53m)

The Gates Learjet 28 Longhorn, an improved version of the Learjet 25, has a redesigned wing with vertical winglets at the tips. The 29 Longhorn is externally similar but with increased fuel capacity. Gates Learjet has now married a new wide-body ten-passenger fuselage to the wing of the 28/29 to produce the 55 Longhorn. The first 55 Longhorn flew in April 1979 and the first production aircraft in August 1980. Deliveries began in April 1981 and a rate of five aircraft per month is planned. The 55 has an economical cruising speed of 462 mph (763km/hr) and a maximum range with four passengers of 2,665 miles (4,290km). *Country of origin:* USA. *Silhouette:* 55 Longhorn. *Picture:* 28 Longhorn.

Power: **2 × TFE731 turbofans**   *Span:* **44ft 9½in (13.65m)**   *Length:* **52ft 3in (15.93m)**

Originally powered by two CJ610 turbojets and known as the IAI 1123, the current production Westwind executive aircraft (1124) has two Garrett-AiResearch turbofans. Produced by Israel Aircraft Industries, the Westwind carries two pilots and up to ten passengers. Economical cruising speed is 460 mph (741km/hr), and with seven passengers range is over 2,785 miles (4,490km). A naval tactical support and coastguard version is available, designated 1124 Sea Scan. A longer-range development is the Westwind II with improved wing and winglets on the tip tanks. Over 50 Westwind IIs have been sold. *Country of origin:* **Israel.** *Silhouette:* **IAI 1124.** *Picture:* **West-wind II.**

Yakovlev Yak-40 Codling   *Confusion:* Citation

Power: 3 × Ivchenko turbofans   *Confusion:* 82ft (25m)   *Length:* 66ft 9in (20.36m)

Around 900 examples of the Yak-40, code-named Codling, have been built and the type is the most widely used aircraft on Soviet internal short-haul services. First flown in 1966, Codling went into service with Aeroflot in 1968 and since then many have been exported. Seating up to 32 passengers, Codling cruises at 292 mph (470km/hr) and has a maximum range of 1,240 miles (2,000km). A cargo version with a large door on the port side has been built. Most of the 800+ Yak-40s built so far are in service with Aeroflot, some as air ambulances carrying patients to medical centres and Black Sea convalescent homes. Production continues at Saratov, about 300 miles (500km) south-east of Moscow. Two examples have been delivered to Aertirrena of Italy, and others are in service in Afghanistan, Bulgaria, Czechoslovakia, France, West Germany, Poland and Yugoslavia. Military users include the Soviet and Polish air forces. *Country of origin:* USSR.

Fairchild Republic A-10 Thunderbolt II

Power: 2 × TF34 turbofans *Span:* 57ft 6in (17.53m) *Length:* 53ft 4in (16.26m)

An entirely new type of battlefield close-support aircraft, the single-seat A-10A Thunderbolt II is heavily armoured and carries massive armament for ground attack. With a combat speed of 443 mph (712km/hr) and a radius of action of 620 miles (1,000km), the Thunderbolt can carry 12,000lb (5,450kg) of weapons externally. In addition to bombs, rockets and guided missiles, the Thunderbolt II has a seven-barrel 30mm gun mounted in the nose. A total of 825 Thunderbolts are being built and the type is in service in the USA and Europe. A combat-readiness trainer version is designated A-10B. *Country of origin:* USA. *Silhouette and picture:* A-10A.

Differentiating between the various delta-wing aircraft is not easy, particularly when they are combat types. The speed at which these triangular shapes streak across the sky leaves very little time to look for finer points.

The Delta Dart interceptor has a planform very like that of the Mirage series, though the intakes appear much smaller from the underside. The Delta Dart also has a different cockpit shape and a broader-chord fin with a large bulge at the base. The Mirage III and 5 look very much like the latest

Saab Viggen

Dassault Mirage 2000

Dassault Mirage III

Dassault design, the Mirage 2000. Intake shape and the fin and rudder are the main points of difference.

The Mirage IV bomber is a good deal bigger than the Mirage III/5 and has a slightly different wingtip shape. The cockpit is a different shape and the fin is broader in chord. Although derived from the Mirage, the Israeli Kfir is distinguished by the canard winglets mounted on its engine intakes and a large dorsal intake at the base of the fin. The underside rear fuselage is also canted down.

A twin-delta wing planform marks the Saab Viggen. The main wing is also an unusual shape, with compound sweep on the leading edge, and the fin is triangular.

Concorde has what is called an "ogive" wing, with compound leading-edge curvature, and the engines are mounted in boxed pairs under the wing.

Sweden's Draken fighter has a double-delta outline and intakes in the wing roots. The fin looks like a half-delta wing with the tip squared.

Delta wings are usually associated with supersonic speeds. An exception is the subsonic Skyhawk attack aircraft, which has a delta wing with curved tips and a delta tailplane similar in shape to the wing.

Another delta with a tailplane is the F-16. The tips are squared off and carry air-to-air missiles. The distinctive feature of the F-16 is the large intake below the forward fuselage.

McDonnell Douglas A-4 Skyhawk

The Soviet Union has three delta-wing fighter/attack aircraft: Flagon, Fishpot and Fishbed. Two have nose intakes (Fishpot and Fishbed), one has compound leading-edge sweep (Flagon) and all three have tailplanes.

The SR-71 is a very unusual delta, with large engine nacelles buried in the wings and a very long, flat forward underfuselage. The vertical surfaces comprise twin inward-canted fins above the wing and one strake on the fuselage centreline.

Sukhoi Su-15 Flagon

Mikoyan MiG-21 Fishbed

General Dynamics/Convair F-106 Delta Dart

Power: 2 × J75 reheated turbojets   *Span:* 38ft 3in (11.67m)   *Length:* 70ft 9in (21.55m)

The F-106A Delta Dart was developed from the earlier F-102 delta-wing fighter. First flown in 1956, the Delta Dart had a very impressive performance for its day, with a maximum speed of over Mach 2 and a combat radius of 600 miles (966km). The Delta Dart continues in service and frequent updating of the nav-attack system and weapons has kept it up to standard. Armament consists of one internal multi-barrel 20mm Gatling gun and external Genie and Falcon air-to-air missiles. Auxiliary fuel tanks can be carried under the wings. *Country of origin:* USA. *Silhouette:* The two-seat version of the Delta Dart (upper side view) is designated F-106B. *Picture:* F-106A.

Power: 1 × Atar reheated turbojet   *Span:* 27ft (8.22m)   *Length* (IIIE): 49 ft 3in (15.03m)

One of the most successful single-seat fighter/ground-attack aircraft produced in Europe, the Mirage III has been sold to many countries. First flown in 1956, it has been built in several versions: IIIC interceptor, IIIE ground attack, IIIB and IIID two-seat trainers and IIIR reconnaissance aircraft. Basic armament consists of two 30mm cannon in the fuselage. Bombs, rockets, guided missiles and long-range tanks can be carried on centreline and underwing pylons. The aircraft is capable of Mach 2.2 and radius of action for ground attack is 745 miles (1,200km). *Country of origin:* France. *Main silhouette:* Mirage IIIE; *lower side view:* Mirage IIID. *Picture:* Mirage IIIS.

Dassault-Breguet Mirage 5

Confusion: Mirage III, Mirage 2000, Kfir

Power: 1 × Atar 9C turbojet   *Span:* 27ft (8.22m)   *Length:* 51ft (15.55m)

The ground-attack version of the Mirage III is designated Mirage 5. Over 1,400 III/5s have been ordered, of which 80 per cent have been sold outside France. The Mirage 5 has simplified avionics and a longer nose than the Mirage III. The prototype was first flown in May 1967. Armament combinations include 2 × 20mm cannon and 10 × 500lb bombs, or 2 × 1,000lb bombs and one AS.30 air-to-surface missile, or 4 × 1,000lb bombs and 2 × AIM-9 Sidewinder air-to-air missiles. Maximum speed of the Mirage 5 is 1,460 mph (2,350km/hr) at 40,000ft (12,000m). Service ceiling is 55,775ft (17,000m). Mirage 5 designations indicate the customer country: 5SDE (*Arabie SaouDitE*—Saudi Arabia) and 5AD (Abu Dhabi), for example. The two-seat trainer has the letter "D" after the country designation. *Country of origin:* France.

Power: 1 × M53 reheated turbofan *Span:* **29ft 6in (9m)** *Length:* **50ft 3in (15.33m)**

Although bearing a superficial resemblance to the Mirage III/5, the Mirage 2000 is a completely new aircraft which will provide the French Air Force with a very advanced Mach 2+ interception capability in the 1980s. Four hundred are likely to be ordered. The controls are electrically signalled ("fly-by-wire"), with computer control. In its primary role the single-seat Mirage 2000 will carry Super Matra 530 and R550 Magic air-to-air missiles and external fuel tanks. A variety of weapons can be carried for ground attack, including rocket projectiles, bombs, laser-guided weapons and a form of cruise missile. A scaled-up, twin-engined development is the Super Mirage 4000, which so far exists only in prototype form. *Country of origin:* France.

Dassault-Breguet Mirage IVA

Confusion: Mirage III/5, Mirage 2000, Kfir

Power: 2 × Atar reheated turbojets   *Span:* 38ft 10in (11.85m)   *Length:* 77ft (23.5m)

The Mirage IVA was designed in the 1950s as France's nuclear deterrent bomber. Its shape owes much to the Mirage III but it is much larger. Seating two in tandem, the Mirage IVA first flew in 1959 and 62 had been completed when production ended in March 1968. Capable of over Mach 2 at high altitude, the Mirage IVA carries either a nuclear weapon recessed into the fuselage underside, or a variety of weapons on pylons under the fuselage and wings. In-flight refuelling equipment is fitted as standard and short take-offs can be achieved by means of auxiliary rockets. *Country of origin:* France.

Power: 1 × J79 reheated turbojet   *Span:* **27ft (8.22m)**   *Length:* **53ft 8in (16.35m)**

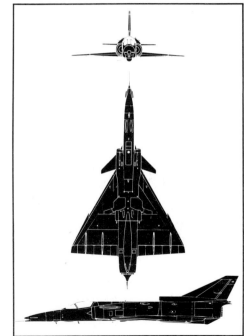

An extensively redesigned Mirage 5 built in Israel and powered by a General Electric J79 engine, the Kfir first went into service with the Israeli Air Force in 1975 as the Kfir-Cl. A modified version, the C2, is the main production aircraft. This has additional small winglets, or canards, just behind the air intakes and an extended wing leading edge. A dual-role interceptor and ground-attack aircraft, the Kfir has two fuselage-mounted 30mm cannon and seven hardpoints for air-to-air and air-to-ground missiles, bombs or drop tanks. The Kfir has a top speed of over 1,450 mph (2,335km/hr). A two-seat trainer derivative is designated Kfir-TC2. *Country of origin:* Israel. *Silhouette and picture:* Kfir-C2.

Saab Viggen *Confusion:* Kfir

Power: 1 × RM8A reheated turbofan   *Span:* 34ft 9in (10.6m)   *Length* (including probe): 53ft 6in (16.3m)

A high-performance Mach 2 multi-role aircraft, the Saab Viggen entered service with the Swedish Air Force in 1971. The Viggen is unusual in having a double–delta layout with the tailplane forward of the wing. The various versions are as follows: AJ37 all-weather attack; JA37 interceptor; SF37 reconnaissance; SH37 maritime reconnaissance; and SK37 two-seat operational trainer with raised rear cockpit. A wide variety of weapons can be carried on three underfuselage and four underwing pylons. The Viggen can operate from unprepared strips and roads. *Country of origin:* Sweden. *Silhouette:* JA37. *Picture:* AJ37.

Power: 4 × Olympus 593 reheated turbojets   *Span:* 83ft 10in (25.56m)   *Length:* 202ft 4in (61.66m)

The world's only fully operational supersonic airliner, the Anglo-French Concorde can carry 128 passengers at a speed of Mach 2 for 3,915 miles (6,300km). It first went into service with British Airways and Air France in 1976. Eighteen Concordes were built, of which 14 entered service. The external layout is unusual: the engines are boxed under the wing in two pairs, while the wing is ogive-shaped in planform and steeply cambered at the leading edge. Concorde's service ceiling is 60,000ft (18,300m), higher than that of any other airliner in service. Concorde commercial services were inaugurated on January 21, 1976, when the fifth and sixth production aircraft (Air France F-BVFA and British Airways G-BOAA) flew Paris-Dakar-Rio de Janeiro and London-Bahrain respectively. *Country of origin:* France/UK.

Saab Draken

Confusion: F-106

Power: 1 × RM6 reheated turbojet   *Span:* 30ft 10in (9.4m)   *Length:* 50ft 4in (15.4m)

With its unusual double-delta wing and Mach 2 performance, the Saab Draken fighter first flew in 1955. It remained in production until 1976 and is in service with Sweden, Denmark and Finland. Apart from its high performance, the Draken can operate from small airfields. Various versions have been produced, including the J35A, B, D and F, plus the SK35C two-seat trainer and S35E reconnaissance aircraft. *Country of origin:* Sweden. *Main silhouette:* J35F; *middle side view:* S35E; *bottom side view:* SK35C. *Picture:* J35F.

McDonnell Douglas A-4 Skyhawk

Power: 1 × J65 or J42 turbojet   *Span:* 27ft 6in (8.38m)   *Length:* 40ft 3in (12.27m)

Designed as a carrierborne attack aircraft, the A-4 Skyhawk was nicknamed the "Bantam Bomber". Although small, it can carry a very heavy weapon load (in later versions over 9,000lb) plus two cannon. Variants have gone from A-4A through to -4S. The two-seat trainer is designated TA-4. All versions from the F model onwards carry a dorsal hump containing avionics equipment, while the -4M was the first sub-type to be known as Skyhawk II. The Skyhawk has a top speed of 670 mph (1,078km/hr) and a range of 920 miles (1,480km). Over 3,000 have been built and production has been completed. *Country of origin:* USA. *Main silhouette:* A-4M; *middle side view:* A-4E; *bottom side view:* TA-4F. *Picture:* A-4M.

General Dynamics F-16 Fighting Falcon   *Confusion:* Skyhawk

Power: 1 × F100 reheated turbojet   *Span:* 31ft (9.45m)   *Length:* 47ft 8in (14.52m)

Highly manoeuvrable and capable of speeds in excess of Mach 2, the F-16 fighter is being built in the USA and in Nato countries and is scheduled to serve with the air forces of the USA, Belgium, Denmark, the Netherlands and Norway. A particular feature is the "shark's mouth" intake. A multi-barrel 20mm cannon is mounted in the fuselage, together with weapons or tanks on four underwing pylons and air-to-air missiles on the wingtips. The production single-seater is known as the F-16A while the tandem two-seat trainer is designated F-16B. A larger tailplane was fitted from late 1981, and the F-16C and D with up-dated systems are under development. *Country of origin:* USA. *Silhouette and picture:* F-16A.

Power: 2 × AL-21F reheated turbojets   *Span* (Flagon-A): 30ft (9.15m)   *Length* (including probe): 68ft (20.25m)

A Mach 2.5 twin-engined all-weather fighter, the Su-15, code-named Flagon, is used in large numbers by the Soviet Air Force. In its early form, Flagon-A, the aircraft had the same wing shape as the Fishpot. The latest variants, Flagon-D, E and F, have wing leading edges with distinctive compound sweep. The Flagon has a massive nose-mounted radome and large air-to-air missiles are carried on the outboard sections of the wing. Like Fishpot, Flagon can carry twin auxiliary tanks under the fuselage. The two-seat version is known as Flagon-C. About a thousand Flagons are believed to be in service with the Soviet air-defence force. Flagon-F is distinguished from the D and E by its ogival, not conical, radome. Flagon can carry a belly gun pack. *Country of origin:* USSR. *Main silhouette:* Flagon-F; *lower side view:* Flagon-C. *Picture:* Flagon-F.

Sukhoi Su-9/Su-11 Fishpot   *Confusion:* Flagon, Fishbed

Power: 1 × AL-7F reheated turbojet   *Span:* 27ft 8in (8.43m)   *Length* (including probe): 56ft (17m)

The Soviet Air Force's first all-weather fighter, Fishpot went into service in 1959 as the Su-9 Fishpot-B with a small radome in the air intake. In the second half of the 1960s an improved version (Su-11 Fishpot-C) reached the squadrons; this has a bigger intake with a larger central radome. Twin auxiliary fuel tanks can be carried under the fuselage and air-to-air missiles under the wings. The tandem two-seat trainer version is known as Maiden. *Country of origin:* USSR. *Silhouette:* Fishpot-C. *Picture:* Fishpot-B.

Power: 1 × R-13 reheated turbojet   *Span:* 23ft 5in (7.15m)   *Length* (including probe): 51ft 8in (15.76m)

The MiG-21 Fishbed fighter is one of the world's most widely used combat aircraft, serving with 28 air forces. Fishbed has been produced in a variety of versions, including the original with a small nose radome (Fishbed-C), all-weather variant with enlarged nose radome (Fishbed-D), main production standard with wider-chord fin (Fishbed-F), deeper dorsal fairing (Fishbed-J), reconnaissance version with pod (Fishbed-H), and latest variants with enlarged dorsal fairing (Fishbed-K, L and N). The two-seater trainer is known as Mongol. Fishbed can fly at over Mach 2 and carries a gun and guided missiles. *Country of origin:* USSR. *Main silhouette:* Fishbed-J; *middle side view:* Fishbed-C; *lowest side view:* Mongol. *Picture:* Fishbed-J.

Lockheed SR-71 *Confusion:* —

Power: 2 × JT11D reheated turbojets   *Span:* 55ft 7in (16.95m)   *Length:* 107ft 5in (32.74m)

The layout of the SR-71A high-altitude strategic reconnaissance aircraft is unique, with the engines mounted on the delta wing and twin canted fins on the engine nacelles. Carrying a crew of two in tandem, the aircraft can fly at up to Mach 3 and has an operational ceiling of over 80,000 (24,384m). A variety of cameras and electronic sensors are carried. Trainer versions are designated SR-71B and -71C. First aircraft in the series was the Falcon missile-armed YF-12A interceptor, which was cancelled when it was decided not to go ahead with the American advanced bomber-defence programme. Three YF-12As and about 30 SR-17s were built. *Country of origin:* USA. *Silhouette and picture:* ST-71A.

Any aircraft with straight wings has better landing, take–off and low-speed characteristics than one which has sharp sweepback. The straight wing is usually not the best configuration for supersonic speeds, however. The modern compromise is to combine straight with swept by pivoting the wing so that it moves to achieve the angle required for the best performance under given conditions. The term generally used to describe this capability is "variable geometry", but such aircraft are also described as "swing wing".

Variable geometry presents special recognition problems, as swept wings can be set at an almost unlimited number of angles, depending on the phase of flight. As a result, special study is needed and other salient features should be well memorised to complete the picture. In addition, certain variable-geometry types can be mistaken for deltas when their wings are fully swept.

Unlike most of the purpose-built variable-geometry types, the Soviet Fitter-C is a conversion of a conventional swept-wing aircraft. As a result, the wing pivot is set outboard of the main undercarriage, leaving the inner wing section fixed. Though the Soviet Union's key strategic bomber, the Tupolev Backfire, also has wings of this type, its size, massive intakes and general shape make it distinctive.

Grumman's Tomcat is the exception to the general variable-geometry rule in that it has twin fins, although this is not apparent in a direct side-on view.

The combination of variable geometry with external loads complicates the recognition puzzle. The F-111, for instance, can carry a massive range of underwing stores which themselves pivot to remain parallel to the centreline as the

General Dynamics F-111

wing moves backwards and forwards. All this tends to blur the general outline.

Key features of variable–geometry aircraft are fuselage shape and thickness, the aspect ratio of the moving wing sections, and tailplane outline. The Panavia Tornado, for instance, is far blunter-looking and more compact than the relatively slender, tapered-wing Flogger.

Panavia Tornado IDS

Confusion: Tornado ADV, Flogger, F-111, Fencer

Power: 2 × RB.199 reheated turbofans   *Span* (wings fully spread): 45ft 7in (13.90m)   *Length:* 54ft 9in (16.70m)

Now entering service, the two-seat Tornado IDS (Interdictor Strike) will form the offensive backbone of the RAF, the West German Air Force and Navy and the Italian Air Force. Total production of the IDS version is scheduled to reach 644, and in the RAF the type is designated Tornado GR1. Capable of twice the speed of sound at altitude, the IDS can fly at up to 920 mph (1,480km/hr) at low level. *Country of origin:* Germany/Italy/UK.

Power: 2 × RB.199 reheated turbofans   *Span* (wings fully spread): 45ft 7in (13.9m)   *Length:* 59ft 3in (18.06m)

Developed by British Aerospace for the RAF, the Tornado ADV (Air Defence Variant) will become the RAF's standard all-weather fighter in the second half of the 1980s. With a longer fuselage and a new airborne interception radar, the Tornado ADV carries a single 27mm cannon and four Sky Flash air-to-air missiles under the fuselage. Two Sidewinder missiles and long-range fuel tanks can be carried under the wings. A Mach 2 aircraft with long endurance, the Tornado ADV will be known in the RAF as the F2, and 165 are to be built. Like the Tornado IDS, the ADV is equipped for in-flight refuelling. *Country of origin:* Germany/Italy/UK.

Grumman F-14 Tomcat

Confusion: F-111, Fencer, Tornado

Power: 2 × TF30 reheated turbofans   *Span* (wings fully spread): 64ft 1in (19.55m)   *Length:* 62ft (18.9m)

The United States Navy's counterpart to the USAF F-15, the two-seat Tomcat is an all-weather carrierborne interceptor. With its powerful fire-control system, Tomcat can engage several targets simultaneously with Phoenix, Sparrow or Sidewinder air-to-air missiles. Tomcat is unusual in having twin fins and variable-geometry wings. Performance includes speeds of just over Mach 1 at sea level and Mach 2+ at high altitude. *Country of origin:* USA.

Power: 2 × TF30 reheated turbofans *Span* (wings fully spread): 63ft (19.20m) *Length:* 73ft 6in (22.40m)

This all-weather two-seat strike/attack aircraft, used by the USAF in Europe and America, carries heavy underwing armament and is capable of over Mach 2 at altitude. Versions are the F-111A (141 built), F-111E (94 built), F-111F (82 built) and FB-111A (77 built). All versions have generally similar outlines. Principal performance figures include maximum speeds of 1,650 mph (2,655km/hr) at 49,000ft (15,000m) and 915 mph (1,472km/hr) at sea level; ceiling of 60,000ft (18,300m); and maximum weapon loads of 24 × 1,000lb or 50 × 750lb bombs. *Country of origin:* USA. *Main silhouette:* FB-111A; *upper side view:* F-111E. *Picture:* EF-111A.

177

Mikoyan MiG-23S Flogger-B/E/G *Confusion:* Flogger-D, Tornado, Fencer, F-111

Power: 1 × Tumansky reheated turbofan *Span* (wings fully spread): 46ft 9in (14.25m) *Length:* 55ft 1in (16.80m)

A standard Soviet interceptor, this Mach 2+ type is in widespread use in Eastern Europe and has been exported to the Middle East. It carries cannon and missile armament. A two-seat variant is known as the Flogger-C, and Flogger-G is an improved interceptor. The Flogger-E export variant is generally similar to the Soviet Air Force version but is equipped to a lower standard. It is fitted with a smaller radar (Nato code-named Blue Jay) in a shorter nose radome and lacks the undernose laser rangefinder and Doppler navigation equipment of Flogger-B. Flogger operators outside the Soviet Union include Czechoslovakia, Egypt and Syria. US press reports suggest that four former Egyptian-operated MiG-23s are being flown by the US Air Force in the USA, and at least one other example is believed to have been presented to China. Further versions can be expected, and it is likely that a seagoing variant of Flogger will operate from any future large aircraft carriers built for the Soviet Navy. *Country of origin:* USSR. *Silhouette and picture:* Flogger-B.

Power: 1 × **Tumansky reheated turbofan**   *Span* (wings fully spread): **46ft 9in (14.25m)**   *Length:* **54ft (16.46m)**

A tactical strike development of Flogger-B, the Flogger-D is one of the major types facing the West in Europe. It differs from Flogger-B in having fixed air intakes and tailpipe nozzle, and a laser rangefinder nose. Flogger-D, with its low-pressure tyres, can operate from unprepared strips. There are five external racks for missiles and bombs. Compared with the MiG-23 Flogger-B, the MiG-27 has a completely redesigned forward fuselage. The ogival radome is replaced with a sharply tapered nose into which is set a small window covering a laser rangefinder and marked-target seeker. A Gatling-type gun replaces the interceptor's twin-barrelled weapon. Other close-support variants are Flogger-F and H. *Country of origin:* USSR. *Silhouette and picture:* Flogger-D.

Sukhoi Su-17 Fitter-C

Power: 1 × Lyulka or 1 × Tumansky reheated turbojet   *Span* (wings fully spread): 45ft (13.7m)   *Length:* 61ft 6in (18.75m)

The single-seat Fitter-C tactical strike fighter is unusual in being a variable-geometry development of a fixed-wing aircraft. Compared with Fitter-A, the outer wings pivot, the engine is more powerful, and armament and fuel have been increased. Export versions are designated Su-20 and Su-22. Certain other Fitters, such as the -J, have a changed fin and a longer tailpipe, associated with the fitting of a Tumansky engine. Operators include the Warsaw Pact countries and Peru. *Country of origin:* USSR. *Silhouette and picture:* Fitter-C.

Power: 2 × Tumansky reheated turbofans   *Span* (wings fully spread): 56ft 6in (17.25m)   *Length:* 69ft 6in (20m)

One of the most advanced types in the Soviet inventory, the Sukhoi Su-24, code-named Fencer, is a low-level supersonic attack aircraft in the same class as is the American F-111. Some 500 two-seat Fencers are in service, with production continuing at the rate of around 100 per year. Armament comprises two 30mm cannon in the lower fuselage and nuclear/conventional bombs, rocket projectiles, or missiles on eight wing and fuselage pylons. With wings fully swept to 70°, maximum speed at altitude is in excess of Mach 2. At lower speeds and low altitude the Fencer can carry a 17,635lb (8,000kg) warload over a radius of 200 miles (322km). *Country of origin:* USSR.

Rockwell International B-1   *Confusion:* Backfire

Power: 4 × F101 reheated turbofans   *Span:* (wings fully spread): 136ft 8in (41.66m)   *Length:* 146ft 8in (44.70m)

First flown in 1974, the B-1 supersonic long-range bomber was to have been the subject of large orders for the US Air Force. These were cancelled by the Carter administration and only four prototypes were completed. President Reagan revived the project and a new programme for 100 B-1Bs was announced in 1981. Externally similar to the B-1, the B-1B carries a crew of four and is armed with up to 22 Air Launched Cruise Missiles (ALCMs) or 38 Short Range Attack Missiles (SRAMs). The B-1B can operate low down at supersonic speeds or can achieve speeds of up to Mach 2 at altitude. Maximum range is 6,100 miles (9,820km). *Country of origin:* USA.

Power: 2 × Kuznetsov reheated turbofans   *Span* (wings fully spread): 115ft (35m)   *Length:* 138ft (42m)

The Soviet strategic bomber force will consist largely of Backfires by the mid-1980s. Carrying either nuclear or conventional weapons, Backfire can fly for over 3,800 miles (6,114km) and is capable of supersonic speeds at all altitudes. Two versions exist: the preliminary Backfire-A and the definitive B. The newer variant differs in having curved wingtips, a main undercarriage without pod fairings, and modified intakes. Production of Backfire-B is running at a rate of about 30 a year, and some 200 are in service. *Country of origin:* USSR. *Silhouette and picture:* Backfire-B.

The majority of straight-wing jets with engines in the fuselage are used for training and light attack work. Those with pilot and pupil side-by-side (Tutor, Dragonfly and Strikemaster) have fatter forward fuselages than those with tandem seating (Iskra, MB.326 and Albatross).

Engine intakes are usually in the wing roots or on the fuselage sides. A notable exception is the Saeta, which has a nose intake. Location of the engine exhausts varies from the tail itself (Strikemaster, Tutor, Hawk) to the wing trailing edge (Dragonfly and Saeta) and the rear underfuselage (Iskra).

Wings tend to be square-cut. Points to look for are aspect ratio, the amount of taper on leading and trailing edges, and fillets at the roots. Note should be taken of whether a particular type can carry wingtip fuel tanks.

Other features to look for are cockpit outline, fin shape and dorsal fairings, and tailplane position. The tailplane can be mounted on top of the fin (Tutor), on top of the rear fuselage (Kiran) or on the fin itself (Saeta).

Two supersonic combat types, the Starfighter and the F-5, have similar plan-view wing shapes. Main points of difference are the marked wing anhedral and T-tail of the Starfighter and the long jetpipe of the F-5.

Although performing widely different roles, the Magister and the Hornet have a V-tail in common. Here the similarity ends, as wing and fuselage shape are quite different and, on the Hornet, the underwing intakes are distinctive. The Hornet's long leading-edge extensions are worthy of note.

While the plan view of the Buckeye looks like those of several other trainers, the fuselage is much deeper.

There are few wing-engined aircraft in this section, and there is little real similarity between the Beagle and the Canberra. Various nose shapes can change the outline of the Canberra itself, while the American-built RB-57F has a wing shape very different to that of the basic Canberra. The U-2 has such a long wingspan that it is difficult to confuse it with anything else.

Finally, in the air the Lear Fan Model 2100 looks more like a jet than a propeller-driven machine.

McDonnell Douglas F-18 Hornet

Power: **1 × J85 turbojet**   *Span:* **38ft 6in (11.13m)**   *Length:* **32ft (9.75m)**

Originally developed as a private venture, the Canadair CL-41 Tutor side-by-side two-seat trainer was adopted by the Royal Canadian Air Force. Production was completed in 1966 after 190 had been built. Twenty CL-41Gs with fuselage pylons were built for Malaysia, in which service the type is known as the Tebuan. Basic armament comprises bombs, rockets and gun pods on wing hardpoints. Maximum speed is 480 mph (774km/hr). *Country of origin:* **Canada**. *Silhouette and picture:* CL-41G.

Morane-Saulnier MS.760 Paris

Confusion: Delfin, Tutor

Power: 2 × Marboré turbojets   *Span:* 33ft 3in (10.15m)   *Length:* 33ft (10.05m)

A four-seat high-speed civil and military communications aircraft, the MS.760 Paris first flew in July 1954. Some 165 Paris Mks I and II were built. The Paris II has higher-powered engines and more fuel capacity. A prototype of the Paris III, with six seats and extended wingtips, was built. The Paris I has a maximum speed of 405 mph (650km/hr) and a range of 930 miles (1,500km). For weapon training the Paris II can carry 7.5mm machine guns and guns and bombs or rockets. The engines are housed in wing-root fairings and the tailplane is mounted on top of the fin. *Country of origin:* France. *Silhouette and picture:* Paris I.

Aero L-29 Delfin (Maya)

Power: 1 × M-701 turbojet   *Span:* 33ft 9in (10.29m)   *Length:* 35ft 5½in (10.81m)

Designed as a Communist-bloc basic trainer, the L-29 Delfin, Nato code-named Maya, first entered service in 1963. The air forces of Czechoslovakia, the Soviet Union, East Germany, Bulgaria, Romania and Hungary use the Delfin, and other countries outside the Warsaw Pact have been supplied with the type. Two underwing pods can carry bombs, rockets, drop tanks or 7.62mm guns. An aerobatic version of the Delfin with a single seat is designated the L-29A Akrobat. *Country of origin:* Czechoslovakia. *Silhouette and picture:* L-29.

Cessna A-37 Dragonfly

Confusion: Saeta

Power: 2 × J85 turbojets   *Span:* 33ft 9in (10.3m)   *Length:* 29ft 3in (8.93m)

The standard USAF basic trainer (T-37B), the Dragonfly originally flew with Continental T69 engines. Many Dragonflies are in service with a number of air forces as trainers, with underwing pylons (T-37C) and with a Minigun in the fuselage and four weapon stations on the wings (A-37). A large number of Dragonflies have been built. Maximum speed is 507 mph (816km/hr) and range with weapon load is 460 miles (740km). *Country of origin:* USA. *Main silhouette:* T-37A; *lower side view:* A-37C. *Picture:* A-37B.

Power: 2 × Marboré turbojets   *Span:* **35ft 10in (10.93m)**   *Length:* **29ft 5in (8.97m)**

The Spanish Air Force's basic jet trainer is the tandem two-seat HA-200 Saeta, first flown in 1955. The basic HA-200 is known as the E-14A, the armed two-seater as the C-10B and the single-seat light strike version as the C-10C. There are two machine guns in the fuselage, and weapons can be carried on two pylons under the forward fuselage and four under the wings. Auxiliary fuel tanks are fitted at the wingtips. Maximum speed is 435 mph (700km/hr). *Country of origin:* **Spain**. *Main silhouette:* **HA-200;** *upper side view* **HA-220 Super Saeta.** *Picture:* **HA-220.**

Lockheed T-33A Shooting Star

Confusion: Seahawk

Power: 1 × J33 or 1 × Nene turbojet   *Span:* 38ft 10½in (11.85m)   *Length:* 37ft 9in (11.48m)

Trainer version of the US Air Force's first operational jet fighter, the T-33A (originally TF-80C) first flew as far back as 1948. A total of 6,600 T-33s were built and the type is still in service in some numbers. Some Shooting Stars were built with noses modified for reconnaissance. Several air forces still operate T-33s, some of them licence-built. Maximum speed is 600 mph (960km/hr) and endurance 3.12hr. *Country of origin:* USA

Power: 1 × Nene turbojet   *Span:* 39ft (11.9m)   *Length:* 39ft 8in (12.1m)

Originally an interceptor with the Royal Navy and the Netherlands and German naval air arms, the Sea Hawk dates back to 1947. The type is now in service only with the Indian Navy, aboard the carrier *Vikrant*. The Sea Hawk has a maximum speed of Mach 0.83 and a radius of action with underwing drop tanks of 386 miles (618km). Armament consists of four 20mm cannon and rockets or bombs. The type is to be replaced in India by the Sea Harrier.*Country of origin:* UK.

WSK-PZL-Mielec TS-11 Iskra

Confusion: Galeb/Jastreb

Power: 1 × SO-1 turbojet   *Span:* 59ft 8in (18.18m)   *Length:* 41ft 9in (12.74m)

The Polish Air Force took delivery of its first TS-11 Iskra tandem two-seat aerobatic trainer in 1963. The layout is unusual, with the engine exhausting under the fuselage and the tail assembly being carried by a long boom. Forward-firing machine guns are housed in the fuselage, and weapons can be carried on four underwing pylons. Several hundred Iskras have been built. Main performance figures include a maximum level speed at 16,400ft (5,000m) of 447 mph (720km/hr); maximum rate of climb at sea level of 2,913ft/min (888m/min); service ceiling of 36,000ft (11,000m); and range with maximum fuel of 907 miles (1,460km). The Iskra is operated by Poland and India. *Country of origin:* Poland.

Power: 1 × **Viper turbojet**   *Span:* **34ft 4in (10.47m)**   *Length:* **33ft 11in (10.34m)**

The first Jugoslav jet to enter production, the Galeb was first flown in 1961 and is now the standard Jugoslav Air Force basic trainer. Also in service is the Jastreb single-seat ground-attack version. This is equipped with three nose machine guns and eight underwing pylons for weapons, compared with the Galeb's two machine guns and smaller weapon load. Maximum speed is 470 mph (756km/hr) and maximum endurance 2hr 30min. *Country of origin:* Jugoslavia. *Silhouette and picture:* Jastreb.

HAL Kiran *Confusion:* Strikemaster, MB.326

Power: 1 × Viper turbojet   *Span:* 35ft 11in (10.70m)   *Length:* 34ft 9in (10.60m)

Designed to replace the Vampire trainers licence-built in India, the HJT-16 Kiran basic trainer was first flown in 1964. The aircraft bears a superficial resemblance to the Jet Provost/Strikemaster but is in fact totally of Indian design. The crew of two are seated side-by-side. A weapon-carrying variant is the Mk IA. A development of the Kiran I is the Orpheus-powered Mk II, intended for counter-insurgency work and weapons training. Two fuselage machine guns and four underwing pylons are fitted. Maximum speed of the Kiran I is 432 mph (659km/hr). *Country of origin:* India. *Silhouette and picture:* Kiran I.

Power: 1 × Viper turbojet   *Span:* 35ft 4in (10.77m)   *Length:* 33ft 8in (10.27m)

A two-seat basic trainer/light strike aircraft, the Strikemaster was developed from the Jet Provost, which was the RAF's first jet trainer. The Strikemaster has improved performance, more power and increased weapon load compared with the Jet Provost. The Jet Provost first flew in 1954 and the Strikemaster in 1967. The Strikemaster has a top speed of 472 mph (760km/hr) and a weapon load of 3,000lb (1,360kg) plus two fuselage-mounted machine guns. The Strikemaster has been widely exported and is still in production. *Country of origin:* UK. *Main silhouette:* Strikemaster; *upper side view:* Jet Provost. *Picture:* Strikemaster.

Aermacchi MB.326

Confusion: Kiran, Galeb, Strikemaster

Power: 1 × Viper turbojet   *Span:* 35ft 7in (10.85m)   *Length:* 34ft 11in (10.64m)

The MB.326 is a highly successful two-seat basic/advanced trainer and single-seat trainer/light attack aircraft (326K). Several hundred 326s of various versions have been built, and licence production has been undertaken in Australia and South Africa; in the latter country the type is called the Impala. Up to 4,000lb (1,815kg) of armament can be carried on underwing pylons, including rockets, bombs, AS.12 missiles and gun pods. A reconnaissance pack can be fitted. Maximum speed is 426 mph (686km/hr). *Country of origin:* Italy. *Main silhouette:* MB.326; *upper side view:* MB.326K. *Picture:* MB.326K.

Confusion: Hawk, MB.326 **Aermacchi MB.339A**

Power: 1 × Viper turbojet   *Span:* 35ft 8in (10.86m)   *Length:* 36ft (10.97m)

Based on and bearing a close resemblance to its predecessor, the MB.326, the two-seat MB.339A basic/advanced trainer has a redesigned forward fuselage. Auxiliary fuel tanks are carried at the wingtips and there are six underwing hardpoints for up to 4,000lb (1,815kg) of bombs and rocket projectiles. Cameras or an armament pod can be carried under the forward fuselage. The prototype was flown in 1976 and the type is in production for the Italian Air Force and for Argentina and Peru. A single-seat tactical support variant is known as the MB.339K Veltro 2. Maximum speed is 558 mph (898km/hr). *Country of origin:* Italy.

Casa C-101 Aviojet *Confusion:* Hawk, MB.339

Power: 1 × TFE731 turbofan   *Span:* 34ft 9in (10.60m)   *Length:* 40ft 2½in (12.25m)

A two-seat basic/advanced jet trainer and light ground-attack aircraft, the C-101EB Aviojet is in production for the Spanish Air Force and went into service in 1980. In the ground-attack role the C-101BB export version can carry two machine guns or a cannon under the fuselage and there are six wing positions for external stores such as bombs, rockets, guided missiles or ECM pods. Maximum speed is 482 mph (775km/hr) and range 1,865 miles (3,000km). *Country of origin:* Spain.

Aero L-39 Albatross

Power: 1 × Walter Titan turbofan   *Span:* 29ft 11in (9.11m)   *Length:* 39ft 9in (12.11m)

Successor to the L-29 Delfin, the tandem two-seat Albatross advanced trainer has engine intakes repositioned in the upper fuselage sides behind the cockpit. A single-seat light ground-attack trainer version, the L-39D, has four underwing pylons and a 23mm cannon in a pod mounted on the belly below the cockpit. The Albatross has a top speed of 379 mph (610km/hr). Deliveries began in 1973 and production (including exports) should total over 700. The L-39 was selected as the standard jet trainer of all the Warsaw Pact countries with the exception of Poland, and first entered service with the Czechoslovak Air Force in the spring of 1974. *Country of origin:* Czechoslovakia. *Silhouette and picture:* L-39.

Northrop T-38A Talon

Confusion: F-5, Starfighter, Hornet, Tigershark

Power: 2 × J85 reheated turbojets   *Span:* 25ft 3in (7.70m)   *Length:* 46ft 4½in (14.13m)

Very similar in outline to the Northrop F-5, the two-seat T-38A Talon was in fact a separate development with a different structure. The Talon was the first supersonic advanced trainer to be put into production, entering service with the USAF in 1961. A total of 1,187 Talons were built before production finished in 1972. The Talon has a maximum range of 1,093 miles (1,759km). *Country of origin:* USA.

Power: **2 × J85 reheated turbojets**   *Span:* **26ft 8in (8.13m)**   *Length:* **48ft 2in (14.68m)**

The most successful lightweight jet combat aircraft ever built, the Northrop F-5 flew for the first time in 1959. It is used for interception, ground attack and reconnaissance. The F-5A is a single-seater with four wing pylons and two 20mm nose guns, the RF-5A is the reconnaissance variant and F-5B is a two-seat trainer. The F-5E Tiger II air-superiority fighter has increased power, improved nav-attack system and a modified wing with leading-edge root extensions. Over 1,500 are expected to be completed. Tiger II has a maximum speed of 1,076 mph (1,732km/hr) and a range of 1,974 miles (3,175km). The reconnaissance version of Tiger II is designated RF-5E and the two-seat version F-5F. *Country of origin:* USA. *Main silhouette:* F-5A; *middle side view:* F-5B; *top side view:* F-5E. *Picture:* CF-5A.

Northrop F-5G Tigershark

Confusion: F-5A/E, Talon, Starfighter, Hornet

Power: 1 × F404 reheated turbofan   *Span* (over missiles): 28ft (8.53m)   *Length:* 46ft 6in (14.19m)

Latest in Northrop's series of lightweight fighters is the F-5G Tigershark, evolved from the Tiger II. In place of the two turbojets of earlier variants the F-5G has a single turbofan. Performance, including acceleration and top speed, is much improved. The F-5G prototype, with systems similar to those of the F-5E, was due to fly in the autumn of 1982 and was to be one of a pre-production batch of six aircraft. Deliveries were to begin in mid-1983. A further development, the F-5G-2, features updated radar, systems and weapons. *Country of origin:* USA.

Lockheed F-104 Starfighter

Power: 1 × J79 reheated turbojet   *Span:* 21ft 11in (6.68m)   *Length:* 54ft 9in (16.69m)

A single-seat all-weather tactical strike and reconnaissance fighter, the Lockheed F-104 Starfighter first flew in 1954 and has since been built in very large numbers. Unlike its swept-wing contemporaries, the Starfighter was designed with a very thin, straight wing. Air-to-air missiles or auxiliary fuel tanks can be carried on the wingtips, while a variety of missiles, bombs or fuel tanks can be accommodated on four underwing pylons. Standard fuselage-mounted armament is a 20mm rotary cannon. Top speed at altitude is 1,320 mph (2,124km/hr) or Mach 2. Main service variant is the multi-role F-104G. The F-104S, licence-built in Italy, carries two Sparrow medium-range air-to-air missiles. The tandem two-seat trainer version, shown in the upper side view, is designated TF-104G. *Country of origin:* USA. *Main silhouette:* F-104S. *Picture:* F-104G.

McDonnell Douglas/Northrop F-18 Hornet

Confusion: Starfighter, Tiger II

Power: 2 × F404 reheated turbofans   *Span:* **37ft 6in (11.43m)**   *Length:* **56ft (17.07m)**

Based on a Northrop private-venture design, the F-18 Hornet is a single-seat carrierborne air-superiority fighter with Mach 1.8 performance and high manoeuvrability. McDonnell Douglas is the prime contractor for the Navy and Marine Corps versions (F-18A fighter, A-18 attack aircraft and TF-18 two-seat trainer), while Northrop has responsibility for the land-based variant (F-18L). In fighter form the Hornet carries a six-barrel 20mm cannon plus air-to-air missiles and other stores on nine wing positions, including the wingtips. Total production for the US Navy and US Marine Corps could be as high as 800, and land-based Hornets have been ordered by Canada and Australia. The first Hornet unit will become operational in 1983. *Country of origin:* **USA.** *Silhouette and picture:* F-18A.

Power: **2 × Marboré turbojets**   *Span:* **37ft 5in (11.40m)**   *Length:* **33ft (10.06m)**

Nearly 1,000 CM.170 Magister two-seat basic trainers were built before production ceased. First flown in 1951, the Magister has a distinctive layout, with high-aspect-ratio wings and V-tail. The CM.170-2 is known as the Super Magister. Top speed is 403 mph (700km/hr) and endurance 2hr 40min. Two machine guns are mounted in the nose, and rockets, bombs or missiles can be carried under the wings. The Magister has been used as a light ground attack aircraft, serving with the Israeli Air Force in the Middle East. A naval-ised version known as the Zephry was produced for shipboard carrier familiarisation duties by the French Navy. *Country of origin:* **France**. *Silhouette and picture:* **Magister**.

Lear Fan Model 2100   *Confusion:* —

Power: 2 × PT6B turboshafts   *Span:* 39ft 4in (12m)   *Length:* 40ft 7in (12.4m)

Radical in both design and construction, the Lear Fan 2100 is a six-passenger V-tail aircraft primarily made of composite materials and powered by two turboshaft engines linked to drive a single propeller at the rear. It has been included in this section as, in the air, it looks exactly like a small rear-engined jet aircraft. Originating in Reno in the USA, the 2100 is being produced in Northern Ireland, where complete assembly and test flying will be conducted from No 43 onward. The 2100 has a remarkable performance, with a maximum speed of 425 mph (684km/hr) and a range of 1,752 miles (3,200km). First flight of the prototype was in January 1981 and deposits on 220 aircraft have been paid. *Country of origin:* USA.

Rockwell International T-2 Buckeye

Power: 2 × J60 or 2 × J85 turbojets   *Span:* 38ft 11in (11.62m)   *Length:* 38ft 3in (11.67m)

A shipborne basic trainer/attack aircraft, the T-2 Buckeye first flew, as the T2J-1 (T-2A) with one J34 engine, in 1958. The T-2B has two J60 engines and the T-2C and D two J85s. The wing was based on that of the early FJ-1 Fury fighter. Armament is carried on underwing stations. Maximum speed is 522 mph (840km/hr) and range, 1,047 miles (1,685km). Buckeyes were exported to two countries: Venezuela (24 examples) and Greece (40). *Country of origin:* USA. *Silhouette and picture:* T-2C.

Ilyushin Il-28 Beagle   *Confusion:* Canberra

Power: 2 × VK-1 turbojets   *Span:* 70ft 5in (21.45m)   *Length:* 57ft 11in (17.65m)

Although it is 29 years since the Il-28 bomber, code-named Beagle, first entered service, it is still in use with various air forces in Africa, Asia and South-east Asia and in small numbers in Eastern Europe. The trainer version, the Il-28U, has a second, lower cockpit and is code-named Mascot. In bomber form the Beagle carries 2,205lb (1,000kg) of bombs internally and two 23mm cannon in the tail. Maximum speed is 559 mph (900km/hr) and maximum range 1,355 miles (2,180km). A three-man crew is carried. Wingtip fuel tanks can be fitted. *Country of origin:* USSR. *Main silhouette:* Il-28; *upper side view:* Il-28U. *Picture:* Il-28.

Power: 2 × Avon turbojets   *Span:* 63ft 11in (19.50m)   *Length:* 65ft 6in (19.96m)

Still in widespread use 30 years after its first flight, the very successful Canberra is used for tactical bombing, reconnaissance, training, electronic warfare and target towing. Production totalled 1,461, including examples licence-built in the USA (as the B-57) and Australia. The internal bomb bay is supplemented by two underwing pylons and, in some versions, four 20mm cannon in a ventral pack. Later versions have a raised offset cockpit. Maximum speed is 580 mph (930km/hr) and range 3,790 miles (6,100km). UK-operated variants are the T4, PR7, PR9, E15, T17, TT18, T19 and T22. Canberras can be seen with various nose radars, used mostly for ECM training. *Country of origin:* UK. *Main silhouette:* B(I)8; *top side view:* B6, *middle side view:* PR9. *Picture:* B58.

Power: 2 × J65 turbojets or 2 × TF33 turbofans   *Span* (RB-57F): 122ft 5in (37.32m)   *Length:* 69ft (21.03m)

Some 500 Canberras were licence-built in the United States, serving as light bombers (B-57A), reconnaissance bombers (RB-57A), intruders (B-57B and C), electronic warfare trainers (EB-57B), reconnaissance aircraft (RB-57D), night interdictors (B-57G) and target tugs (B-57E). A later development is the RB-57F strategic reconnaissance aircraft, with a much larger wing, nose radome, auxiliary underwing jets, turbofan engines and a large square-cut fin. At least a dozen RB-57Fs were converted from B-57Bs. Ceiling of this variant is 75,000ft (22,875m) and range is in excess of 4,000 miles (6,435km). *Country of origin:* USA. *Silhouette and picture:* B-57B.

Power: 1 × J57 or 1 × J75 turbojet   *Span:* 80ft (24.38m)   *Length:* 49ft 7in (15.11m)

A high-altitude special-purpose reconnaissance aircraft, the single-engined U-2 came to the world's attention in 1960 when one was shot down over the Soviet Union. A very-high-aspect-ratio wing gives the U-2 a service ceiling of about 80,000ft (24,384m); cruising speed is 460 mph (740km/hr) and endurance over eight hours. Variants include the U-2A, B, C, D and R. The D has two seats. Special sensing equipment and cameras are carried and there are two large integral wing pods. The production line was reopened to turn out 12 much modified U-2s (U-2R) and 35 aircraft with improved sensors and designated TR-1A and B. One example was supplied to Nasa as the ER-2. *Country of origin:* USA. *Silhouette:* U-2. *Picture:* U-2R.

A wide variety of different types, both civil and military, are covered in this section. Most of them are light transport/executive aircraft and short-range twin-engined airliners.

The Dove, Saunders ST-27 and Merlin IV/Metro have many characteristics in common, as have "oldies" such as the Guarani, Convair 340/640, Martin 4-0-4, Crate and Azor. Wing shape and aspect ratio, engine nacelle outline and fin shape are the points to look for.

Swearingen Merlin IIIB

The DC-3/Dakota and the Commando have a lot in common, including rectangular wing centre-sections and backward-tapered outer wings. The Commando's fuselage is deeper and wider than that of the DC-3 and the former does not have a stepped windscreen.

Among the anti-submarine types the Atlantic bears a superficial resemblance to the Neptune, though the Atlantic's fuselage is shorter and fatter and its wing is low-set, while that of the Neptune is in the high-mid position.

While the Mohawk, with its external pods and triple fins, is very unusual, the Aero 45 is typical of a long series of light twins which are difficult to tell apart when they are airborne.

The Beech, Piper and Cessna light twins and the Cougar can be sorted out by concentrating on small wing-shape differences, undercarriage retraction arrangements and window layout. In one case the engine nacelles are oval in cross-section rather than flat. There are also varying degrees of sweepback on fins and tailplanes. Piper's Aerostar is unusual in having a mid-wing and a long, curved fuselage underside.

Piper Aerostar

Cessna 310

Further up the size scale are the BAe 748, YS.11, Saab-Fairchild 340 and Gulfstream I. Length is the key to the YS.11, while the Gulfstream I has a different fin shape and slight dihedral on the tailplane.

From the Seminole to the Xingu, wing planforms and ·fuselage shapes resemble those of aircraft that appeared earlier in the section. They differ in having T-tails, with the tailplane mounted at the top of the fin.

Though the last three types in this section all have twin fins and rudders, their overall outlines are very different.

The Beech B99 Airliner has a long fuselage aft of the wing, together with a prominent keel and a long, drooping nose. This compares with the Cessna Conquest, which has engines spaced widely apart.

The Navajo Chieftain has a broad-chord wing, deep fuselage, straight tailplane and close-in engine nacelles, while the Cessna Titan has a narrow-chord wing, widely spaced nacelles, slim fuselage and dihedral tailplane. Family resemblances are evident within various manufacturers' series, particular examples being the Cessna 421/414 and the Cessna 401/402. Minor differences have to be noted carefully.

Though they come from totally different design offices, the Metro/Merlin and the Jetstream are at first sight very similar. But close examination reveals narrower-chord wings, slimmer, shorter engine nacelles and oval windows on the Jetstream. The Jetstream tailplane is straight, while the Metro/Merlin unit is swept.

FMA IA 58 Pucara

Embraer EMB-111 Bandeirante

de Havilland Dove *Confusion:* ST-27, Metro/Merlin IV

Power: 2 × Gipsy Queen piston engines   *Span:* **57ft (17.40m)**   *Length:* **39ft 3in (11.96m)**

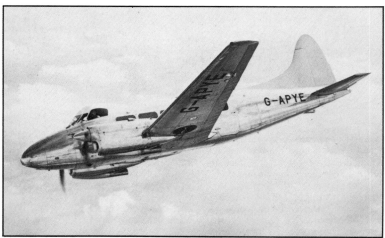

A total of 534 Dove 8/11-seat light transports were built over nearly 20 years. Series numbers were allotted largely to signify power increases in the Gipsy Queen engines. The military version of the Dove, the Devon, remains in service in a number of countries. The Royal Navy uses the name Sea Devon. Economical cruising speed is 187 mph (310km/hr) and range 880 miles (1,415km). A small number of Doves were re-engined by Riley and fitted with a swept fin and rudder. *Country of origin:* **UK.** *Main silhouette:* **Dove;** *upper side view:* **Riley Dove.** *Picture:* **Dove.**

Power: 2 × PT6A turboprops   *Span:* 71ft 6in (21.79m)   *Length:* 59ft (17.98m)

A much modified version of the British four-engined Heron light transport, the Saunders ST-27 is a 23-passenger commuter transport. With two turboprops instead of four piston engines, the S-27 has a maximum cruising speed of 230 mph (370km/hr) and a range with maximum payload of 115 miles (185km). Alternative interior layouts allows the carriage of mixed passengers and cargo or, with the rear bulkhead removed, all cargo. Usable volume of the all-passenger and passenger/cargo versions is 723ft³ (20.47m³), compared with the 828ft³ (23.45m³) of the all-cargo arrangement. Only a small number had been produced before financial support for the project dried up. *Country of origin:* Canada.

Fairchild Swearingen Metro   *Confusion:* ST-27

Power: 2 × TPE331 turboprops   *Span:* 57ft (17.37m)   *Length:* 59ft 4in (18.09m)

Developed from the Merlin, the Metro is a 20-passenger commuter airliner with a range of 500 miles (804km). The Metro II has deeper windows than the Metro, and both versions are characterised by long noses. An executive transport version of the Metro II is designated Merlin IVA and has seating for 12/15 passengers. The Metro III and IIIA have a new, longer-span wing, while the IIIA also has PT6A engines. The III has a range of 714 miles (1,149km). Introduced in 1981, the Metro IIIC incorporates the wing introduced on the Metro III, as well as the latter's streamlined nacelles and new main landing gear doors. It also offers improved handling, a redesigned cabin with new passenger seats and other detail refinements. Over 200 Metros of all types have been sold to some 40 operators. *Country of origin:* **USA**. *Silhouette:* Metro IIIA. *Picture:* Merlin IVA.

FMA IA 50 Guarani

Power: **2 × Bastan turboprops**   *Span:* **64ft 3in (19.59m)**   *Length:* **50ft 2½in (15.30m)**

Developed from the Huanquero, the IA 50 Guarani seats up to 15 passengers or can be used for navigation training or air ambulance work. Compared with the Huanquero, the Guarani has a swept single fin. Both types can carry tip tanks. Cruising speed is 280 mph (450km/hr) and range 1,240 miles (1,995km). First flown as the Guarani I, embodying 20 per cent of the structural components of the Huanquero, this type was developed into the Guarani II, the definitive standard. The Guarani II features more powerful engines, de-icing equipment, a single swept fin and rudder in place of the Guarani I's twin-fin arrangement, and a shorter rear fuselage to save weight. The type was phased out of production in 1973. *Country of origin:* Argentina. *Silhouette and picture:* Guarani II.

Convair CV-240/340/440 Metropolitan

Confusion: DC-3, Guarani, 4-0-4, Crate

Power: 2 × R-2800 piston engines   *Span:* 105ft 4in (32.12m)   *Length:* 79ft 2in (24.14m)

Originally built as the 40-seat Convair 240, the Metropolitan was developed into a number of variants. The 340 had a lengthened fuselage seating 44 passengers, while the 440 ultimately had accommodation for up to 52. Versions were also produced for the US Air Force and US Navy for air ambulance work, transport, crew training and ECM training. Altogether 1,081 240/340/440s were completed. The 440 cruises at 289 mph (465km/hr) for 1,300 miles (2,092km). *Country of origin:* USA. *Silhouette:* CV-340. *Picture:* CV-440.

Power: 2 × Allison 501 or 2 × Dart turboprops   *Span:* 105ft 4in (32.12m)   *Length:* 79ft 2in (24.14m)

The Convair 340 and 440 both proved capable of conversion to turboprop power. Pacific Automotive converted more than 115 to Allison 501 turboprops (CV-580), while kits were produced for refitting 340/440s with Rolls-Royce Darts to produce the CV-600/640. Canadair built 10 CV-540s and 10 CC-109 Cosmopolitans (RCAF) with Napier Eland turboprops. The 640 with Darts can carry 56 passengers for 1,230 miles (1,975km) at a speed of 300 mph (482km/hr). Original operators included Caribair, Hawaiian Airlines and Pacific Western. *Country of origin: USA. Silhouette and picture:* CV-640.

Martin 4-0-4 *Confusion:* Convair 340/640

Power: 2 × R-2800 piston engines   *Span:* 93ft 3in (28.44m)   *Length:* 74ft 7in (22.75m)

Developed from the Martin 2-0-2, which first flew in 1946, the 4-0-4 pressurised twin-engined transport entered service in 1951. The type was a rival to the Convair 340/440, which it resembles in outline. Over one hundred 4-0-4s were built and a number remain in use in the USA and South America. Forty passengers are carried, cruising speed is 280 mph (448km/hr) and range is 1,080 miles (1,730km). Other performance figures include a maximum speed of 312 mph (500km/hr) at 14,500ft (4,420m); initial rate of climb of 1,905ft/min; service ceiling of 29,000ft (8,845m); and a maximum range of 2,600 miles (4,160km). *Country of origin:* USA.

Power: 2 × ASh-82 piston engines   *Span:* **104ft (31.69m)**   *Length:* **73ft 2in (22.30m)**

Some 3,600 Il-14 Crate transports were built for both civil and military use. The civil version seats 18/26 passengers, while the military Crate has port-side double freight doors. A stretched version, the Il-14M, carries 24/28 passengers. A line in Czechoslovakia produced a 32-passenger variant, the Avia 14-32, the freighter 14T and the photographic survey 14FG. In 1960 the Czechs produced a pressurised 42-passenger Crate with circular windows known as 14-42. The -14M has a cruising speed of 193 mph (310km/hr) and a range of 810 miles (1,304km). The Crate is still in service in the Eastern Bloc and has been widely exported. *Country of origin:* USSR. *Silhouette and picture:* Il-14M.

Casa 207 Azor

Confusion: Crate, DC-3

Power: 2 × Hercules piston engines   *Span:* 91ft 2½in (27.80m)   *Length:* 68ft 5in (20.85m)

Used by the Spanish Air Force as a troop transport, freighter, crew trainer and air ambulance, the Casa 207 Azor first flew in 1955. Up to 36 passengers can be carried over 1,150 miles (1,850km) at a cruising speed of 266 mph (428km/hr). Other performance figures include a maximum speed of 285 mph (458km/hr) at 6,100ft (1,860m), and a service ceiling of 28,200ft (8,600m). Designed originally for commercial use as a DC-3 replacement, the Azor failed to attract civil interest and was built solely for the Spanish Air Force. Only 20 Azors were produced. The Azor succeeded a smaller transport, the 14-passenger Casa 202 Halcon. *Country of origin:* Spain.

Power: 2 × R-1830 piston engines   *Span:* 95ft (28.96m)   *Length:* 64ft 5in (19.63m)

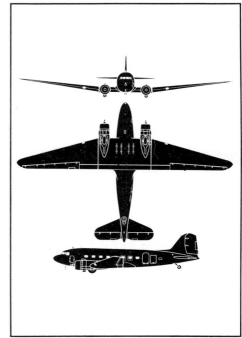

Probably the most famous of all airliners, the DC-3/Dakota first flew in 1935 and nearly 13,000 were built, including some 2,000 in Russia and Japan. Some 700 DC-3/Dakotas are still in use and there have been many variants, including turboprop developments. The basic DC-3 seats up to 36 passengers and cruises at 194 mph (312km/hr) for 1,510 miles (2,430km). *Country of origin:* **USA**. *Silhouette and picture:* **DC-3**.

Curtiss C-46 Commando

Confusion: DC-3, Crate, Azor, Atlantic

Power: 2 × R-2800 piston engines   *Span:* 108ft (32.92m)   *Length:* 76ft 4in (23.26m)

Like the ubiquitous DC-3/Dakota, the Curtiss Commando twin radial-engined transport has remained in service continuously since the Second World War. The type is in civil and military use, carrying either passengers or freight. Passenger versions can carry up to 62 passengers for 1,170 miles (1,880km) at a cruising speed of 187 mph (301km/hr). A total of 3,180 Commandos were built, of which some 100 are still operating. Freight is loaded through a large door on the aft port side. *Country of origin:* USA.

Power: 2 × Tyne turboprops   *Span:* 119ft 1in (36.30m)   *Length:* 104ft 2in (31.75m)

A multi-national European product, the Atlantic long-range maritime patrol aircraft is in service in France, West Germany, Italy, the Netherlands and Pakistan. First flown in 1961, the Atlantic has a 12-man crew and can cruise at 195 mph (320km/hr) for 18hr. The weapon load of acoustic torpedoes, depth charges or mines is carried internally. An updated version is the Atlantic NG (*Nouvelle Génération*), with improved systems and structure, and capable of carrying Exocet missiles in the weapons bay. Some Atlantics are specially equipped for electronic countermeasures duties. *Country of origin:* France. *Silhouette:* Atlantic Mk 1. *Picture:* Atlantic NG.

Kawasaki/Lockheed P-2 Neptune *Confusion:* Atlantic

Power: 2 × T64 turboprops plus 2 × J3 turbojets   *Span:* 97ft 8½in (29.78m)   *Length:* 95ft 11in (29.23m)

Originally designed and built by Lockheed in America, the P-2 Neptune maritime patrol and anti-submarine aircraft was subsequently manufactured under licence in Japan. After completing a number of P-2H Neptunes, Kawasaki developed a longer, higher-powered and longer-range version, the P-2J. Carrying 12 crew, the P-2J cruises at 230 mph (370km/hr) and has a range of 2,765 miles (4,450km). Up to 8,000lb (3,630kg) of weapons can be carried in the internal bomb bay, while rocket projectiles may be fitted under the wings. Details of the P-2J's operational equipment remain classified but this is known to be comparable in standard to that carried by the P-3 Orion and to include APS-80J search radar, exhaust-gas detector, and magnetic anomaly detector (MAD) in the tail boom. A total of four P-2Js have been converted to UP-2J target tugs. The Japan Air Self-Defence Force has over 80 P-2Js in service at present. *Country of origin:* Japan/USA. *Silhouette and picture:* P-2J.

Grumman OV-1 Mohawk

Power: 2 × T53 turboprops   *Span:* 48ft (14.63m)   *Length:* 41ft (12.50m)

Developed as a US Army battlefield surveillance aircraft, the OV-1 Mohawk carries a wide range of cameras and electronic sensors, and can operate from small, rough sites. OV-1A has cameras, OV-1B sideways-looking radar (SLAR), OV-1C cameras and infra-red sensors, and OV-1D cameras and sideways-looking radar or infra-red. The SLAR is mounted in a long, rectangular under-fuselage pod which extends well forward of the nose. Large auxiliary fuel tanks are carried under the wings. The crew of two are seated side by side and maximum speed is 305 mph (491km/hr). *Country of origin:* USA. *Silhouette:* OV-1B. *Picture:* OV-1A.

Aero 145 *Confusion:* Baron

Power: 2 × M332 piston engines   *Span:* 40ft 2½in (12.25m)   *Length:* 25ft 6in (7.77m)

The original Aero 4/5-seat light twin was flown in 1947. It was followed by the Super Aero 45 and later by the 145 with uprated engines. The 45/145 remained in production until 1961, by which time some 700 had been built, of which over 600 had been exported. A particular recognition point is the streamlined, unstepped nose. The 145 cruises at 155 mph (250km/hr) for up to 1,055 miles (1,700km). Other performance figures include a maximum speed of 175 mph (280km/hr); initial climb rate of 985ft/min (400m/min); and service ceiling of 19,360ft (5,900m). Empty weight is 2,116lb (960kg) and normal loaded 3,306lb (750kg). *Country of origin:* Czechoslovakia. *Silhouette and picture:* Aero 145.

Power: 2 × Continental piston engines   *Span:* 37ft 10in (11.53m)   *Length:* 29ft 10in (9.09m)

The B55 Baron four-passenger light transport was developed from the D95 Travel Air, which was itself a scaled-down Twin Bonanza. First flown in 1960, the Baron has been steadily updated over the years and has appeared under a variety of designations: A55, B55, C55, D55, E55, Turbo Baron and Baron 58/58TC. A pressurised variant is called the Baron 58P; over 300 examples have been delivered. Maximum cruising speed is 230 mph (370km/hr) and range 1,212 miles (1,950km). *Country of origin:* USA. *Main silhouette:* D55; *upper side view:* Baron 58. *Picture:* Baron 58.

Piper PA-31 Navajo *Confusion:* Apache, Baron

Power: 2 × Lycoming piston engines   *Span:* 40ft 8in (12.4m)   *Length* (-31C): 32ft 7½in (9.94m)

There have been several variants of the PA-31 Navajo since it was first introduced in 1964. Seating 6/8, the Navajo is used as an executive aircraft and a commuter airliner. When fitted with turbo-supercharged engines the type is called the Turbo-Navajo. The PA-31P, produced in 1970, has a pressurised cabin with fewer windows, and a longer fuselage. The PA-31C can fly 1,226 miles (1,973km) at a cruising speed of 238 mph (383km/hr). *Country of origin:* USA. *Main silhouette:* PA-31; *upper side view:* PA-31P. *Picture:* PA-31.

Power: 2 × Lycoming piston engines   *Span:* 37ft 2in (11.33m)   *Length:* 27ft 7in (8.41m)

Originally known as the Twin-Stinson, the Piper PA-23-160 Apache first flew in 1952. In this form it had a curved fin, rudder and tailplane. Ten years later it was followed on the line by the PA-23-235 with a more bulbous cabin, a larger, square-cut fin and rudder, and square-cut tailplane. The Apache is similar to the Aztec but has 4/5 seats, a shorter nose and lower-powered engines. The 235 cruises at 191 mph (307km/hr) for up to 980 miles (1,900km). *Country of origin:* USA. *Silhouette:* PA-23-160. *Picture:* Apache 235.

Piper PA-23 Aztec

Confusion: Cougar, Cessna 310

Power: 2 × Lycoming piston engines   *Span:* 37ft 2½in (11.34m)   *Length:* 31ft 3in (9.52m)

Originally built as the five-seat Aztec A in 1959, the Piper PA-23 evolved into the six-seat, longer-nosed Aztec B in 1962. The Aztec C, introduced in 1970, had redesigned engine nacelles and a longer nose, and Aztec D was externally similar. The latest version is the Aztec F. Aztecs of various marks are fitted with turbo-superchargers. As is the case with many American light aircraft, new designations often denote updated equipment and fittings rather than any change in outline. The Aztec F cruises at 210 mph (338km/hr) for 830 miles (1,335km). *Country of origin:* USA. *Main silhouette:* Aztec D; *lower side view:* Aztec B. *Picture:* Turbo Aztec F.

Power: 2 × Lycoming piston engines   *Span:* 36ft 10½in (11.23m)   *Length:* 29ft 10in (9.10m)

Originally a Grumman product, the GA-7 Cougar is intended for business and training use and can seat 4/6 people. First flown in 1974, the Cougar was significantly re-engineered before the production prototype flew in 1977. Gulfstream American's first entry into the lightweight twin-engined market, the Cougar was intended mainly for business use and for private pilots who already have instrument-flying experience. It can also be used as an economical twin-engined trainer. The production prototype flew for the first time on January 14, 1977, and delivery of production aircraft began in February 1978. Production has now ceased. The Cougar has a maximum range of 1,265 miles (2,035km) and cruises at 190 mph (305km/hr). *Country of origin:* USA.

Cessna 310 *Confusion:* Cougar, Twin Comanche

Power: 2 × Continental piston engines   *Span:* 36ft 11in (11.25m)   *Length:* 31ft 11½in (9.74m)

First flown in 1953, the Cessna 310 four-seat twin had a straight fin in its original form. In addition to hundreds of civil sales, the type was adopted by the USAF as the U-3A. With engine improvements incorporated, the 310 was marketed as the Riley 65 Rocket and Turbo Rocket. In 1960 the Cessna Model 310 appeared with a swept fin and more windows. Over 5,000 310s have been built and a large number of variants are flying, including some with turbo-supercharged engines and a further USAF version, the U-3B. Another development is the 320C Skyknight, seating up to seven. Cruising speed is 166 mph (267km/hr) and range is up to 709 miles (1,141km). *Country of origin:* USA. *Silhouette and picture:* Cessna 310.

Power: 2 × Lycoming piston engines   *Span:* 36ft 9½in (11.22m)   *Length:* 25ft 2in (7.67m)

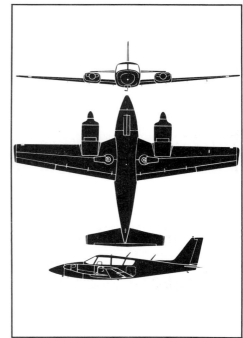

Developed as a twin version of the PA-24 Comanche single-engined light aircraft, the Twin Comanche first flew in 1961 and has been built in large numbers. A four/six-seater, it cruises at 198 mph (319km/hr) and has a range of 830 miles (1,335km). There are many variants, differing mainly in engine power, propellers and internal layout. Some are fitted with wingtip fuel tanks. From 1971 the PA-30 was succeeded by the externally similar PA-39. Refinements introduced with the later Twin Comanche variants include turbo-supercharging, first applied to the Turbo Twin Comanche B and C, and counter-rotating propellers (to eliminate torque effects) on the Twin Comanche C/R. *Country of origin:* USA. *Silhouette:* PA-39. *Picture:* PA-30C.

Piper PA-34 Seneca *Confusion:* Twin Comanche

Power: 2 × Continental piston engines   *Span:* 38ft 11in (11.85m)   *Length:* 28ft 7½in (8.73m)

The PA-34 Seneca six-passenger light transport and trainer was introduced in 1971. It has twin turbo-supercharged Continental engines, cruises at 177 mph (285km/hr) and has a range of 1,016 miles (1,635km). Poland holds a licence to build the Seneca II and distribute it in Eastern Europe. These aircraft are powered by PZL-Franklin engines and designated PZL-112 M-20 Mewa (Gull). Latest version of the PA-34 has detail modifications and is called the Seneca III. *Country of origin:* USA. *Silhouette:* Seneca II. *Picture:* Seneca III.

Power: 2 × Continental piston engines   *Span:* **38ft 1in (11.6m)**   *Length:* **34ft 4in (10.46m)**

Developed from the Cessna 310, the Model 340A is a four-passenger pressurised business aircraft. The layout is similar to that of the 310 but the fuselage cross-section is different and the windows are circular. The 340 in effect replaced the 320C Skyknight. As with other similar types in the Cessna range, the powerplants are Continental flat-four piston engines, which have a distinctive rectangular appearance in the head-on view. Range of the 340A is 1,580 miles (2,543km) at an economical cruising speed of 206 mph (332km/hr). Latest 340A variants feature a number of improvements, including better forward view as a result of structural changes, and a new strobe lighting system. *Country of origin:* USA.

Piper Aerostar   *Confusion:* Duke, Beech 99

Power: 2 × Lycoming piston engines   *Span:* 36ft 8in (11.18m)   *Length:* 34ft 10in (10.61m)

The first of the Aerostar series of light transport aircraft flew in 1967 as the Model 600. The 601P has more wingspan and a pressurised fuselage. A six-seater, the Aerostar 601 is one of a small number of types with a straight wing and swept tail surfaces. A new model, the 7/8-seat 800, flew in 1976. Several hundred Aerostars have been delivered. The 601B cruises at 270 mph (434km/hr) and has a range of 1,435 miles (2,309km). Aerostars have set a number of world records in their class. A total of more than 600 Aerostars of all models have been built. Latest model, introduced in 1981, is the Aerostar 602P. *Country of origin:* USA. *Silhouette:* 601P. *Picture:* 602P.

Power: 2 × Continental piston engines   *Span:* 38ft 10in (11.48m)   *Length:* 30ft 5in (9.27m)

First flown in 1978 as the four-seat Model 303, the Crusader is now designated T303. With six seats and turbo-supercharged engines, the Crusader is the first completely new twin-engined type to be put into production by Cessna for a decade. Deliveries began in September 1981. Cruising speed is 207 mph (333km/hr) and maximum range 1,156 miles (1,861km). *Country of origin:* USA.

Beechcraft Duke

Confusion: Queen Air, Seminole

Power: 2 × Lycoming piston engines   *Span:* 39ft 3in (11.96m)   *Length:* 33ft 10in (10.31m)

A pressurised, turbo-supercharged light transport, the Beech B60 Duke seats 4/6 passengers, cruises at 268 mph (431km/hr) and has a range of 1,163 miles (1,872km). Several hundred Dukes have been built in two versions, the A60 and B60. The B60, powered by Lycoming TIO-541-E1C4 engines, entered production in 1974. *Country of origin:* USA. *Silhouette and picture:* B60.

Power: 2 × Lycoming piston engines   *Span:* 50ft 3in (15.32m)   *Length:* 35ft 6in (10.82m)

Like the rest of the Beech range, the Queen Air has been built in very large numbers for both civil and military use. A four/nine-passenger twin, the Queen Air has been produced as the 65/A65, U-8F (US Army), Model 70/80/A80/B80 and U-21A, B, C, E and G (US Army). The U-8F, characterised by a straight fin, is called the Seminole. The Queen Air is in service both as an executive aircraft and a feederliner. The B80 seats 11 passengers and is called the Queen Airliner. It has a maximum cruising speed of 224 mph (360km/hr) and a range of 1,550 miles (2,494km). *Country of origin:* USA. *Main silhouette:* B80; *top side view:* B88; *bottom side view:* U-21. *Picture:* B80.

241

Beechcraft King Air

Confusion: Beechcraft 99, Queen Air

Power: 2 × PT6A turboprops   *Span* (100): 45ft 10½in (13.98m)   *Length:* 39ft 8½in (12.10m)

Based on the 65-80 Queen Air but with a redesigned pressurised fuselage, the King Air is a 16-seat twin-turboprop business aircraft. Models include the 90/A90/B90/C90/E90/100/B100 and T-44 advanced trainer for the USAF. Over 1,000 King Air 90s have been built and the type is in use in many countries. Maximum cruising speed is 285 mph (460km/hr) and range 1,507 miles (2,425km). *Country of origin:* USA. *Silhouette:* B100. *Picture:* E90.

Power: **2 × PT6A turboprops**   *Span:* **45ft 10½in (14m)**   *Length:* **44ft 7in (13.58m)**

The B99 Airliner is a twin-turboprop unpressurised 17-seat feederliner/air taxi. It first flew in 1966 and deliveries began in 1968. Similar in outline to other Beech twins of similar size, the B99 has a particularly long nose. A main cargo door allows the aircraft to be used for all-cargo or passenger/cargo operations. Maximum cruising speed is 282 mph (454km/hr) and range 531 miles (853km). Offering increased power and systems refinements, the C99 is known as the Commuter. Deliveries began in 1981. *Country of origin:* USA.

Cessna 441 Conquest *Confusion:* Navajo, Chieftain, Titan

Power: 2 × TPE331 turboprops   *Span:* 49ft 4in (15.04m)   *Length:* 39ft (11.89m)

Designed to fill a slot between piston-engined and turbofan business aircraft, the Cessna 441 Conquest seats eight/ten passengers in a pressurised cabin. It has a high-aspect-ratio wing, while the general layout is similar to that of other Beech twins. Range is 1,291 miles (2,077km) and maximum cruising speed 319 mph (513km). The prototype Conquest flew in 1975 and over 200 have been delivered. *Country of origin:* USA.

Power: 2 × Lycoming piston engines   *Span:* 40ft 8in (12.4m)   *Length:* 34ft 8½in (10.55m)

The PA-31-350 Chieftain has a longer fuselage than the Navajo and is a 6/10-seat executive/commuter/cargo aircraft. Cargo can be carried both in the cabin and in the nose. The Lycoming engines have turbo-superchargers. Cruising speed is 251 mph (404km/hr) and range 1,019 miles (1,640km). *Country of origin:* USA.

Cessna Titan *Confusion:* Chieftain, Chancellor

Power: 2 × Continental piston engines   *Span:* 46ft 4in (14.12m)   *Length:* 39ft 6in (12.04m)

Intended to provide greater payload/range performance than the Cessna 402, the Cessna Titan was originally known as the 404. The cabin is convertible to cargo, feederliner and executive configurations and double doors can be fitted for loading large cargo. The all-passenger Titan is called the Ambassador, while the utility passenger/cargo version is known as the Courier. There are no significant external differences between the two variants. Maximum cruising speed is 229 mph (369km/hr) and range 1,598 miles (2,572km). Several hundred Titans have been delivered. *Country of origin:* USA.

Power: 2 × Continental piston engines   *Span:* 41ft 1in (12.53m)   *Length:* 36ft 4½in (11.09m)

This series of pressurised business aircraft began in 1967 with the Model 421, which was developed into the 421B Golden Eagle and the 421B Executive Commuter. In 1975 came the 421C Golden Eagle, which had a new outer wing without the distinctive wingtip fuel tanks. The 421C Executive Commuter seats up to 11 as a feederliner and has a maximum cruising speed of 279 mph (450km/hr) and a range of 1,440 miles (2,317km/hr). Baggage is carried at the back of the cabin and in the long nose. *Country of origin:* USA. *Main silhouette:* Model 421A; *lower side view:* Model 421B. *Picture:* Model 421C.

Cessna 425 Corsair

Confusion: Golden Eagle, Cessna 401

Power: 2 × PT6A turboprops   *Span:* 44ft 1in (13.45m)   *Length:* 35ft 10in (10.9m)

A turboprop six/eight-seat pressurised business executive transport, the Corsair is based on the airframe of the 421 Golden Eagle. Design began on November 1, 1977, and construction of a prototype was initiated three months later on January 30, 1978. This flew for the first time on September 12, 1978, and construction of a pre-production aircraft was started during 1979. FAA certification was gained by mid-1980. Initial deliveries of definitive aircraft were made in November 1980 and the type is now in full production. At a cruising speed of 242 mph (389km/hr) the Corsair has a range of 1,895 miles (3,050km). A total of 1,100lb (499kg) of baggage and up to six passengers can be carried. *Country of origin:* USA.

Power: 2 × Continental piston engines   *Span:* 39ft 10in (12.15m)   *Length:* 36ft 1in (11m)

The Cessna 401 and 402 have basically similar airframes, the series having the names Utililiner and Businessliner for the six/eight-seat feeder and nine-seat executive versions. Several variants with differing cockpit, cabin and equipment standards have been built. Production of the 401 finished in 1972 and thereafter the 402 was standard. The 402 Businessliner has a maximum range of 1,639 miles (2,637km) and a maximum cruising speed of 218 mph (351km/hr). Wingtip tanks are fitted as standard. *Country of origin:* USA. *Silhouette:* Model 401B. *Picture:* Model 402.

Piper PA-31T Cheyenne II *Confusion:* T-1040, Merlin III

Power: 2 × PT6A turboprops   *Span:* 42ft 8in (13.01m)   *Length:* 34ft 8in (10.57m)

The first turboprop-powered Piper aircraft, the PA-31T Cheyenne II light transport first flew in 1969. The airframe is similar to that of the pressurised Navajo. Seating is provided for eight including the pilot. Large wingtip fuel tanks are fitted. Economical cruising speed is 244 mph (393km/hr) and range is 1,702 miles (2,739km). A lower-powered version is known as the Cheyenne I, while the Cheyenne II XL has a 2ft fuselage stretch. *Country of origin:* USA. *Silhouette:* Cheyenne I. *Picture:* Cheyenne II XL.

Power: 2 × Continental piston engines   *Span:* **44ft 1in (13.4m)**   *Length:* **36ft 4in (11.09m)**

Cessna introduced the pressurised twin-engined Model 414 on December 10, 1969, as a 'step-up' aircraft for owners of Cessna or other light unpressurised twins. It combined the basic fuselage and tail unit of the Model 421 with the wing of the Model 402 and had 310 hp turbocharged engines. Successor to the 414, the 414A Chancellor is a utility transport seating up to six passengers in a pressurised cabin. Major changes from the Model 414 included a new 'wet' wing of increased span, and extended nose and baggage area. First introduced in 1978, the Chancellor is available in I, II, and III versions with differing equipment. Maximum speed is 275 mph (443km/hr) and range at 166 mph (267km/hr) is 1,490 miles (2,340km). No wingtip tanks are fitted. *Country of origin:* USA.

Fairchild Swearingen Merlin III   *Confusion:* Jetstream 31

Power: 2 × TPE331 turboprops   *Span:* 46ft 3in (14.10m)   *Length:* 42ft 2in (12.85m)

Produced in large numbers, the Swearingen Merlin series of executive transports has been steadily developed since its introduction in 1966. The original version was an eight-seater with two PT6 engines (IIA). Re-engined with TPE331s, this became the Merlin IIB. Merlin IIIA is an 8/11 passenger stretched version with four large side windows. The IIIB is powered by uprated TPE331s. The pressurised IIIA has a cruising speed of 288 mph (463km/hr) and a range of 1,968 miles (3,167km). The latest version, the Merlin IIIC, was introduced in 1981. *Country of origin:* USA. *Silhouette:* Merlin IIIC. *Picture:* Merlin IIIB.

Power: **2 × PT6A turboprops**   *Span:* **41ft 1in (12.5m)**   *Length:* **36ft 8in (11.18m)**

A commuter airliner, the nine-passenger T-1040 combines the wings, nose and tail of the Cheyenne with the fuselage of the Chieftain and is powered by two 500 shp turboprops. The prototype T-1040 (T = transportation) first flew in July 1981 and production deliveries have now started. The aircraft is a product of the recently created Airline Division of Piper, which hopes to sell 100 – 150 units per year. With full payload the T-1040 has a range of 450 nautical miles (724km), flying at a cruising speed of 238kt (441km/hr). *Country of origin:* **USA**.

BAe Jetstream 31 *Confusion:* Merlin II/III

Power: 2 × TPE331 turboprops   *Span:* 52ft (15.85m)   *Length:* 47ft 1in (14.37m)

In its original form the Jetstream was developed by Handley Page and then Scottish Aviation. Thirty Astazou-powered Jetstreams 1 and 2 are still in civil service, while T1s and T2s are used by the RAF and the Royal Navy. British Aerospace Scottish Division (formerly Scottish Aviation) has now produced a much modified version called Jetstream 31, powered by two Garrett turboprops and aimed at the commuter and light business markets. A flight development aircraft flew in March 1980 and the first production aircraft was rolled out in January 1982. Production is being built up to 25 per annum in 1984. Jetstream 31 can carry eight passengers for 1,025 miles (1,649km) and has a maximum cruising speed of 303 mph (488km/hr). In executive shuttle layout the 31 carries 12 passengers. *Country of origin:* UK.

Power: 2 × Dart turboprops　　*Span:* 78ft 6in (23.92m)　　*Length:* 63ft 9in (19.43m)

A long-range twin-engined business aircraft, the Grumman Gulfstream I seats up to 24 passengers. The layout is similar to that of the BAe 748, particularly in the engine/undercarriage nacelle arrangement. Maximum cruising speed is 348 mph (560km/hr) and range with maximum fuel is 2,540 miles (4,088km). Military versions include the TC-4C for the US Navy and the VC-4A for the US Coast Guard. Over 200 Gulfstream Is have been built. Now in production is the 37-passenger Gulfstream I-C commuter airliner, with a 10ft 8in (3.25m) fuselage extension. *Country of origin:* USA. *Main silhouette:* Gulfstream I; *lower side view:* Gulfstream I-C. *Picture:* Gulfstream I.

BAe 748 *Confusion:* YS-11A, Gulfstream I

Power: 2 × Dart turboprops *Span:* **98ft 6in (30.02m)** *Length:* **67ft (20.42m)**

First flown in 1960, the 748 is still in production and over 360 examples have been sold so far. Seating up to 58 passengers and with a maximum cruising speed of 278 mph (448km/hr), the 748 has been sold to many civil and military operators around the world. India has built a large number of 748s under licence. The Andover C1 cargo version has an upswept rear fuselage with loading doors, while some variants have a large aft side-loading door. The latest military 748 is the Coastguarder for maritime patrol, with a radome under the nose. Other role equipment includes a chute for the dropping of dinghies and smoke floats. *Country of origin:* UK. *Main silhouette:* 748 Military Transport; *upper side view:* Andover C1. *Picture:* Coastguarder.

Power: **2 × Dart turboprops**   *Span:* **105ft (32m)**   *Length:* **86ft 3½in (26.3m)**

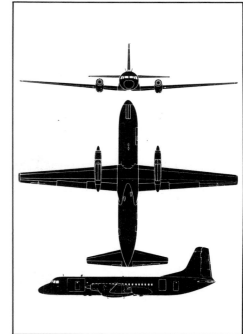

The YS-11A short/medium-range airliner went into service in 1965 and a total of 174 were built, including 22 for the Japan Maritime and Air Self-Defence Forces. The variants are designated -100, -200, -300, -400, -500 and -600. Up to 60 passengers can be carried at 290 mph (466km/hr) for 680 miles (1,090km). A big freight door can be fitted on the forward port side. The YS-11A is particularly large for a twin-engined machine. The type has been exported and some are in service in the United States. *Country of origin:* Japan. *Silhouette:* YS-11A-300. *Picture:* JMSDF YS-11A.

Saab-Fairchild 340

Confusion: Gulfstream I, Bandeirante

Power: 2 × CT7 turboprops   *Span:* 70ft 4in (21.44m)   *Length:* 64ft 8in (19.72m)

The first jointly designed and developed US-European transport aircraft, the Saab-Fairchild 340 is a 34-seater intended for economical operation over short-haul, low-density routes. To fly late in 1982, the aircraft is scheduled to be certificated in 1984, when it will go into service. Over 100 orders and paid options have been placed and production is to rise to six per month in 1986. Fairchild is building wings, tail and engine nacelles, while Saab makes the fuselage and undertakes final assembly. The 340 cruises at 243 mph (391km/hr) and has a range of 1,115 miles (1,795km) with maximum payload. *Country of origin:* Sweden/USA.

Embraer EMB-110 Bandeirante

Power: 2 × PT6A turboprops   *Span:* 50ft 3in (15.32m)   *Length:* 49ft 9in (15.08m)

A very successful commuter transport, the EMB-110 Bandeirante seats 21 passengers (in 110P2 form), cruises at 224 mph (360km/hr) and has a range of 1,191 miles (1,916km). First deliveries went to the Brazilian Air Force in 1973. There are twelve versions of the Bandeirante, including the 110P1 (quick-change passenger transport), B1 (aerial photography), S1 (geophysical survey), K1 (military transport with longer fuselage), 110A (navigation/landing aid calibration), 110E (eight-seat executive transport) and 111 (radar-equipped maritime patrol aircraft). Over 400 Bandeirantes are now in service. *Country of origin:* Brazil. *Silhouette:* EMB-110K1. *Picture:* EMB-111.

Piper PA-44 Seminole *Confusion:* Duchess

Power: 2 × Lycoming piston engines   *Span:* 38ft 6½in (11.75m)   *Length:* 27ft 7in (8.41m)

Bearing a close resemblance to the Beechcraft Duchess 76, the T-tail PA-44 Seminole is one of a new generation of American light aircraft intended for training and light transport duties. First flight was in 1976 and deliveries began in the spring of 1978. Although similar in appearance to other Piper aircraft, the Seminole is in fact a new design. Turbo Seminole is the name given to the turbo-supercharged version. Range is 960 miles (1,546km) and cruising speed 178 mph (286km/hr) *Country of origin:* USA. *Silhouette:* Seminole. *Picture:* Turbo Seminole.

Power: 2 × Lycoming piston engines   *Span:* 38ft (11.59m)   *Length:* 29ft (8.84m)

Embodying some parts from the single-engined Beechcraft Sierra, the Duchess 76 is a four-seat T-tail cabin monoplane designed for transport and training. The accent is on low cost and ease of production, and an unusual feature is the fitting of pilot doors on both sides of the aircraft. The Duchess first flew in production form in 1977. Several hundred have been delivered. Maximum cruising speed is 185 mph (298km/hr) and range is over 800 miles (1,290km). *Country of origin:* USA.

Piper PA-42 Cheyenne III *Confusion:* Super King Air 200, Duchess

Power: 2 × PT6A turboprops   *Span:* 47ft 8in (14.6m)   *Length:* 38ft (11.58m)

The latest addition to the Cheyenne family is the PA-42 Cheyenne III, with more wingspan, longer fuselage, uprated engines, more windows and a prominent T-tail. Wingtip fuel tanks are standard. Up to eight passengers can be carried in the cabin. Deliveries of the Cheyenne III began in 1978. Range is 1,968 miles (3,167km) and maximum cruising speed is 347 mph (558km/hr). *Country of origin:* USA.

Power: 2 × PT6A turboprops *Span:* 54ft 6in (16.61m) *Length:* 43ft 9in (13.34m)

The Super King Air 200 represents a major departure in Beech twin design, with a wing of much higher aspect ratio and a T-tail. The prototype flew in 1972 and deliveries continue. In addition to civil applications as a feederliner/executive aircraft, the type has been ordered by the USAF, US Navy and US Army as the C-12A/C/D, UC-12B and RU-21J. A geographic survey version is the Model 200T, and a further variant is known as the Maritime Patrol 200T. The Super King Air 200 cruises at 313 mph (503km/hr) and has a range of 2,172 miles (3,495km). *Country of origin:* USA. *Silhouette and picture:* Super King Air 200.

Embraer EMB-121 Xingu

Confusion: Super King Air 200, Pucara

Power: 2 × PT6A turboprops   *Span:* 46ft 1in (14.05m)   *Length:* 40ft 2in (12.25m)

A pressurised 5/6-passenger business aircraft, the EMB-121 Xingu first flew in 1976 and deliveries began in 1977. In addition to civilian sales, the Xingu has been bought by the Brazilian Air Force. Maximum cruising speed is 304 mph (489km/hr) and range is 1,343 miles (2,160km). The uprated Xingu II flew in 1981, and is now in production, while the Xingu III with more wingspan and a further increase in power is in flight test. *Country of origin:* Brazil. *Silhouette and picture:* Xingu I.

Power: 2 × Astazou turboprops   *Span:* 47ft 7in (14.50m)   *Length:* 46ft 9in (14.25m)

The IA 58 Pucara counter-insurgency (Coin) aircraft first flew in 1969. Highly manoeuvrable, the Pucara is capable of using very short rough fields. Two 20mm cannon and four machine guns are fitted in the fuselage and 3,307lb (1,500kg) of bombs, rockets or missiles are carried on one underfuselage and two underwing pylons. The Pucara is in service with the Argentinian Air Force. Maximum speed is 310 mph (500km/hr) and range is 1,890 miles (3,042km). The Argentinian Air Force has two squadrons equipped with the type and plans to acquire an eventual total of 100. The IA 58B Bravo version has two 30mm cannon instead of the 20mm weapons fitted to the initial version, and a redesigned fuselage. *Country of origin:* Argentina.

Beech 18 *Confusion:* Huanquero

Power: **2 × R-985 piston engines** *Span:* **49ft 8in (15.14m)** *Length:* **32ft 2½in (10.7m)**

The original Beech 18 entered production in 1937 and several thousand had been completed by the end of the Second World War. Civil manufacture recommenced after the war and development led to the E18, G18 and H18 Super models, of which over 750 were built. Compared with early marks, the later 18s have extended rectangular wingtips, various nose lengths and changed window shapes. The H18 Super 18 carries nine passengers for 1,530 miles (2,460km). Long-nose turboprop conversions of the Beech 18 by Hamilton Aviation are called the Westwind III and Westwind II STD. *Country of origin:* USA. *Silhouette:* Beech 18. *Picture:* H18 Super 18.

Power: 2 × IA 19R piston engines   *Span:* 64ft 3in (19.6m)   *Length:* 45ft 10in (13.98m)

A light seven-passenger military transport and trainer, the IA 35 Huanquero first flew in 1953 and production totalled 31 examples. They have been used for bombing and gunnery training, crew training and ambulance and photographic work in addition to their basic transport role. Maximum cruising speed is 217 mph (350km/hr) and range is 975 miles (1,570km). When carried, armament consists of two machine guns and 440lb (200kg) of underwing weapons. *Country of origin:* Argentina.

Let L-200 Morava   *Confusion: —*

Power: 2 × M337 piston engines   *Span:* 40ft 4½in (12.31m)   *Length:* 28ft 3in (8.61m)

The successor to the Aero 145, the L-200 Morava is a four/five-seat light business aircraft first flown in 1957. Over 400 have been built and many have been exported within Eastern Europe. The three versions—the L-200, L-200A and L-200D—are all similar in external appearance. The Morava can be converted to carry two stretchers. Cruising speed is 159 mph (256km/hr) and range 1,063 miles (1,710km). *Country of origin:* **Czechoslovakia**. *Silhouette and picture:* L-200.

With only two exceptions, the aircraft in this class are basically transports, though varying widely in size.

The Partenavia Victor and MU-2 look alike, the points of difference being the depth of the fin, nose and engine nacelle shape, and the wingtip tanks on the MU-2.

There is a superficial resemblance between the Commander and the P.166, but close examination reveals that the P.166 has a "gull" wing, clearly seen in the head-on view. The P.166's engines are also mounted pusher-fashion on the wing trailing edge. The Turbolet and the Frégate have similar layouts, including the mounting of the main undercarriage in fuselage sponsons. The Frégate fuselage is longer, however, and the fin is unswept. These two types could also be confused with the Pembroke. The Dornier 228 is characterised by a long nose and sharply backward-tapered wingtips.

The Tracker anti-submarine aircraft can look like some of the transports but it is usually seen with underwing stores.

The Herald, Friendship, Coke, Clank and Cline can all be confused. Points to note are wing planforms, nose/cockpit shape and engine nacelle shape; the last-mentioned is most significant on Cline, which has very deep nacelles perched on top of the wing.

The Caribou and Buffalo have a distinctive "sit," with long, upswept rear fuselages. Buffalo is further distinguished by a tall T-tail.

The Provider, G.222, Transall and Aviocar are similar in general layout but vary in size and have various particular points of difference. With its auxiliary turbojets and fuel tanks under the wing, the Provider can at times look as if it has six engines. The Transall has much more fuselage forward of the wing than the others, and the Aviocar has a fixed undercarriage.

The veteran Bristol Freighter is almost in a class of its own, with its box-like fuselage and stalky fixed undercarriage. It might however be confused with the much smaller Islander

de Havilland Canada DHC-6 Twin Otter

Pilatus Britten-Norman Trislander

The designers of the Clod, Clash, Skyvan and Shorts 330 all chose a high-aspect-ratio strutted wing and twin fins. Fuselage shapes are nevertheless very different, and the 330 has a retractable undercarriage. The Shorts 360 is more streamlined than the 330 and has a single, swept fin.

Everything about the Hawkeye is bulky, including fuselage, nacelles and fins. The massive radar scanner, mounted over the fuselage, completes the picture.

and Trislander, although fuselage and wing shapes are very different. Apart from its very long fuselage, Trislander is unique in having a third piston engine mounted high on the fin.

Dornier has put its own particular stamp on the Do 28B and the Skyservant, leaving the wing clear by mounting the engines and main undercarriage on stub wings protruding from the fuselage. Like the Freighter, the two Dornier designs have tailwheel undercarriages.

While the Twin Otter and Nomad have some points in common, the Twin Otter's fixed undercarriage looks very different from the Nomad's stub-wing-mounted arrangement.

Grumman E-2 Hawkeye

Power: 2 × Lycoming piston engines   *Span:* 46ft 7in (14.2m)   *Length:* 43ft (13.10m)

Beginning in 1948 with the Aero Commander, the Commander range is very extensive and many hundreds have been produced. From the 520 six-seater the design progressed to the Grand Commander with a longer fuselage and accommodation for nine passengers. Also in the series are the Shrike Commander four-seater, the shorter-wing, pressurised, eight-seat Hawk Commander, and a Garrett AiResearch turboprop version of the Hawk, the Commander Jetprop 840. Other versions are the Jetprop 980 and 1000. The 840 has a range with maximum payload of 1,233 miles (1,985km) at 285 mph (460km/hr). *Country of origin:* USA. *Silhouette:* Aero Commander. *Picture:* Commander Jetprop 900.

Mitsubishi MU-2 *Confusion:* Turbolet

Power: 2 × TPE331 turboprops *Span:* 39ft 2in (11.94m) *Length:* 39ft 5in (12.02m)

A utility transport first flown in 1963, the MU-2 seats up to 11 passengers. Various versions, from the MU-2A to P, vary in power, weights and performance. The MU-2E, fitted with a thimble-shaped nose radome, is used by the Japan Air Self-Defence Force for rescue work. Wingtip tanks are standard. MU-2s are now assembled in the United States at a plant in Texas. The MU-2N has a cruising speed of 300 mph (480km/hr) and a range of 1,450 miles (2,330km). The MU-2N is called the Marquise and the MU-2P the Solitaire. *Country of origin:* Japan/USA. *Main silhouette:* MU-2B; *upper side view:* MU-2J. *Picture:* MU-2J.

Power: 2 × M601 or 2 × PT6A turboprops   *Span:* 57ft 4in (17.48m)   *Length:* 44ft 8in (13.61m)

A light passenger/freight transport, the L-410 Turbolet first flew in 1969. Cruising at 236 mph (380km/hr) for up to 124 miles (200km), the Turbolet carries 17/19 passengers. The first production version, the L-410A, is powered by American PT6A engines, while the L-410M has two Czech M601A turboprops. A survey/photographic version, the L-410AF, has a large glazed nose on which is mounted a non-retractable nosewheel. Current production model is the L-410UVP, with increased span, larger fin and tailplane dihedral. *Country of origin:* Czechoslovakia. *Silhouette:* L-410A. *Picture:* L-410UVP.

Piaggio P.166 *Confusion:* MU-2

Power: 2 × Lycoming piston engines or 2 × Lycoming turboprops   *Span:* 48ft 2½in (14.69m)   *Length:* 39ft 3in (11.9m)

Produced in large numbers, the P.166 with two pusher engines was first flown in 1957. This light transport, seating up to nine passengers, has been built in both military and civil forms. Current versions are the P.166-DL2 with piston engines and P.166-DL3 with turboprops; the latter first flew in 1976. Wingtip tanks are fitted as standard. A maritime surveillance version is known as the P.166-DL3-MAR. Economical cruising speed of the -DL3 is 186 mph (300km/hr) and range with maximum payload 460 miles (741km). *Country of origin:* Italy. *Silhouette:* P.166-DL3. *Picture:* P.166M.

Power: 2 × TPE331 turboprops   *Span:* 55ft 7in (16.97m)   *Length* (-200): 54ft 3in (16.55m)

The Dornier Do 228 commuter transport is a combination of a new-technology wing with the modified fuselage of the Do 128 and a retractable undercarriage. The basic Do 228-100 has a length of 49ft 4in (15.03m) and seats 15 passengers, while the -200 is longer and seats 19. Both versions are fitted with Garrett AiResearch turboprops. The 228-100 was due to go into service in Norway in the summer of 1982, following first flights by the -100 and -200 in 1981. Over 20 Do 228s have been ordered and production at a rate of five per month is planned. Economical cruising speed is 206 mph (332km/hr) and range (Do 228-200) is 715 miles (1,150km). *Country of origin:* West Germany. *Silhouette:* -200. *Picture:* -100.

Aérospatiale N 262/Frégate

Confusion: Turbolet, Pembroke

Power: 2 × Bastan turboprops   *Span:* 71ft 10in (21.90m)   *Length:* 63ft 3in (19.28m)

Descended from an earlier unpressurised transport, the Nord N 260 Super Broussard, the pressurised N 262/Frégate short-range airliner is used by civil and military operators. First flown in 1962, the 262 has been produced in four series: A, B, C and D. Only four Bs were built and the standard basic production version was the 262A. A few Series C with more powerful engines were built; military counterpart of the C is the Series D for the French Air Force. The 262C cruises at 247 mph (397km/hr) over a range of 1,490 miles (2,400km) with 26 passengers. *Country of origin:* France. *Silhouette and picture:* Series C.

Power: 2 × Leonides piston engines   *Span:* 64ft 6in (19.6m)   *Length:* 46ft (14m)

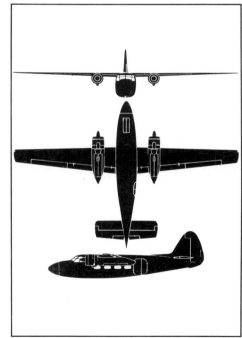

Still in service with the RAF as a six/ten-seat communications and light transport, the Pembroke C1 first flew in 1952. Derived from the civil Prince transport, the Pembroke was supplied to a number of air forces. Some Pembrokes were used for photographic purposes. Double freight doors are fitted on the port side. Cruising speed is 155 mph (255km/hr) and range 1,150 miles (1,850km). The RAF's Pembroke C1s were fitted with new wing main spars during the early 1970s to prolong their service lives. The Royal Swedish Air Force operates two ten-passenger Pembroke 52s. *Country of origin:* UK. *Silhouette and Picture:* C1.

277

Grumman S-2/C-1 Tracker/Trader   *Confusion:* Pembroke, Herald

Power: 2 × R-1820 piston engines   *Span* (S-2D to -2G): 72ft 7in (22.13m)   *Length:* 43ft 6in (13.26m)

Used on land or aboard aircraft carriers, the Grumman S-2 Tracker is an anti-submarine aircraft. A carrier on-board delivery version, the C-1 Trader, can seat nine passengers. The Tracker first flew in 1953 and carries homing torpedoes, depth bombs and depth charges internally and torpedoes, rockets or bombs under the wings. Various versions were built, from the S-2A to the -2G, and over 1,000 of the type were produced. With a normal crew of four, the Tracker has a maximum speed of 265 mph (426km/hr) and nine hours' endurance. Non-US Tracker operators include the Australian Navy, Canada, Argentina, Turkey, Peru, Brazil, South Korea and the Japan Maritime Self-Defence Force. *Country of origin:* USA. *Silhouette:* S-2D. *Picture:* S-2A

Power: 2 × Dart turboprops   *Span:* 94ft 9in (28.88m)   *Length:* 75ft 6in (23.01m)

Produced in prototype form with four Leonides piston engines, the Herald short-haul airliner was put into production with two Rolls-Royce Dart turboprops. Initial version was the Series 100, followed by the Series 200 seating up to 50 passengers. The military transport version, carrying freight or troops, is known as the Series 400. The Herald cruises at 275 mph (443km/hr) for up to 700 miles (1,125km). Range with maximum fuel, standard tankage, and no reserves is 1,760 miles (2,830km). Maximum payload is 11,700lb (5,300kg), and service ceiling at an all-up weight of 35,000lb (15,875kg) is 27,900ft (8,500m). Some 48 Heralds were built. *Country of origin:* UK. *Silhouette and picture:* Series 200.

279

Fokker F.27 Friendship

Confusion: Herald, Coke/Curl, Tracker

Power: 2 × Dart turboprops   *Span:* **95ft 2in (29m)**   *Length* (Mk 500): **82ft 2½in (25.06m)**

Orders for the F.27 Friendship short/medium-haul airliner have totalled over 750 since it first flew in 1955, and the type remains in production. The Friendship was built under licence in the USA as the FH-227. Variants are the Mks 100, 200, 300, 400/600 and the long-fuselage, 52-passenger 500. The Mk 500 also has a large side freight door. Friendships are in use as military and civil transports, and underwing long-range tanks can be fitted. For maritime patrol Fokker offers the F.27 Maritime with a radome under the fuselage. The Mk 500 has a cruising speed of 298 mph (480km/hr) and a range of 1,082 miles (1,741km/hr). *Country of origin:* **Netherlands.** *Main silhouette:* Mk 500; *upper side view:* FH-227. *Picture:* F.27 Maritime.

Antonov An-24/An-26 Coke/Curl

Power: 2 × Ivchenko turboprops   *Span:* 95ft 9½in (29.2m)   *Length:* 77ft 2½in (23.53m)

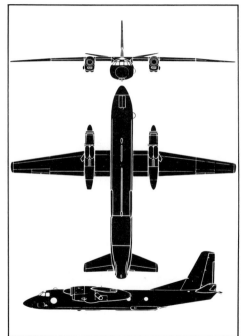

Over 1,000 Antonov An-24 transports, code-named Coke, have been built since the type first flew in 1960. Initially fitted with 44 seats, the aircraft was developed to accommodate 50 passengers as the -24V. A subsequent variant was fitted with higher-powered engines and modified wing. An under-fuselage rear door is fitted to the -24T, while the -24RT and -24RV each have an auxiliary turbojet in the starboard nacelle. The An-26 Curl is a development with an upswept rear fuselage and enlarged rear loading ramp. The basic An-24V Series II has a range of 1,490 miles (2,400km) and a cruising speed of 280 mph (450km/hr). *Country of origin:* USSR. *Silhouette and picture:* An-26.

Antonov An-30 Clank

Confusion: Coke/Curl, Cline, Friendship

Power: 2 × Ivchenko turboprops   *Span:* 95ft 9½in (29.2m)   *Length:* 79ft 7in (24.26m)

Designed for aerial survey, the An-30, code-named Clank, is a direct development of the An-24 Coke. It is fitted with a longer glazed nose and a raised flight deck. Cameras are mounted in the fuselage, which has its own darkroom, and a computer controls the flight profile. The An-30 has fewer windows than the passenger versions of the An-24. An auxiliary turbojet is mounted in the starboard nacelle. This is used for engine starting, and for take-off, climb and cruise power in the event of main engine failure. The An-30's primary role is aerial photography for map-making, for which it is equipped with large survey cameras mounted above four apertures in the cabin floor. The openings are covered by doors which can be opened under remote control from the crew photographer's station. *Country of origin:* USSR.

Power: 2 × Ivchenko turboprops   *Span:* 95ft 9½in (29.2m)   *Length:* 78ft 1in (23.8m)

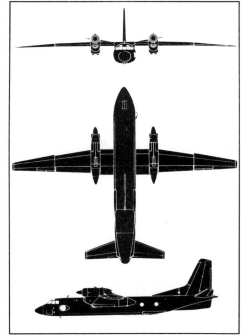

A major increase in power is the main feature of the An-32 Cline, which is a direct development of the An-24 Coke. Main differences are bigger engine nacelles mounted over the wings and a greatly enlarged ventral fin. Higher power gives the Cline better airfield performance, particularly at high altitudes and temperatures. Payloads include 39 passengers, 30 parachutists or 24 stretchers. A rear loading door is fitted. Range is 1,367 miles (2,200km). Operating from airfields 12,125-14,750ft (4,000-4,500m) above sea level, the An-32 can carry 6,600lb (3,000kg) of freight for 680 miles (1,100km). *Country of origin:* USSR.

DHC DHC-4A Caribou *Confusion:* Buffalo

Power: 2 × R-2000 piston engines   *Span:* 95ft 7in (29.15m)   *Length:* 72ft 7in (22.13m)

A short take-off and landing (Stol) utility transport, the DHC-4A Caribou first flew in 1958. The civil variant accommodates 30 passengers, while in military service 32 troops, three tons (3,050kg) of freight, two jeeps or stretchers can be carried. Under the upswept rear fuselage there is a large single loading door. In Canadian Forces service the Caribou is known as the CC-108. The US Army ordered 159 CV-2 Caribous. These aircraft were later taken over by the USAF, which designated them C-7A. Range is 1,307 miles (2,103km) and cruising speed 182 mph (293km/hr). *Country of origin:* Canada.

DHC DHC-5 Buffalo/Transporter

Power: 2 × CT64 turboprops   *Span:* 96ft (29.26m)   *Length:* 79ft (24.08m)

Originally called the DHC-5 Caribou II, the Stol turboprop development of the Caribou was renamed Buffalo. A military transport, the Buffalo carries 41 troops, jeeps, stretchers or freight loaded through an underfuselage rear door. The Caribou first flew in 1964. In USAF service it is known as the C-8A, and as the CC-115 with the Canadian Forces. Specially equipped Buffalos are used for maritime patrol. Range is 691 miles (1,112km) at a maximum cruising speed of 261 mph (420km/hr). The 44-seat civil passenger/cargo version of the DHC-5D Buffalo is the DHC-5E Transporter. *Country of origin:* Canada.

Fairchild C-123 Provider *Confusion:* G.222, Transall

Power: 2 × R-2800 piston engines and 2 × J44 turbojets   *Span:* 110ft (33.53m)   *Length:* 76ft 3in (23.93m)

A tactical assault transport, the C-123 Provider can carry up to 60 equipped troops, stretchers or cargo. It was first flown in 1949 and production totalled 307. Originally produced as C-123Bs, 183 Providers were later converted to C-123K standard with underwing auxiliary jets. A further 10 were fitted with wingtip jets as the C-123H. Equipped with spraying gear for mosquito control, the Provider becomes the UC-123B. Underwing fuel tanks are standard, while some Providers have nose radomes. C-123s were supplied to air forces in the Far East and South America. *Country of origin:* USA. *Silhouette:* C-123K. *Picture:* C-123H.

Power: 2 × T64 turboprops *Span:* 94ft 2in (28.7m) *Length:* 74ft 5½in (22.7m)

A general-purpose pressurised military transport, the G.222 is in production for the Italian Air Force and export customers. Capable of operating from rough strips, the 222 can carry 44 equipped troops, 36 stretchers or freight loaded through a large underside rear door. The prototype 222 first flew in 1970 and the type can also be used for firefighting, cropspraying and maritime surveillance. A version re-engined with Rolls-Royce Tyne turboprops for export is known as the G.222T. Range of the G.222 is 435 miles (700km) and continuous cruising speed is 224 mph (360km/hr). *Country of origin:* Italy. *Silhouette:* G.222. *Picture:* G.222T.

Transporter Allianz C-160 Transall

Confusion: G.222, Provider, Aviocar

Power: 2 × Tyne turboprops   *Span:* 131ft 3in (40m)   *Length:* 106ft 3½in (32.4m)

A joint Franco-German development, the C-160 Transall is a general-purpose military transport. It can carry up to 93 troops, freight or vehicles. A total of 179 were produced before production ceased in 1972. The line has since been reopened and production resumed. The aircraft of the new batch have updated electronics, increased maximum take-off weight, and a reinforced wing embodying an optional fuel tank. Surveillance, electronic warfare and airborne command versions are on offer. As well as France and Germany, South Africa and Turkey also use the Transall. The aircraft can operate from semi-prepared surfaces. Cruising speed is 306 mph (492km/hr) and range 730 miles (1,175km). *Country of origin:* France/Germany.

Power: 2 × TPE331 turboprops   *Span:* **62ft 4in (19m)**   *Length:* **49ft 9in (15.16m)**

Used for both military and civil purposes, the Aviocar is a Stol utility transport, trainer and survey aircraft. More than 300 have been sold, and there are production centres in Spain and Indonesia. The C-212-5 Series 100, the first production version, has now been superseded on the line by the Series 200 with more powerful engines and greater weight. In civil transport form the Aviocar seats up to 26 passengers, cruises at 216 mph (347km/hr) and has a range of 230 miles (370km) with full payload. An anti-submarine and maritime patrol version with a nose radome has been developed. *Country of origin:* Spain. *Silhouette:* Series 200. *Picture:* Series 100.

Bristol Freighter/Wayfarer *Confusion:* —

Power: 2 × Hercules piston engines   *Span:* 108ft (32.92m)   *Length* (Mk 31): 68ft 4in (20.83m)

Following a first flight in 1945, a total of 214 Bristol 170 short-range freighter aircraft were built. Originally intended for military use as the Freighter, the 170 was known as the Wayfarer in civil passenger and mixed passenger/freight form. The type has been widely used as a car ferry, loading through clamshell doors in the nose. Most of the civil 170s produced were Mks 31E and 31M. The Mk 32, of which 20 were built, features a long nose and enlarged fin. The Mk 31 has a range of 820 miles (1,320km) and a cruising speed of 164 mph (264km/hr). Instone Air Line uses 170s for carrying racehorses and cargo in the UK, and the type is also in service in New Zealand. *Country of origin:* UK. *Silhouette and picture:* Mk 31E.

Power: 2 × Lycoming piston engines   *Span:* 49ft (14.94m)   *Length* (long nose): 39ft 5in (12.02m)

First flown in 1965, the 10-passenger BN-2 Islander light transport has sold all over the world and over 900 have been ordered. Licence production is going on in Romania and the Philippines. Compared with earlier versions, the BN-2A-85 Islander has a longer nose and an extra rear cabin window on each side. Military variants with underwing stores are the Defender and the Maritime Defender. Tip tanks can be fitted. Range at a cruising speed of 160 mph (257km/hr) is 870 miles (1,400km). Latest version is the BN-2-T Turbine Islander, powered by two Allison turboprops and offering 10kt more cruising speed. *Country of origin:* UK.*Silhouette:* BN-2A-85. *Picture:* BN-2-T.

Pilatus Britten-Norman Trislander *Confusion:* Islander

Power: 3 × Lycoming piston engines   *Span:* 53ft (16.15m)   *Length* (Mk III-2): 43ft 9in (13.33m)

The BN-2A Trislander is derived from the twin-engined Islander and has 75 per cent of its components in common. Essential difference is the fitting of a third engine in the redesigned fin. Some Trislanders have been produced with a short nose, while the Mk III-2 has a long nose. The Mk III-4 embodies a rocket motor for use in the event of engine failure on take-off. Trislanders were produced in Belgium for a time. The aircraft carries 16/17 passengers, cruises at 175 mph (282km/hr) and has a range with maximum payload of 160 miles (257km). Over 80 Trislanders have been delivered to operators in the UK, Africa, Australia, USA, Canada, Indonesia and South America. *Country of origin:* UK. *Silhouette and picture:* Mk III-2.

Power: 2 × Lycoming piston engines or 2 × Allison 250 turboprops   *Span:* 39ft 4½in (12m)   *Length:* 30ft 8in (9.35m)

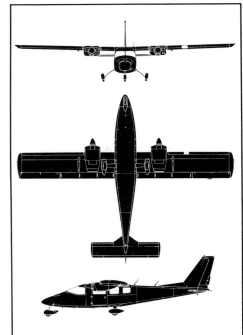

A streamlined light transport, the original P.68 was first put into production in 1964. A variety of versions have emerged, including the six-passenger P.68B, the P.68R with retractable undercarriage, P.68C, currently in production, and P.68TC with turbosupercharged engines. An Italian/German development, the P.68 Observer, has a transparent nose and is designed for police and observation duties. Cruising speed of the P.68B is 184 mph (296km/hr) and range 1,029 miles (1,656km). Aeritalia is now developing a turboprop, retractable-undercarriage version designated AP.68B. *Country of origin:* Italy. *Silhouette:* P.68C. *Picture:* P.68R.

Dornier Do 28B

Confusion: Skyservant

Power: 2 × Lycoming piston engines   *Span:* 45ft 3½in (13.80m)   *Length:* 29ft 6in (9m)

A twin-engined version of the Do 27, the Do 28 seven-passenger light transport retains the basic wings and fuselage of the single-engined type. Some 120 Do 28s were built, including military aircraft and six floatplanes. First flight was in 1959. The nose was redesigned, the tailplane enlarged and wingspan increased to produce the Do 28B1. The B2 has supercharged engines. Maximum cruising speed of the B1 is 170 mph (274km/hr) and range 768 miles (1,235km). *Country of origin:* West Germany. *Silhouette:* Do 28B1. *Picture:* Do 28B2

Dornier Do 28D/Do 128 Skyservant

Power: 2 × Lycoming piston engines or 2 × LTP101 turboprops   *Span:* 51ft (15.55m)   *Length:* 37ft 5in (11.41m)

Retaining the same layout as the Do 28 but virtually a complete redesign, the Do 28D Skyservant first flew in 1966. A Stol utility transport, the Skyservant seats up to 14 passengers or can carry freight. Six air forces have bought Skyservants, the largest operator being the Luftwaffe with 101. Now on the line are the Do 128-2 Skyservant and the turboprop-powered Do 128-6. *Country of origin:* West Germany. *Silhouette:* Do 28D2. *Picture:* Do 128-6.

GAF Nomad   *Confusion:* Skyvan, Twin Otter

Power: 2 × Allison 250 turboprops   *Span:* 54ft (16.46m)   *Length:* 47ft 1in (14.35m)

A twin-turboprop high-wing utility transport and feederliner, the GAF Nomad first flew in 1971. The prototype was known as the N2, while the initial production variant is the 17-passenger N22B. Patrol and surveillance versions of the N22B are known as the Search Master B and L. For general-purpose military work the N22B is known as the Mission Master. Latest version of the Nomad is the N24 with increased fuselage length and seating for 19 passengers. The N24 Nomad has a range of 985 miles (1,585km) and a cruising speed of 167 mph (269km/hr). *Country of origin:* Australia. *Silhouette:* N22B. *Picture:* N24A.

DHC DHC-6 Twin Otter

Power: 2 × PT6A turboprops   *Span:* 65ft (19.81m)   *Length:* 51ft 9in (15.77m)

A general-purpose civil and military transport, the DHC-6 Twin Otter can operate from short, rough fields and accommodate up to 20 passengers or freight. First flown in 1965, the Twin Otter has been built in three forms, the 100, 200 and 300 series. Service designations are CC-138 (Canadian Forces) and UV-18A (US Army). Maximum cruising speed is 210 mph (337km/hr), at which the range is 1,103 miles (1,775km). The floatplane version has a short nose and small additional fins above and below the tailplane. A Twin Otter Series 300 supplied to China for survey work has a nose probe and wingtip pods. *Country of origin:* Canada. *Silhouette:* Series 200. *Picture:* UV-18A.

Antonov An-14 Clod *Confusion:* Skyvan, Cash

Power: 2 × Ivchenko piston engines   *Span:* 72ft 2in (21.99m)   *Length:* 37ft 6in (11.44m)

A rough-field Stol utility transport, the An-14, code-named Clod, was produced in quantity, mainly for Aeroflot. With a one-man crew, the Clod has seating for seven passengers. The prototype flew in 1958 but production was delayed for a major redesign to the present standard, with a high-aspect-ratio wing and large endplate fins. In the Soviet Union the Clod is known as the Pchelka ("Little Bee"). Clamshell rear doors simplify freight loading. Cruising speed is 112 mph (180km/hr). *Country of origin:* USSR.

Power: 2 × Isotov turboprops   *Span:* 72ft 2in (22m)   *Length:* 42ft 7in (12.98m)

A development of the An-14 Clod, the An-28 Cash is a 19-passenger light utility transport intended to replace the old An-2 biplane. Like the Clod, the Cash has a high-aspect-ratio braced wing, sponson-mounted undercarriage and rear doors. The fuselage is however a completely different shape, as are the twin fins. Cash is also used for parachute training, rescue, cropspraying and firefighting. Cargo can be carried. *Country of origin:* USSR.

Shorts Skyvan

Confusion: Shorts 330, Shorts 360, Skyservant, Clod, Cash

Power: 2 × TPE331 turboprops   *Span:* 64ft 11in (19.79m)   *Length:* 40ft 1in (12.21m)

A rugged Stol general-purpose transport, the Skyvan originally flew in 1963 with piston engines. It was then fitted with French Astazou turboprops and finally with Garrett AiResearch turboprops. Some 130 Skyvans have been built for military, paramilitary and civil use. The Skyliner feederliner can carry up to 19 passengers, while freighter versions can lift 4,600lb (2,085kg) of cargo or vehicles. Freight is loaded through an underside rear door. Skyvan Series 3 has a range of 694 miles (1,115km) and a maximum cruising speed of 195 mph (314km/hr). *Country of origin:* UK. *Silhouette and picture:* Series 3.

Power: **2 × PT6A turboprops**   *Span:* **74ft 8in (22.76m)**   *Length:* **58ft (17.69m)**

A 30-seat feederliner and utility transport, the Shorts 330 is similar in basic configuration to the smaller Skyvan. The fuselage is rectangular in cross-section and the wing has a high aspect ratio. Unlike the Skyvan, the 330 has a retractable undercarriage. The 330 has been sold in the UK, Canada, the USA and Germany. A military version for troop/freight/vehicle transport is proposed, as is a maritime surveillance variant with nose radar. The 330-200, now on the line, has uprated engines and offers as standard a number of features which are available only as options on the basic 330. Maximum take-off weight is increased by 300lb (135kg) from the 22,600lb (10,250kg) of the 330. *Country of origin:* **UK**. *Silhouette and picture:* 330.

Shorts 360 *Confusion:* Shorts 330, Nomad

Power: 2 × PT6A turboprops   *Span:* 74ft 8in (22.75m)   *Length:* 70ft 6in (21.49m)

Retaining the high-aspect-ratio wing of the Shorts 330, the new 360 differs from the former in having a 3ft extension in the forward fuselage and a redesigned rear fuselage with a single swept fin. Flown for the first time in 1981, the 360 is now in production at Belfast alongside the 330. A short-range commuter transport, the 360 carries 36 passengers and cruises at 243 mph (391km/hr), and has a maximum range of 655 miles (1,054km). Deliveries began in the last quarter of 1982. *Country of origin:* UK.

Power: 2 × T56 turboprops   *Span:* 80ft 7in (24.56m)   *Length:* 57ft 7in (17.55m)

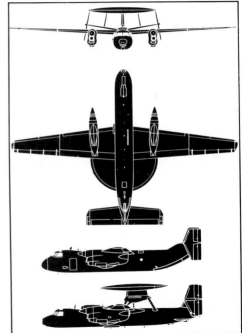

The first US Navy turboprop-powered type to enter service, the E-2 Hawkeye is a carrierborne early-warning aircraft. Virtually an airborne radar station, the Hawkeye carries a massive oval radome mounted above the fuselage and houses complex electronic gear operated by a five-man crew. The differences between the various Hawkeye versions (E-2A, B and C) lie in the radar and internal equipment. The transport version of Hawkeye is the C-2A Greyhound, which can accommodate 39 passengers, stretchers or cargo. The aircraft has a range of 1,650 miles (2,660km). *Country of origin:* USA. *Main silhouette:* E-2C; *upper side view:* C-2A. *Picture:* E-2C.

Four propellers

The Shackleton apart, this class of aircraft is made up of transports and their derivatives. The types range from the Heron light transport to giants like the Guppy and the An-22 Cook.

From some angles the Heron can be mistaken for the larger, tubbier Viscount. One quick clue is the length of the engine nacelles forward of the leading edge on the Viscount. The Viscount's Dart turboprops and the Heron's Gipsy Queen piston engines also sound very different.

Though the Viscount and Vanguard obviously come from the same stable, the Vanguard is larger, longer and has deeper inner nacelles. The Vanguard can also be mistaken for the Soviet Coot, which is slimmer and lacks the dihedral tailplane of the former. May is like its stablemate the Coot, with the addition of a belly radome and the long magnetic anomaly detector in the tail.

Lockheed P-3 Orion

The Orion maritime reconnaissance aircraft and the Electra transport parallel the May and Coot. A particular feature of the Orion/Electra is the wide spacing of the engines on a relatively short wing.

de Havilland Canada Dash 7

The DC-4, DC-6 and DC-7 all have a family resemblance, differing in length and nose, nacelle and fin shape. The DC-7's rival, the Britannia, is much more square-cut and has longer engine nacelles.

Canadair's CL-44 makes no secret of its Britannia ancestry.

The Shackleton has distinctive twin fins and the large radome of the AEW variant is clearly visible.

Boeing's Stratofreighter has a deep double-bubble fuselage. Students should be wary of relying on a sight of the tail flight-refuelling boom, as in some cases it is missing. The newest Stratofreighter/Stratocruiser derivative, the Guppy, is so unusual as to be virtually impossible to mistake for anything else.

The Hercules and the Cub require careful study, one useful feature being the marked anhedral on the Cub's outer wing panels. The Dash 7 is notable for its T-tail and massive flap arrangement, while the very large Soviet Cock freighter is in a class on its own.

Power: 4 × Gipsy Queen piston engines   *Span:* 71ft 6in (21.8m)   *Length:* 48ft 6in (14.8m)

A scaled-up, four-engined Dove, the Heron first flew in 1950 and altogether 150 were built. As a short-range light transport the Heron seats 14/17, cruises at 225 mph (362km/hr) and has a range of 1,180 miles (1,900km). Herons are used as executive aircraft and there have been a variety of re-engined conversions, including the Shin Meiwa DH 114TAW, the Saunders ST-27 and the Riley Turbo Skyliner. Powered by four 290 hp Lycoming engines with Rajay turbo-superchargers, the Turbo Skyliner has a maximum level speed at 12,000ft (3,660mph) of 285 mph (495km/hr); cruising speed at 75 per cent power of 225 mph (362km/hr); service ceiling of 20,000ft (6,100m); and a two-engines-out service ceiling of 15,000ft (4,570m). A total of 18 Riley Turbo Skyliners were converted from Heron Series 2X, 2A and 2DA aircraft. *Country of origin:* UK. *Silhouette:* Heron. *Picture:* Riley Turbo Skyliner.

Vickers Viscount *Confusion:* Heron, Vanguard

Power: 4 × Dart turboprops *Span* (700): 93ft 8½in (28.56m) *Length* (700): 81ft 10in (25.04m)

The world's first turboprop transport to go into service, the Viscount short-range airliner first flew in 1948 and 441 were built. The first production version was the Series 700 with up to 59 passengers. This was followed by the stretched 800 series with seating for up to 65 passengers. The Viscount remains in service in many countries. Several 700s and 800 were built or converted for executive use. Scottish Aviation designed a convertible passenger/cargo interior for Series 800 Viscounts. Nine pallets can be loaded and maximum cargo weight is 14,900lb (6,759kg). The 700 cruises at 312 mph (502km/hr) and has a range of 1,750 miles (2,815km). *Country of origin:* UK. *Main silhouette:* Viscount Series 800; *upper side view:* Viscount Series 700. *Picture:* Viscount Series 700.

Power: 4 × Tyne turboprops   *Span:* 118ft 7in (36.15m)   *Length:* 122ft 10½in (37.45m)

Designed to a British European Airways specification, the Type 951 Vanguard first flew in 1959. It was expected to be a major successor to the Viscount, but the advent of pure-jet aircraft like the Caravelle precluded large-scale production. Altogether 43 Vanguards were built, of which nine were converted into Merchantman freighters. As a passenger-carrying aircraft the Vanguard seats up to 139 passengers, has a maximum cruising speed of 425 mph (684km/hr) and a range of 1,830 miles (2,945km). *Country of origin:* UK. *Silhouette and picture:* Vanguard.

Ilyushin Il-18 Coot

Confusion: Vanguard, May, Orion, Electra

Power: 4 × Ivchenko turboprops   *Span:* 122ft 8½in (37.40m)   *Length:* 117ft 9in (35.9m)

Over 800 Il-18 Coot medium-range airliners were built and the type was exported to a number of countries. It first came into service in 1959 and was known in Russia as the Moskva. Several versions were produced, including the Il-18V with 89/100 passengers and the Il-18D with 122 passengers. The Il-18D cruises at 388 mph (625km/hr) over ranges of up to 4,040 miles (6,500km). A military development is the electronic surveillance Coot-A, with forward fuselage side bulges, a large underfuselage pannier and dorsal aerial fairings. The pannier, measuring 33ft 7½in (10.25m) long by 3ft 9in (1.15m) deep, is believed to house sideways-looking radar. Similar containers, measuring 14ft 5in (4.4m) long by 2ft 10½in (0.88m) deep, are mounted on either side of the forward fuselage. They are assumed to contain cameras or other sensors. *Country of origin:* USSR. *Silhouette and picture:* Il-18.

Power: 4 × Ivchenko turboprops   *Span:* 122ft 9in (37.4m)   *Length:* 131ft (39.92m)

Like the American Orion, the Il-38, code-named May, is a civil airliner developed for maritime reconnaissance and anti-submarine warfare. The May marries the wings and tail assembly of Coot to a new fuselage with a bulbous radome under the forward section and a magnetic anomaly detector (MAD) fairing extending from the tail. May has a cruising speed of 370 mph (595km/hr) and a range of 4,500 miles (7,240km). Armament includes homing torpedoes and depth charges. *Country of origin:* USSR.

Lockheed L-188 Electra *Confusion:* Orion, Coot, May

Power: 4 × Allison 501 turboprops   *Span:* 99ft (30.18m)   *Length:* 104ft 6½in (31.81m)

A medium-range four-turboprop airliner, the Lockheed Electra first flew in 1957. Early in its career the Electra suffered two disastrous crashes, the result of metal fatigue. A number of modifications were required by the airworthiness authorities, including strengthening of the wing and engine nacelle structure, and the provision of thicker wing skins. Two versions of the Electra were built: the L-188A and the longer-range L-188C. A total of 168 Electras were completed. The Orion maritime reconnaissance aircraft was evolved from the Electra. The L-188C seats 98 passengers, cruises at 405 mph (652km/hr) and has a range of 2,770 miles (4,458km). *Country of origin:* USA. *Silhouette:* L-188C. *Picture:* L-188A.

Power: **4 × T56 turboprops**   *Span:* **99ft 8in (30.37m)**   *Length:* **116ft 10in (35.61m)**

A development of the civil Lockheed Electra, the P-3 Orion long-range anti-submarine aircraft first flew in 1958. Carrying a crew of ten, the Orion is equipped with sophisticated search equipment, including the distinctive tail-mounted magnetic anomaly detector (MAD) probe. Armament includes torpedoes and depth charges, and part of the warload can be carried on outer-wing pylons. A number of versions of the Orion have been built, the latest being the CP-140 for Canada. The P-3C Orion has a four-engine loiter endurance of 12.3hr and patrol speed is 237 mph (381km/hr). *Country of origin:* USA. *Silhouette and picture:* P-3C.

Douglas DC-4/C-54 Skymaster

Confusion: DC-6, DC-7

Power: 4 × R-2000 piston engines   *Span:* 117ft 6in (35.8m)   *Length:* 93ft 11in (28.6m)

First flown as long ago as 1938, the DC-4 was widely used in military as well as civil forms. The Air Force variant was known as the C-54 Skymaster and the naval version as the R-5D. As an airliner the DC-4 seats 44 passengers, cruises at 227 mph (363km/hr) and has a range of 1,500 miles (2,480km). Military versions have a large freight door on the port side. Many Skymasters later found their way onto the civil market. A British conversion known as the Carvair combined a new forward fuselage with a raised cockpit and clamshell doors for vehicle loading. The Carvair has a maximum cruising speed of 213 mph (342km/hr); sea-level maximum rate of climb of 650ft/min (198m/min); service ceiling at 73,000lb (33,110kg) all-up weight of 18,700ft (5,700m); and maximum-payload range of 2,300 miles (3,700km). *Country of origin:* USA. *Main silhouette:* **DC-4**; *upper side view:* **Carvair**.Picture: **DC-4**.

Power: 4 × R-2800 piston engines   *Span:* 117ft 6in (13.58m)   *Length:* 100ft 7in (30.66m)

A stretched, pressurised version of the DC-4, the DC-6 first flew in 1946 and 176 were built. Some air forces also acquired DC-6s. The DC-6A was a freighter with a new fuselage, while the DC-6B was a 54-passenger airliner version of the DC-6A. The military DC-6A was designated C-118A. Cruising speed of the DC-6 is 313 mph (501km/hr) and range 3,820 miles (6,112km). The C-118 Liftmaster, still widely used by air forces around the world, can carry 76 fully equipped troops, 60 stretchers or 27,000lb of cargo. Large freight loading doors are fitted fore and aft of the wing. With a maximum level speed at 18,100ft (5,520m) of 360 mph (579km/hr), the C-118 has a normal range of 3,860 miles (6,212km). A total of 167 Liftmasters were built. *Country of origin:* USA. *Main silhouette:* DC-6B; *upper side view:* DC-6. *Picture:* C-118.

Douglas DC-7B/C *Confusion:* DC-4, DC-6, Britannia

Power: 4 × R-3350 piston engines   *Span* (-7C): 127ft 6in (38.86m)   *Length:* 112ft 3in (34.21m)

A stretch of the DC-6B fuselage produced the DC-7, seating up to 95 coach-class passengers. A change to Wright turbo-compound engines raised weight and improved performance. More fuel was provided on the -7B, which had intercontinental range. The last of the DC-4/DC-7 line was the -7C with increased wingspan and a longer fuselage. Some 120 DC-7Cs were built and a number were converted to DC-7CF freighters. The DC-7C cruises at 310 mph (499km/hr) for up to 4,100 miles (6,595km). Maximum payload is 21,500lb (9,750kg) and service ceiling 21,700ft (6,615m). Production of the DC-7 series ran to 120 DC-7s, 96 DC-7Bs and 120 DC-7Cs; these totals include some aircraft converted to DC-7F freighters. *Country of origin:* USA. *Silhouette and picture:* DC-7C.

Bristol Britannia

Power: 4 × Proteus turboprops   *Span:* 142ft 3½in (43.38m)   *Length:* 124ft 3in (37.87m)

A long-range turboprop transport, the Britannia first flew in 1952. It went into service in 1957 as the 90-passenger Britannia 102, and was followed by the longer, 133-passenger Britannia 300. A military version, the Britannia C1, was used by the RAF to carry passengers and freight. Some 82 Britannias were completed and the type continues in service as a civil airliner. Maximum cruising speed of the Series 300 is 402 mph (647km/hr) and range is 4,268 miles (6,868km). *Country of origin:* UK. *Silhouette:* Series 310. *Picture:* Series 253F.

Canadair CL-44 *Confusion:* Britannia, DC-7C

Power: 4 × Tyne turboprops   *Span:* 142ft 3½in (43.38m)   *Length:* 151ft 10in (46.28m)

The CL-44 is a lengthened and re-engined version of the Britannia. In its initial form, as the CC-106 Yukon, the aircraft first flew in 1959 and went into service with the Royal Canadian Air Force. The type then evolved into the civil CL-44D, the world's first swing-tail long-range transport. The whole rear fuselage hinges to allow freight to be loaded. A total of 40 CL-44s were built. Cruising speed is 380 mph (612km/hr) and range 5,260 miles (8,460km). Maximum payload is 64,372lb (29,200kg) of cargo, or 45,685lb (20,800kg) in passenger configuration. Up to 214 passengers can be accommodated by the short-haul version, and 189 by the transatlantic variant. Convertible passenger/cargo variants have also been built. *Country of origin:* Canada. *Silhouette and picture:* CL-44.

Power: 4 × Griffon piston engines   *Span:* 119ft 10in (36.52m)   *Length:* 87ft 4in (26.62m)

Originally produced for maritime reconnaissance, the Shackleton was converted for airborne early warning as the AEW2. Fitted with a large radome under the forward fuselage, the AEW2 carries a crew of 12 and can remain on station for up to 15hr. The type is due to be superseded in the RAF by the Nimrod AEW3. The Shackleton is still used in its basic maritime/anti-submarine MR3 form by the South African Air Force. *Country of origin:* UK. *Silhouette and picture:* MR3.

Boeing KC-97 Stratofreighter

Confusion: Guppy

Power: 4 × R-4360 piston engines + 2 × J47 turbojets   *Span:* 141ft 3in (43.05m)   *Length:* 117ft 5in (35.79m)

Combining the wings, tail and landing gear of the Boeing B-29/B-50 Superfortress with a large double-bubble fuselage, the KC-97 Stratofreighter was produced in very large numbers. The airliner version is called the Stratocruiser. The type is used as a convertible tanker transport and has a large aerial refuelling boom under the rear fuselage. Various versions were built, including the KC-97E, F, G, K and L. Earlier marks did not have underwing auxiliary turbojets but could be fitted with auxiliary fuel tanks in the same positions. As a tanker the KC-97L can carry 10,825gal (49,210lit) of fuel, and up to 96 troops as a transport. Cruising speed is 301 mph (485km/hr). *Country of origin:* USA. *Silhouette and picture:* KC-97L.

Power: 4 × R-4360 piston engines or 4 × Allison 501 turboprops   *Span:* 156ft 3in (47.62m)   *Length:* 143ft 10in (43.84m)

Retaining the wings and engines of the Boeing Stratocruiser airliner, the Aero Spacelines Guppy has a vast fuselage originally designed to accommodate spacelauncher stages. Subsequently the type has been used to airlift other specialised freight, including wings for the Airbus A300. In 1980 Airbus Industrie acquired production rights to the design, and is currently having two further examples built. Range with maximum payload is 505 miles (813km) and maximum cruising speed is 288 mph (463km/hr). The normal flight crew is four. Variants are known as Pregnant Guppy, Super Guppy and Mini-Guppy. *Country of origin:* USA. *Silhouette and picture:* Guppy.

Lockheed C-130 Hercules *Confusion:* Belfast, Cub

Power: 4 × T56 turboprops   *Span:* 132ft 7in (40.41m)   *Length:* 97ft 9in (29.78m)

One of the most successful military transports built in the West, the C-130 Hercules first flew in 1954 and has been in production since 1955. Over 1,650 have been built for operators in 30 nations. There are many versions, including the C-130D for Arctic work, WC-130B and -130E for weather reconnaissance, AC-130E gunship, KC-130F Marine Corps tanker, C-130F for the US Navy, -130H and -130N for rescue, -130P for helicopter refuelling and EC-130Q for Navy communications. The Hercules can also be fitted with skis and various loads can be carried under the wings, including recce drones. A civil version is designated L-100. Main current production version is the C-130H, which carries 92 troops or freight, cruises at 340 mph (547km/hr) and has a range with maximum payload of 2,450 miles (3,943km). *Country of origin:* **USA**. *Silhouette and picture:* L-100.

Power: 4 × Tyne turboprops *Span:* 158ft 9½in (48.42m) *Length:* 136ft 5in (41.69m)

A long-range strategic freighter, the Shorts Belfast C1 first flew in 1964 and ten were produced for the RAF. The single squadron of Belfasts was disbanded in 1976 and the aircraft were sold to commercial operators. Up to 250 equipped troops or freight and vehicles could be carried. The Belfast cruises at 336 mph (540km/hr) for 3,985 miles (6,413km) with 30,000lb (13,608kg) of payload. British independent freight operator HeavyLift Cargo Airlines has acquired three Belfasts and is using them to transport large loads worldwide. The first of these aircraft to be delivered is based at Stansted, Essex, and the second in Singapore. *Country of origin:* **UK.**

Antonov An-12 Cub

Confusion: Hercules, Belfast

Power: **4 × Ivchenko turboprops** *Span:* **124ft 8in (38m)** *Length:* **121ft 4½in (37m)**

Produced in very large numbers, the An-12, code-named Cub, is used in both military and civil forms. The Cub has a crew of five and can carry 100 paratroops, vehicles, guns or missiles, loaded through the large rear ramp. Cubs serving with the Soviet and other air forces have a twin 23mm gun turret in the tail. This is replaced by a fairing on the civil version, which is known as the An-12V. Electronic intelligence and electronic countermeasures versions are coded Cub-B and Cub-C respectively. The Cub cruises at 342 mph (550km/hr) and has a range of 2,110 miles (3,400km). *Country of origin:* USSR. *Silhouette and picture:* An-12V.

Power: 4 × PT6 turboprops   *Span:* 93ft (28.35m)   *Length:* 80ft 8in (24.58m)

Capable of very short take-offs and landings, the DHC-7 Dash 7 seats 50 passengers or carries a mixture of passengers and freight. First flown in 1975, the Dash 7 went into airline service in 1977. The Dash 7 operates over short routes and, in addition to its good airfield performance, is very quiet in operation. Cruising speed is 235 mph (379km/hr) and range is 696 miles (1,120km). A maritime reconnaissance version with belly radome is known as the DHC-7R Ranger. This variant differs principally from the airliner in having increased fuel tankage, providing 10–12hr of endurance at normal patrol speeds; two observer's stations with bubble windows; nose-mounted Texas Instruments search radar; and equipment for maritime surveillance. An all-cargo version is designated Series 101. *Country of origin:* **Canada.** *Silhouette and picture:* Dash 7.

Antonov An-22 Cock   *Confusion:* Cub

Power: 4 × Kuznetsov turboprops   *Span:* 211ft 3½in (64.4m)   *Length:* 189ft 8in (57.8m)

The second largest transport in the world (after the C-5A Galaxy), the Antonov An-22 Antheus, code-named Cock, is a heavy freighter for military and civil use. A crew of five/six, 28/29 passengers and a wide variety of vehicle, gun, missile and freight loads can be carried. Cargo is loaded by means of a large rear ramp. The first Cock flew in 1965 and the type went into service with the Soviet Air Force in 1967. An unusual feature is the fitting of two radomes in the nose. The four turboprop engines drive large contra-rotating propellers. Cock has a range of 6,800 miles (10,950km) and cruises at 422 mph (679km/hr). The An-22 has set a number of world records, including no fewer than 14 payload-to-height marks on one occasion in 1967, when 100,000kg (220,500lb) of metal blocks were carried to a height of 25,748ft (7,848m). *Country of origin:* USSR.

Single propeller, low wing, retractable undercarriage

This class consists almost exclusively of trainers and light sports/touring/business aircraft. Side and plan views require special study. Points to look for include wing taper, faired or raised canopies, engine cowling and fin shape, and undercarriage-retraction direction.

The Zlin 526 and Meta-Sokol display marked backward wing taper, and the main undercarriage legs retract rearwards, with the wheels only partially submerged in the wing. The Safir has an extremely short undercarriage. The differences between the Neiva Universal and the Pilatus P-3 lie in fuselage depth, wing shape and fin height.

The PC-7 Turbo-Trainer has a particularly long fuselage and a very large fin fillet; the air intake is large and there are conspicuous single exhaust pipes on each side of the engine cowling, just behind the spinner. Two new trainers, the Tucano and Epsilon, are similar in outline but differ in wing, cockpit and fin shape.

Head-on, the Siai-Marchetti SF.205 looks similar to the Mooney Ranger, but thereafter the similarity ends. Of particular note is the forward-raked fin of the Ranger. The Gardan Horizon has a very short fuselage and, like the Zlin 526 and Meta-Sokol, has rearward-retracting main legs with partially submerged wheels.

The Bellanca Viking's tailplane is braced by V-struts and the undercarriage is housed in small blisters. Of the two versions of the Bonanza, the V35 stands out because of its "butterfly" V-tail.

Both the Piper Cherokee Arrow and the Robin HR 100 have similar broad-chord wing planforms, but their cabin window and fin shapes are different. On the Rockwell Commander the tailplane is mounted half-way up the fin.

The P.149 has a curious canopy shape and outwards-retracting undercarriage. On the Wassmer Super IV the wing is plank-like, and the Siai-Marchetti SF.260 has a bubble canopy and wingtip tanks.

Beech Bonanza V35

The Bellanca SkyRocket can be recognised by its long cabin and long-span tailplane, while the Beechcraft Sierra has a squat fuselage, square wings and a most unusual main undercarriage which retracts outwards.

Sportavia's RF-4B has a high-aspect-ratio wing, small cockpit canopy, tall fin and large tailplane cut-outs. The RF-5B has a larger cockpit and longer fuselage. The Soviet Yak-18 has a long nose, radial engine, raised cockpit and tricycle undercarriage. By contrast, the Texan has a deeper fuselage, shorter nose and a tailwheel undercarriage.

Although produced by entirely different design teams, the T-CH-1 and the T-28 Trojan look very much alike. Points of difference lie mainly in the deep cowling of the Trojan's radial engine and its larger cockpit canopy. The Piper Turbo Lance II has a distinctive look by reason of its T-tail.

Of entirely different concept to the light aircraft is the Alizé, which is used for anti-submarine work and has large wing bulges.

Zlin 526/726 *Confusion:* Meta-Sokol

Power: 1 × Avia piston engine   *Span:* 32ft 5in (9.88m)   *Length:* 26ft 2in (7.98m)

The Zlin Trener, Trener-master and Akrobat series has been in production in Czechoslovakia since 1947; more than 1,400 aircraft have been built. First of the series to feature a retractable undercarriage was the Z 326 of 1957. The single-seat competition aircraft were designated Akrobats and scored a number of successes in international aerobatics contests. Various engines have been used but all models have the distinctive swept wing leading edge and large, angular rudder. Last of the series is the Z 726, which first flew in 1973. Generally similar to the Z 526F, it has a slightly shorter wing and metal-covered rudder and elevators. Production ended in 1977 after 32 had been built. Maximum cruising speed of the 526F is 130 mph (210km/hr). *Country of origin:* Czechoslovakia. *Silhouette:* Zlin 526. *Picture:* Zlin 526A Akrobat.

Power: 1 × Walter Minor piston engine   *Span:* 33ft (10.06m)   *Length:* 24ft 9in (7.54m)

The four-seat L-40 Meta-Sokol first flew in 1954 and is a development of the earlier all-wood M-1 Sokol tourer. On the ground the type's most easily identifiable feature is its unique reverse tricycle undercarriage. Most Meta-Sokols were exported, production having exceeded 200 by the end of 1961. Features to look out for are the tall, almost parallel fin and rudder and the half-concealed main wheels when the gear is retracted. Cruising speed is 137 mph (220km/hr), maximum range 688 miles (1,107km), maximum rate of climb at sea level 630ft/min (192m/min), and service ceiling 14,765ft (4,500m). *Country of origin:* Czechoslovakia.

Saab Safir *Confusion:* Neiva Universal

Power: 1 × Lycoming piston engine   *Span:* 34ft 9in (10.60m)   *Length:* 26ft 4in (8.03m)

The Saab-91 Safir four-seat primary trainer first flew in 1945. Four main versions have been built: the Saab-91A, powered by a 145hp de Havilland Gipsy Major 10 and originally operated by Sweden and Ethiopia; the Saab-91B, powered by a 190hp Lycoming and first flown in 1949; the Saab-91C, first flown in 1953 and widely used for private and light commercial work and as an air force trainer; and the Saab-91D, generally similar to the -91C but powered by a 180hp Lycoming driving a constant-speed propeller. Maximum speed at sea level is 165 mph (266km/hr). Operators of the -91D included Finland, the Netherlands and Tunisia. *Country of origin:* Sweden. *Silhouette and picture:* Saab-91D.

Power: 1 × Lycoming piston engine   *Span:* 36ft 1in (11m)   *Length:* 28ft 2½in (8.6m)

Designed as a replacement for Brazilian Air Force Fokker S-11/S-12s and North American T-6 Texans, the Neiva flew for the first time in 1966. Brazilian Air Force designation for this tricycle-undercarriage 2/3-seater is the T-25. In addition to the 140 or so delivered in Brazil, a further 10 are being used by the Chilean Air Force. Two underwing hardpoints are provided for mounting 7.62mm machine-gun pods. A developed version with a more powerful Lycoming engine is under consideration. Maximum cruising speed is 177 mph (285km/hr). *Country of origin:* Brazil.

Pilatus P-3 *Confusion:* Universal

Power: 1 × Lycoming piston engine   *Span:* 34ft 1in (10.40m)   *Length:* 28ft 8in (8.75m)

The Pilatus P-3 is an all-metal tandem two-seat trainer built primarily for the Swiss Air Force; another six aircraft went to Brazil. First flight was in 1953, with the first of 18 pre-production aircraft following the next year. Powered by a 260hp Lycoming, the P-3 has a cruising speed of about 155 mph (249km/hr). Suitable for primary and advanced training, including aerobatics, night flying and instrument flying, the P-3 can be equipped for weapon training with one 7.9mm machine gun in an underwing pod, four practice bombs or two air-to-ground rockets. The P-3 will be superseded in Swiss Air Force service by the PC-7. *Country of origin:* Switzerland.

Laverda Super Falco F8L

Power: 1 × Lycoming piston engine   *Span:* 26ft 3in (8m)   *Length:* 21ft 4in (6.50m)

The Falco first flew in 1955, powered by a 90hp Continental. Since then four production versions have been built: F8L Series I, an initial production batch of ten built by Aviamilano in 1956 and powered by 135hp Lycomings; F8L Series II, also built by Aviamilano, with a 150hp Lycoming; F8L America, built by Aeromere for the US market; Super Falco Series IV, generally similar to the F8L America but powered by a 160hp Lycoming and built by Laverda (the former Aeromere company). An extremely clean design, the Super Falco seats two side-by-side and is fully aerobatic. Maximum cruising speed is 180 mph (290km/hr), and maximum sea-level climb rate 984ft/min (300m/min). *Country of origin:* Italy. *Silhouette and picture:* Super Falco.

Navion Rangemaster *Confusion:* Super Falco

Power: 1 × Continental piston engine   *Span:* **34ft 9in (10.59m)**   *Length:* **27ft 6in (8.38m)**

The five-seat Navion Rangemaster is a much modified development of the original Navion, produced first by North American Aviation and later, between 1948 and 1950, by Ryan, which acquired the rights in 1947. The Rangemaster retains the original Navion wing and undercarriage but is otherwise completely re-engineered. First flight was in 1960, with production commencing the next year. Fitted with wingtip fuel tanks, the type has excellent range and cruises at more than 185 mph (298km/hr) on its 260hp Continental. A large number of Navions of all types are still active, particularly in the US. *Country of origin:* USA.

Confusion: PC-7, Mentor, Epsilon   **Embraer EMB-312 (T-27) Tucano**

Power: 1 × PT6A turboprop   *Span:* 36ft 6in (11.14m)   *Length:* 32ft 4in (9.86m)

Due to enter service in 1983, the two-seat T-27 Tucano will become the standard basic trainer in the Brazilian Air Force. Turboprop-powered, the Tucano will combine the characteristics of a basic piston trainer and a light jet. In addition to its flying training role, the Tucano will be available for armament training and counter-insurgency work, with underwing 0.5in machine guns and bombs or rocket projectiles. Top speed is 296 mph (476km/hr). First flown in August 1980, the Tucano is the subject of a Brazilian Government order for 112, with a further 50 on option. *Country of origin:* Brazil.

Aérospatiale TB 30 Epsilon

Confusion: Tucano, PC-7

Power: 1 × Lycoming piston engine   *Span:* 26ft (7.92m)   *Length:* 24ft 10in (7.59m)

To be used as a two-seat tricycle-undercarriage primary trainer by the French Air Force, the TB 30 Epsilon first flew in December 1979 and some 60 have so far been ordered. During its development the Epsilon underwent extensive modifications to fuselage, tail and wingtips. Maximum speed is 238 mph (383km/hr) and endurance 3.75hr. Pupils trained on the Epsilon will progress to the Alpha Jet and then to operational types. *Country of origin:* France.

Pilatus PC-7 Turbo-Trainer

Power: 1 × PT6A turboprop   *Span:* 34ft 1½in (10.40m)   *Length:* 32ft (9.75m)

This two-seat all-metal aircraft is suitable for basic, intermediate and aerobatic training. A tactical trainer version is also available with six underwing hardpoints for up to 2,300lb (1,000kg) of stores. First flight of the prototype was in 1966 and the first production aircraft eventually flew in mid-1978. Several countries have ordered the type, including Bolivia, Burma, Jordan, Mexico, Abu Dhabi, Chile and Guatemala, and Switzerland will replace its P-3s with up to 60 Turbo-Trainers by the mid-1980s. Powered by a 550hp Pratt & Whitney turboprop, the PC-7 has a cruising speed of more than 186 mph (300km/hr). *Country of origin:* Switzerland.

Beechcraft T-34 Mentor/T-34C

Confusion: PC-7, KM-2B, Tucano, Epsilon

Power: 1 × Lycoming piston engine or 1 × P & W turboprop (T-34C) *Span* (T-34): 32ft 10in (10m) *Length* (T-34): 25ft 11in (7.90m)

Derived from the Bonanza 33 series, the Mentor tandem two-seat trainer first flew in 1948. More than 450 T-34As were built for the USAF and a further 420 T-34Bs for the US Navy. The type is still in widespread use throughout South America. A new version, the T-34C, first flew in 1973. Re-engined with a 715shp Pratt & Whitney turboprop, it is an extensively re-engineered variant with improved performance and is suitable for forward air control and light strike missions as the T-34C-1. The US Navy has ordered 184 T-34Cs against an anticipated requirement for more than 300. Nearly 70 of the armed T-34C-1 version have been ordered. *Country of origin:* USA. *Silhouette and picture:* T-34C.

Power: 1 × Lycoming piston engine   *Span:* **32ft 10in (10m)**   *Length:* **26ft 4in (8.04m)**

The KM-2B is a modification of the original KM-2 development of the Beechcraft Mentor, combining the airframe and powerplant of the KM-2 with the two-seat tandem cockpit of the T-34A Mentor. The KM-2B first flew in 1974 and was selected by the Japan Air Self-Defence Force (JASDF) to replace its T-34As in the primary training role the following year. The JASDF ordered 50 examples of the type, designating them T-3. The first of these made its first flight on January 17, 1978, and 44 had been delivered to the JASDF by February 1981. Powered by a 340hp Lycoming flat-six engine, the KM-2B has a cruising speed of about 158 mph (254km/hr), maximum level speed of 228 mph (367km/hr), maximum rate of climb of 1,520ft/min (463m/min) and service ceiling of 26,8000ft (8,170m). *Country of origin:* Japan. *Silhouette:* **KM-2.** *Picture:* **KM-2B.**

Siai-Marchetti S.205/S.208 *Confusion:* Ranger

Power: 1 × Lycoming piston engine   *Span:* 35ft 7½in (10.86m)   *Length:* 26ft 3in (8m)

The S.205 four-seat all-metal light aircraft first flew in 1965. The type was designed from the outset to take a variety of engines, from 180 to 300hp, and there is also a version with fixed undercarriage. A new version, the S.205AC powered by a 200hp Lycoming, has been ordered by the Italian Aero Club. The first of 140 were delivered in 1977. The S.208, a five-seater based on S.205 components, flew for the first time in May 1967. In addition to an order for 40 from the Italian Air Force (S.208M), the S.208 has also been delivered to customers in Europe and Africa. A version designated S.208AG has been developed for general duties and features a fixed undercarriage. Maximum cruising speed is 187 mph (300km/hr). *Country of origin:* Italy. *Silhouette:* S.208. *Picture:* S.208M.

Power: 1 × Lycoming piston engine   *Span:* 35ft (10.67m)   *Length:* 23ft 2in (7.06m)

The four-seat all-metal Mooney Ranger is one of several Mooney light aircraft featuring the distinctive fin and rudder with its unswept leading edge. Originally known as the Mark 21, the Ranger first flew in 1961, although the earlier M-20 had flown in 1953. Other models in the series are the Executive, with a 200hp Lycoming, and the Mooney 201 (M20J), which first flew in 1976. The Mark 22 (originally known as the Mustang) is a five-seat pressurised version which first flew in 1964. Powered by a 310hp Lycoming turbosupercharged engine, it has the basic wing of the Ranger but is rather longer than the earlier version. *Country of origin:* USA. *Silhouette:* Ranger. *Picture:* Mooney 201.

Gardan/Socata GY-80 Horizon   *Confusion:* Ranger, Picchio

Power: 1 × Lycoming piston engine   *Span:* 31ft 10in (9.70m)   *Length:* 21ft 9½in (6.64m)

Designed by Yves Gardan, this four-seat all-metal light aircraft was put into series production by Sud Aviation from 1963. Four versions with engines of different power were originally offered. By mid-1968 more than 260 Horizons had been delivered to customers, mainly in Europe. Design and construction are conventional and the tricycle undercarriage retracts rearwards, with the wheels half concealed. Powered by a 160hp Lycoming, the Horizon has a cruising speed of about 145 mph (233km/hr). Other performance figures include a sea-level rate of climb of 660ft/min (201m/min), service ceiling of 13,450ft (4,100m), and range with 44 Imp gal (200lit) fuel of 590 miles (950km). *Country of origin:* France.

Power: 1 × Continental piston engine   *Span:* 34ft 2in (10.41m)   *Length:* 26ft 4in (8.02m)

The Viking series of light aircraft consists of three models developed from the earlier Bellanca 260C and Standard Viking 300: the Model 17-30A Super Viking 300A, powered by a 300hp Continental; Model 17-31A Super Viking 300A, identical to the Model 17-30A with the exception of engine and propeller; and the Model 17-31ATC Turbo Viking 300A, which has two Rajay turbochargers added to its 300hp Lycoming. Total production of all models of Viking had reached more than 1,500 by the beginning of 1978. Production ceased in 1980. Accommodation is provided for four persons and top speed of all models is more than 222 mph (357km/hr). *Country of origin:* USA. *Silhouette:* Viking 300. *Picture:* Super Viking.

General Avia F15F/F15E Picchio *Confusion:* Viking

Power: 1 × Lycoming piston engine   *Span:* 32ft 6in (9.90m)   *Length:* 25ft 5in (7.75m)

The F15F four-seat light aircraft is a derivative of the Procaer F15E Picchio. First flight was in October 1977 and a pre-production batch was under construction during 1978. The F15E Picchio is slightly shorter than the F15F and features a conventional enclosed cabin compared with the new aircraft's fully glazed sliding canopy. The first F15 Picchio flew in 1959 and successive models built since then have featured a number of detail design changes, including the addition of wingtip fuel tanks. Most important change was the switch to all-metal construction with the F15E, which first flew in 1968. Cruising speed of the F15F is 174 mph (280km/hr). *Country of origin:* Italy. *Silhouette:* F15E. *Picture:* F15F.

Power: 1 × Continental piston engine   *Span:* 33ft 6in (10.21m)   *Length:* 26ft 8in (8.13m) (F33); 27ft 6in (8.38m) (A36)

The Bonanza Model F33 is a four/five-seat executive aircraft, similar to the Bonanza Model V35 but featuring a conventional tail unit with swept fin and rudder. Originally known as the Debonair, it first flew in September 1959. An aerobatic version is available and is in service as a trainer in several air forces. Other Model F33s are used as trainers by US and European airlines. Production of the Model 33 had reached more than 2,100 by early 1978. The Bonanza Model A36 is a six-seat utility version and, like the Model 33, is powered by a 285hp Continental. Slightly longer than the Model 33, it is distinguished by an additional cabin window on each side of the rear fuselage. Production had reached more than 1,200 by early 1978. The Bonanza 36 has a maximum cruising speed of 196 mph (315km/hr). *Country of origin:* USA. *Silhouette:* A36. *Picture:* F33A.

343

Beechcraft Bonanza Model V35B *Confusion:* Bonanza 33/36

Power: 1 × Continental piston engine   *Span:* 33ft 6in (10.21m)   *Length:* 26ft 5in (8.05m)

This four/five-seat V-tail light aircraft first flew in December 1945 and production had reached more than 10,000 by 1977. Current production version is the V34B. Powered by a 285hp Continental driving a two-blade constant-speed propeller, the V35B has a cruising speed of about 200 mph (322km/hr). Externally the V35 Bonanza has changed little over the years and is immediately identifiable by the distinctive arrangement of the tail. Internal refinements continue to mirror changing tastes and advances in avionic equipment. *Country of origin:* USA. *Silhouette and picture:* V35B.

Power: 1 × Lycoming piston engine   *Span:* 32ft 2½in (9.82m)   *Length:* 24ft 7in (7.50m)

The Cherokee Arrow II is generally similar in appearance to the Cherokee Archer II but has a retractable undercarriage, more powerful engine and the untapered wings of the PA-28-180 Archer. First flown in 1975, it was superseded in 1977 by the PA-28R-201 Arrow III, which has the new longer-span tapered wings. Third in the Arrow series is the Turbo Arrow III, which is identical to the Arrow III but has a 200hp turbocharged Continental engine driving a two-blade constant-speed propeller. The Turbo Arrow III is a few inches longer than the standard aircraft and has a remodelled cowling with a larger airscoop and more pointed spinner. The Arrow IV (see page 359) has a T-tail. *Country of origin:* USA. *Silhouette and picture:* Arrow II.

Robin HR 100 *Confusion:* Arrow

Power: 1 × Lycoming piston engine   *Span:* 29ft 9½in (9.08m)   *Length:* 24ft 11in (7.59m)

There are three basic models in the HR 100 series of French light aircraft. The fixed-undercarriage four-seat HR 100/210 Safari II is a development of the original all-metal production HR 100/200, of which 31 were built. It first flew in 1971 and remained in production until 1976, some 78 having been built. The retractable-undercarriage four/five-seat HR 100/285 Tiara first flew in 1972 and featured a new vertical tail and wing structure. Powerplant was a 285hp Lycoming driving a three-blade constant-speed propeller. The HR 100/250TR is similar to the Tiara but has a lower-powered engine. Third of the basic models is the six-seat HR 100/4+2, which first flew in May 1975. It is one foot longer than the Tiara and features an additional set of cabin windows. Powerplant is a 320hp Lycoming driving a three-blade propeller. Maximum cruising speed is 168 mph (270km/hr). *Country of origin:* France. *Silhouette:* HR 100 Tiara. *Picture:* HR 100/280.

Power: 1 × Lycoming piston engine   *Span:* 35ft 7in (10.85m)   *Length:* 25ft (7.63m)

These attractive four-seat light aircraft are all basically similar, the differences lying in equipment and powerplants. The Commander 112 first flew in December 1970, with production aircraft being delivered from 1972. Successive models were improved in exterior and interior detail but retained the same exterior shape. The Commander 114 was introduced in 1976 and differs from the Model 112 principally in having a 260hp engine rather than the 112's 210hp unit. All aircraft have the characteristic mid-set tailplane and sharply tapered rear cabin windows. Cruising speed is 175 mph (281km/hr). Other performance figures include a maximum rate of climb at sea level of 1,000ft/min (305m/min), and a range with maximum fuel, no reserves, of 1,130 miles (1,818km). *Country of origin:* USA. *Silhouette:* Commander 112. *Picture:* Commander 114.

Piaggio P.149 *Confusion:* Guepard

Power: 1 × Lycoming piston engine   *Span:* 36ft 6in (11.12m)   *Length:* 28ft 9½in (8.80m)

The P.149, developed from the P.148, is a four/five-seat all-metal light aircraft. First flown in 1953, the type was built in quantity as a liaison and training aircraft for the Federal German Air Force and was subsequently built under licence by Focke-Wulf in Germany. Some East African countries have small numbers of ex-German P.149Ds. Powered by a 270hp Lycoming driving a three-blade constant-speed propeller, the P.149D cruises at 165 mph (266km/hr). Other performance figures include a maximum level speed at sea level of 192 mph (309km/hr); maximum rate of climb at sea level of 980ft/min (300m/min); service ceiling of 19,850ft (6,050m); and range (including allowance for starting, warm-up, take-off and climb, plus 30min reserves) of 680 miles (1,095km). *Country of origin:* Italy. *Silhouette and picture:* P.149D.

Wassmer WA-40/Super IV/CE.43 Guepard

Power: 1 × Lycoming piston engine   *Span:* 32ft 9½in (10m)   *Length:* 26ft 6½in (8.09m)

Several versions of the Wassmer WA-40 four/five-seat cabin light aircraft have been built since the first flew in 1959. Later aircraft introduced a swept fin and rudder (WA-40A) and improved engine cowling. The Super IV/21 is externally similar to the Super IV but is powered by a 250hp Lycoming driving a constant-speed propeller. The Cerva CE.43 Guepard is an all-metal derivative of the Super IV/21 and first flew in 1971. Production ended in 1976 after 43 had been built. Wassmer went into liquidation in 1977 and responsibility for Wassmer and Cerva products passed to Issoire-Aviation. *Country of origin:* France. *Silhouette:* WA-40A. *Picture:* Super IV.

Siai-Marchetti SF.260 *Confusion:* Guepard

Power: 1 × Lycoming piston engine   *Span:* 27ft 5in (8.35m)   *Length:* 23ft 3½in (7.10m)

The SF.260 has been built in both civil and military versions since it first entered production in 1964. Derived from the Aviamilano F.250, it is of conventional construction and is fully aerobatic. Military versions are the SF.260M two/three-seat trainer, first flown in 1970, and the SF.260W Warrior weapons trainer/tactical support aircraft, first flown in 1972. This version is fitted with two or four underwing stores pylons. Both types are widely deployed throughout the world. Civil versions are the SF.260A, B and C. The SF.260A was marketed in the US as the Waco Meteor. Outwardly similar to the military versions, civil SF.260s are also widely distributed throughout the world. *Country of origin:* Italy. *Silhouette:* SF.260. *Picture:* SF.260M.

Power: 1 × Lycoming piston engine　　*Span:* 31ft 2in (9.5m)　　*Length:* 25ft 4in (7.7m)

With side-by-side forward seats and an additional seat behind, the HTP-32 is to be the standard basic trainer for the Indian Air Force. Following an initial order for 24 machines, a total of 160 HTP-32s are expected to be procured. Four underwing store points are provided for weapon training, and the type can also be used for observation, liaison and sports flying. Maximum speed is 135 mph (217km/hr) and endurance 4hr. *Country of origin:* India.

Beechcraft Sierra 200 *Confusion:* SkyRocket II

Power: 1 × Lycoming piston engine   *Span:* 32ft 9in (9.98m)   *Length:* 25ft 9in (7.85m)

Originally known as the Musketeer Super R, this type was first introduced in 1969. In 1971 the manufacturer renamed the entire Musketeer range and the Super R became the Sierra 200. Since then several detail improvements have been made, including the fitting of a more powerful engine and general aerodynamic cleaning-up. With accommodation for four to six persons, the Sierra can be identified by its four cabin windows on each side (against three in the similar but fixed-undercarriage Sundowner 180). Powered by a 200hp Lycoming flat-four, the Sierra has a cruising speed of about 160 mph (257km/hr). *Country of origin:* USA.

Power: 1 × Continental piston engine   *Span:* 35ft (10.67m)   *Length:* 28ft 11in (8.81m)

Design of this sleek six-seat executive aircraft was begun as long ago as 1956 by the late G. M. Bellanca. The choice of innovative materials for the type's construction lengthened development time, but it is claimed that the glass-fibre epoxy laminate used has a higher strength/weight ratio than aluminium and is also aerodynamically extremely smooth. The prototype first flew in March 1975 and has since set a number of speed records. By early 1978 orders for some 70 aircraft had been recorded. Cruising speed is 255 mph (410km/hr). Other performance figures include a maximum cruising speed (83 per cent power) of 331 mph (532km/hr); rate of climb at sea level of 1,900ft/min (579m/min); and a range at 15,000ft (4,570m) and 75 per cent power of over 1,215 miles (1,955km). *Country of origin:* USA.

Yakovlev Yak-18 Max/Yak-18P Moose

Confusion: Texan

Power: 1 × Ivchenko or 1 × Vedeneev piston engine   *Span:* 34ft 9in (10.60m)   *Length:* 27ft 5in (8.35m)

Several versions of this Russian two-seat basic trainer have been built since it first appeared in 1946. The original aircraft was a tailwheel-undercarriage type with a five-cylinder radial engine closely cowled with individual cylinder helmets. Introduced in 1957, the Yak-18A was a cleaned-up version of the Yak-18U with a tricycle undercarriage and a more powerful nine-cylinder radial engine. Widely used as a club aircraft, the Yak-18A has been exported in large numbers throughout the Communist world. A further development, the Yak-18P Moose, is a single-seater specifically designed for advanced training and competition aerobatics. A four-seat tourer development is the Yak-50, used extensively for Aeroflot training. The powerplant is a Vedeneev radial. *Country of origin:* USSR. *Silhouette and picture:* Yak-18P.

North American T-6 Texan

Power: 1 × R-1340 piston engine   *Span:* 42ft (12.80m)   *Length:* 29ft 6in (8.99m)

The extremely long-lived T-6 Texan was first produced before the Second World War and was widely used as an advanced trainer in that conflict, more than 10,000 being built in North America. The type was known as the Harvard in RAF service. The Texans to be seen today are virtually the same as the wartime aircraft. The type is still in wide use throughout South America and elsewhere as an air force trainer and racing aircraft. *Country of origin:* USA. *Silhouette:* T-6G. *Picture:* SNJ-3 (naval version).

AIDC T-CH-1 *Confusion:* Trojan

Power: 1 × T53 turboprop   *Span:* 40ft (12.19m)   *Length:* 33ft 8in (10.26m)

This tandem two-seat trainer was designed to fill a Nationalist Chinese Air Force requirement for an advanced trainer/ground attack aircraft. It first flew in November 1973 and entered series production in May 1976, 50 having been ordered. Powered by a licence-built 1,450hp Lycoming turboprop, the T-CH-1 cruises at more than 250 mph (402km/hr). Externally, the design owes much to the North American T-28A, particularly in the arrangement of the cockpit and tail assembly. Cruising speed is 196 mph (315km/hr). *Country of origin:* Taiwan.

Confusion: T-CH-1 **North American T-28 Trojan**

Power: 1 × R-1820 piston engine *Span:* 40ft 7½in (12.38m) *Length:* 32ft 10in (10m)

Originally designed as a replacement for the T-6 Texan, this tandem two-seat trainer first flew in September 1949. First operated by the US Air Force and US Navy, the type has since been used by a number of air forces throughout the world. The T-28A, T-28B and T-28C were all trainers, but the T-28D, slightly larger and fitted with a more powerful engine, has been widely used in the counter-insurgency role. A total of six underwing stations can accommodate a variety of armament. T-28s of all versions can still be seen in South America, South-east Asia and North Africa, as well as in the US. *Country of origin:* USA. *Main silhouette:* T-28C; *lower side view:* T-28D. *Picture:* T-28D.

Piper Lance I/Lance II/Turbo Lance II

Confusion (Lance): Cherokee

Power: 1 × Lycoming piston engine   *Span:* 32ft 10in (10m)   *Length:* 27ft 8½in (8.44m)

There are three main versions of the Piper Lance. The original model, first flown in August 1974, was essentially a retractable-undercarriage Cherokee Six and featured a conventional tail unit. The Lance II and Turbo Lance II both have the now fashionable T-tail arrangement, while the Turbo Lance also has the extra power of a 300hp turbocharged Lycoming engine. The T-tail is claimed to reduce drag and to increase performance. Main distinguishing point of the Turbo Lance is the large air inlet for the turbocharger located beneath the propeller spinner. *Country of origin:* USA. *Silhouette:* Turbo Lance II. *Picture:* Lance.

Power: 1 × Lycoming piston engine   *Span:* 35ft 5in (10.8m)   *Length:* 27ft (8.23m)

Developed from the fixed-undercarriage Archer II, the Arrow IV is a four-seat monoplane with a T-tail and retractable tricycle undercarriage. The T-tail was introduced in 1979 and two versions of the type are now available, the Arrow IV and the Turbo Arrow IV. The Arrow IV has a cruising speed of 193 mph (311km/hr) and a range of 840 miles (1,353km). *Country of origin:* USA.

Breguet BR 1050 Alizé   *Confusion: —*

Power: 1 × Dart turboprop   *Span:* 51ft 2in (15.60m)   *Length:* 45ft 6in (13.86m)

The three-seat Alizé (Tradewind) is a carrier-based anti-submarine aircraft currently in service with the navies of France and India. First flight was in 1956 and two prototypes and three pre-production aircraft preceded 75 production Alizés into Aéronavale service from mid-1959. Armament includes a torpedo or depth charges, AS.12 air-to-surface missiles or rockets. The Alizé has a large retractable radome underneath the rear fuselage. Noticeable also are the large landing gear/weapons nacelles on the wing leading edges. *Country of origin:* France.

Power: 1 × T53 turboprop   *Span:* 45ft 1in (13.74m)   *Length:* 39ft 6in (12.03m)

Conversion of a number of C-3603 fighter-bombers of 1940s vintage for target towing began in 1967. Even after 25 years' service with the Swiss Air Force the type still had at least another ten years of useful airframe life remaining, and it was decided that the C-3603 could best be used as a target tug for air-to-air gunnery training. Produced under the direction of Ing Jean-Pierre Weibel, the first conversion flew in August 1968, followed by 23 production aircraft; the first aircraft entered service in 1971. The modification involved fitting an additional section to the front fuselage to accommodate the 1,100hp Lycoming turboprop, and the addition of a third, central fin. Accommodation is provided for two beneath a continuous transparent canopy. Cruising speed is about 260 mph (418km/hr). *Country of origin:* Switzerland.

This large section embraces touring, training and agricultural aircraft, and it is split into two groups: tricycle and tailwheel undercarriage.

In the first group major points to look for are cabin/cockpit canopy shape, fin contours and whether the undercarriage wheels are covered by spats. The "flat" piston engine is the most usual powerplant, giving a streamlined look to the nose. Wing shapes in general tend to be rectangular, often with fillets at the root leading edge.

On the Gulfstream American AA-5 and the Lynx the nosewheel leg is unusual in being curved forward. The Chiensou is the first of a series with swept fin and rudder and, in this case, wingtip fuel tanks. Differences in undercarriages are brought out on the Robin 400 and the Cherokee. The former has streamlined struts on the main undercarriage and an offset noseleg, while the latter has spindly legs and a centrally mounted nosewheel strut.

The Robin Dauphin has an unusual wing planform with taper at the root on the leading edge, then a rectangular section and finally outer wings with taper on leading and trailing edges. There is dihedral on the outer panels only, as on other types such as the Fletcher FU-24.

The Beech Skipper and the Piper Tomahawk have T-tails but in other respects are conventional.

The first four of the tailwheel-undercarriage types—Nord 3203, Chipmunk, HT.2 and I-115—all feature raised cockpits and square-cut wings, though the Chipmunk's curved fin is a useful recognition feature. An elliptical wing planform, reminiscent of the Spitfire's, distinguishes the Mudry CAP 10B/20L and the Emeraude. The three Jodel types have the same basic wing planform, with a rectangular centre section and tapered outer panels.

Agricultural aircraft from the IAR 822/826 through to the UTVA-65 are all characterised by small cockpit hoods and very long, fairly slim noses, while the remainder have the bluntness of radial engines. The Fieldmaster is noteworthy for having a tricycle undercarriage.

Socata Rallye

Power: 1 × Lycoming piston engine   *Span:* **32ft 9in (9.98m)**   *Length:* **25ft 9in (7.85m)**

The Beechcraft Musketeer series began with the Model 23 Musketeer, which first flew in 1961. The series has been progressively improved over the years, although the basic exterior appearance has remained largely unchanged. In 1974 Beech renamed the series as follows: the original Musketeer Super R became the rectractable-undercarriage Sierra 200; the Musketeer Custom became the Sundowner 180; and the Musketeer Sport became the Sport 150. These new designations reflect the engine power. Main external difference between the Sundowner 180 and the Sport 150 is the former's extra cabin window on each side. Cruising speeds are about 140 mph (225km/hr) for the Sundowner and 125 mph (200km/hr) for the Sport. *Country of origin:* USA. *Silhouette:* Sierra 200. *Picture:* Sundowner 180.

Gulfstream American AA-5A/AA-5B   *Confusion:* Lynx, Sundowner

Power: 1 × Lycoming piston engine   *Span:* 31ft 6in (9.60m)   *Length:* 22ft (6.71m)

A larger development of the AA-1 series, the AA-5 first flew in 1970. This all-metal four-seat aircraft is built in four versions; the basic AA-5A with 150hp Lycoming engine; the de luxe Cheetah, externally identical to the AA-5A but with additional internal equipment; the AA-5B with 180hp Lycoming; and the de luxe Tiger, which has the same internal equipment as the Cheetah. The AA-5B series first flew in 1974. The Cheetah was known as the Traveler until 1976. Cruising speeds are 145 mph (235km/hr) for the AA-5A and 160 mph (260km/hr) for the AA-5B. *Country of origin:* USA. *Silhouette:* AA-5A. *Picture:* Tiger.

Power: 1 × Lycoming piston engine   *Span:* 24ft 5½in (7.46m)   *Length:* 19ft 3in (5.86m)

Designed originally as a trainer version of the American Aviation AA-1 Yankee, the AA-1A first flew in 1970. It was re-designated AA-1B Trainer in 1973. The AA-1C was introduced in 1977 and incorporated a number of minor design changes as well as a more powerful 115hp Lycoming engine. The T-Cat is externally identical to the AA-1C but includes a number of internal equipment changes. The Lynx is designed to be both a trainer and sports aircraft and is equipped with a de luxe interior and exterior finish, and wheel fairings. Cruising speed of the T-Cat and Lynx is about 130 mph (210km/hr). *Country of origin:* USA. *Silhouette:* AA-1. *Picture:* Lynx (upper) and T-Cat.

Aerospace of New Zealand Airtrainer CT4   *Confusion:* Sundowner

Power: 1 × Continental piston engine   *Span:* 26ft (7.92m)   *Length:* 23ft 2in (7.06m)

The original Victa Airtourer was a two-seat all-metal fully aerobatic light aircraft which first flew in 1959. Production aircraft were powered by a 100hp Continental engine. A four-seat development, the Aircruiser, was flown in 1967 but not produced in quantity. Aerospace of New Zealand acquired the Australian company's Airtourer and Aircruiser designs in 1971 and re-engineered the latter into a two/three-seat military trainer. Called the Airtrainer CT4, it is powered by a 210hp Continental and cruises at about 160 mph (260km/hr). Fourteen Airtrainer CT4As are being rebuilt for use by the Royal New Zealand Air Force. *Country of origin:* New Zealand.

Power: 1 × Lycoming piston engine   *Span:* 28ft (8.53m)   *Length:* 19ft 8in (5.99m)

The PL-1B is a Taiwan-built version of the PL-1 Laminar, an amateur-designed two-seat light aircraft. First flown in 1962, this conventional tricycle-undercarriage all-metal light aircraft was adopted for use by the Taiwanese Air Force after an example was built and flown at Taichung in 1968. The production version is designated PL-1B Chiensou; a total of 55 were built. Powered by a 150hp Lycoming piston engine, the PL-1B cruises at about 130 mph (210km/hr). Other variants of the basic Pazmany PL-1 include the PL-2, with wing dihedral increased from 3° to 5°, wider cockpit and extensively changed internal structure to simplify construction, and the Indonesian-built Lipnur LT-200. *Country of origin:* Taiwan/USA.

Robin HR 200 *Confusion:* DR 400

Power: 1 × Lycoming piston engine   *Span:* 27ft 4in (8.33m)   *Length:* 21ft 9½in (6.64m)

Although the all-metal two-seat HR 200 series bears an external resemblance to the HR 100/210 it is an entirely new design. Slightly smaller overall, it is intended for schools and clubs. First flight was in 1971 and there are four versions: HR 200/100S, basic version; HR 200/100 Club, similar to the HR 200/100 with 108hp Lycoming engine but with wheel fairings and Hoffmann propeller; HR 200/120B with 118hp Lycoming engine; and HR 200/160 with 160hp Lycoming engine. Main distinguishing feature is the large forward-sliding clear canopy giving almost all-round vision. Cruising speed ranges from about 120 mph (195km/hr) for the HR 200/100 to 155 mph (250km/hr) for the HR 200/160. Latest generation of Robin aircraft is the 2000 series. *Country of origin:* France. *Silhouette and picture:* HR 200/100 Club.

Power: 1 × Lycoming piston engine   *Span:* 28ft 7¼in (8.72m)   *Length:* 22ft 10in (6.96m)

There are several aircraft in the DR 400 all-wood series of light aircraft. The DR 400/100 2+2 is a development of the earlier DR 220 2+2 and first flew in 1972. It is powered by a 100hp Lycoming engine. The DR 400/120 Petit Prince also flew for the first time in 1972 and is powered by a 118hp Lycoming engine. The DR 400/140B Major is powered by a 160hp Lycoming engine and is externally the same as the 2+2 and Petit Prince. The DR 400/600 Chevalier replaced the earlier DR 360 Major 160 and is powered by a 160hp Lycoming engine. Most powerful aircraft in the range is the DR 400/180 Regent (together with the DR 400/180R Remorqueur glider tug), which replaced the earlier DR 235 Regent and DR 380 Prince. This four/five-seater is powered by a 180hp Lycoming. *Country of origin:* **France.** *Silhouette and picture:* DR 400/180.

Piper PA-28/PA-32 Cherokee *Confusion:* Cherokee, DR 400

Power: 1 × Lycoming piston engine   *Span:* 30ft (9.14m)   *Length:* 23ft 6in (7.16m)

The PA-28 Cherokee series embraces several two, two/four and four-seat light aircraft. The original PA-28-140 Cherokee 140 two-seater was announced in 1964. The PA-28-180 Cherokee 180 is a four-seater powered by a 180hp Lycoming engine. Slightly longer than the 140, it has three cabin windows each side. The PA-28-235 is slightly larger than the Model 180 and is powered by a 235hp Lycoming. The introduction of the PA-28-161 Warrior in 1973 saw the first use of a new increased-span tapered wing. The 1977 versions, designated Warrior II, have the original 150hp engine replaced by a 160hp unit. Last of the PA-28 fixed-undercarriage series is the PA-28-181 Archer, with the new tapered wings of the Warrior. This four-seater was introduced in 1972. The Cherokee Six (PA-32) has a longer fuselage and four windows per side. *Country of origin:* USA. *Silhouette:* Cherokee 180. *Picture:* Warrior II.

Power: 1 × Continental piston engine   *Span:* 30ft 10in (9.40m)   *Length:* 24ft 7¼in (7.50m)

The IA 80 Piranha two-seat light training and general-purpose aircraft was developed by the former Wassmer company as the WA 80 Piranha and first flew in 1975. With a fuselage similar to that of the four-seat WA 51 Pacific, it is a particularly roomy aircraft. Of all-plastic construction, it has an extremely smooth finish. Powered by a 100hp Rolls-Royce Continental engine, the IA 80 has a cruising speed of about 120 mph (190km/hr) and a range of 435 miles (700km). Other performance figures include a never-exceed speed of 187 mph (302km/hr); maximum speed at sea level of 149 mph (240km/hr); flaps-up stalling speed of 59 mph (95km/hr); flaps-down stalling speed of 50 mph (80km/hr); sea-level rate of climb of 690ft/min (210m/min); service ceiling of 13,125ft (4,000m); take-off run of 655ft (200m); take-off to 50ft (15m) of 985ft (300m); landing from 50ft (15m) of 985ft (300m); landing run of 495ft (150m); and load factors of +4.4g/–2.2g. Planned production rate is one Piranha per month. *Country of origin:* France.

FWA AS 202 Bravo *Confusion:* Sportsman

Power: 1 × Lycoming piston engine   *Span:* 31ft 11¾in (9.75m)   *Length:* 24ft 7¼in (7.50m)

Following an agreement with the Italian company Siai-Marchetti in 1967, FFA has developed and produced the two/three-seat AS 202 Bravo light trainer and sporting aircraft. First flown in 1969, the Bravo is currently available in two versions: AS 202/15 powered by a 150hp Lycoming engine, of which some 28 had been delivered by the beginning of 1978; and the AS 202/18A powered by a 180hp Lycoming. This aerobatic version first flew in 1974 and over 100 have been ordered, of which 48 are for the Iraqi Air Force. FFA has also flown the prototype of a 260hp Lycoming-engined version, the AS 202/26A. Cruising speed of the AS 202/15 is about 130 mph (210km/hr), and maximum range is 553 miles (890km). *Country of origin:* Switzerland. *Silhouette and picture:* AS 202/15.

Fournier RF-6B/RFB RS 180 Sportsman

Power: 1 × Lycoming piston engine/
1 × Continental piston engine

Span: **34ft 5½in (10.50m)**   *Length* (RS 180): **23ft 5½in (7.15m)**

Designed by René Fournier, the four-seat RS 180 Sportsman first flew in 1973, powered by a 125hp Lycoming engine. Early production aircraft were designated RF6-180 and had the tailplane positioned on the top of the fuselage; in early 1978 the designation was changed to RS 180 and the tailplane was repositioned midway up the fin. The Fournier RF-6B, a generally similar but smaller two-seat version, first flew in 1974. Intended primarily for aerobatics and training, it has a one-piece transparent canopy and is powered by a 100hp Rolls-Royce Continental engine. Cruising speed of the RS 180 is about 145 mph (235km/hr) and that of the RF-6B about 120 mph (190km/hr). Load factors for the RF-6B are +9g and –4.5g. Production was suspended in 1981. *Country of origin:* **France/West Germany.** *Silhouette:* RF-6-180. *Picture:* RS-180.

Fuji FA-200 Aero Subaru   *Confusion:* Vinka

Power: 1 × Lycoming piston engine   *Span:* 30ft 11in (9.42m)   *Length:* 26ft 9½in (8.17m)

Design of this all-metal four-seat light aircraft began in 1964 and the type first flew in the following year. First production version was the FA-200-160 with a 160hp Lycoming engine. Two other versions have been built: the FA-200-180 with 180hp Lycoming engine, and the FA-200-180AO with a 180hp Lycoming and fixed-pitch propeller. Total production all versions had reached 296 by early 1981, when production ceased. *Country of origin:* Japan.

Valmet L-70 Vinka/Miltrainer

Power: 1 × Lycoming piston engine   *Span:* 32ft 4in (9.85m)   *Length:* 24ft 7in (7.50m)

This two/four-seat training/touring light aircraft was first flown in 1975 and was produced to meet a requirement of the Finnish Air Force for a basic trainer to replace its Saab Safirs. Thirty were ordered, with deliveries to be completed by the end of 1982. Of conventional appearance and construction, the Vinka has a large one-piece rearward-sliding canopy and forward-swept wing-root leading edges. Powered by a 200hp Lycoming engine, the Vinka cruises at about 140 mph (225km/hr). The Vinka is known as the Miltrainer for export purposes. *Country of origin:* Finland.

Aerotec A-122 Uirapuru *Confusion:* Vinka

Power: 1 × Lycoming piston engine *Span:* 27ft 11in (8.50m) *Length:* 21ft 8in (6.60m)

The two-seat Uirapuru first flew in 1965, powered by a 108hp Lycoming engine; it was followed by a second aircraft powered by a 150hp engine. An order for 30 A-122As was placed by the Brazilian Air Force in 1967, the aircraft being designated T-23 by the military. Powered by a 160hp Lycoming engine, the type was subsequently ordered by both Bolivia and Paraguay, while the quantity in Brazilian service was increased to 100. The civil version is designated A-122B and is similar to the A-122A but with a revised canopy. A total of 155 Uirapurus of all versions had been built by early 1977, when production ended. Cruising speed of the A-122A is about 115 mph (185km/hr), that of the A-122B about 120 mph (195km/hr). *Country of origin:* Brazil. *Silhouette and picture:* A-122A.

Power: 1 × Avia piston engine   *Span:* 29ft 10¾in (9.11m)   *Length:* 23ft 2½in (7.07m)

The two-seat Zlin 42, the first of a series of sporting and touring aircraft to be developed by the Moravan factory, fist flew in 1967. Initial production aircraft were powered by a 180hp M137A engine and the principal operator was East Germany. Production of the Zlin 42M began in 1974. The Zlin 43, a larger, two /four-seat version of the Zlin 42, is powered by a 210hp Avia M337A. Latest version, with altered cockpit hood and more powerful engine, is the 142. *Country of origin:* Czechoslovakia. *Silhouette:* Zlin 43. *Picture:* Zlin 42M.

BAe Bulldog/Pup

Confusion: Dauphin, Zlin 42/43

Power: 1 × Continental or
1 × Lycoming piston engine

Span (Pup): 31ft (9.45m)   *Length* (Pup): 22ft 11in (6.99m)

Three versions of the all-metal Pup were built. The B-121 Series 1 Pup 100, a two-seater powered by a 100hp Rolls-Royce Continental, first flew in 1967. The B.121 Series 2 Pup 150 was powered by a 150hp Lycoming engine and first flew in 1968. This version was fitted with an optional seat for a third adult or two children. Final variant was the Series 3 Pup 160, six of which were built for Iran. The Bulldog was developed in 1968 as a military trainer version and differed externally in being slightly larger and in having a fully transparent sliding canopy. It first flew in 1969 and production aircraft were fitted with a 200hp Lycoming. Customers include the RAF, Ghana, Nigeria, Jordan, Lebanon, Kenya and the Royal Hong Kong Auxiliary Air Force. Production continues on a small scale. *Country of origin:* UK. *Silhouette:* Bulldog. *Picture:* Pup 150.

Robin DR 221 Dauphin

Power: 1 × Continental or 1 × Lycoming piston engine   *Span:* 28ft 7in (8.72m)   *Length:* 22ft 11½in (7m)

The three/four-seat DR 221 Dauphin, a development of the DR 220 2+2 range, first flew in 1967. All of the aircraft in this range have the characteristic cranked wing of Jodel-inspired light aircraft. The basic DR 220 and the strengthened DR 220A are both powered by a 100hp Rolls-Royce Continental, while the DR 220/108 is fitted with a 115hp Lycoming. The Dauphin is powered by a 115hp Lycoming and cruises at about 125 mph (205km/hr). Other performance figures include a maximum rate of climb at sea level of 650ft/min (198m/min); service ceiling of 12,800ft (3,900m); and a maximum range of 565 miles (910km). More than 140 DR 220s and DR 221s were built before production switched to later Robin designs. *Country of origin:* France. *Silhouette:* DR 220. *Picture:* DR 221.

Socata Rallye

Confusion: FU-24

Power: 1 × Continental piston engine   *Span:* 31ft 11in (9.74m)   *Length:* 22ft 10½in (6.97m)

The Rallye family of light aircraft embraces several different aircraft, all originating from the Morane-Saulnier company's 90hp Rallye-Club of 1959. About 580 Rallyes were built by Morane-Saulnier. Current Socata versions are: Rallye 100S, Rallye 100T, Rallye 100ST, Rallye 150GT, Rallye 150T, Rallye 150ST, Rallye 180GT, Rallye 180T, Rallye 235GT, Rallye 235CA and Rallye 235G. In all cases the designation includes the power of the engine fitted. Total production of Socata-built aircraft has reached at least 1,650. With engine powers of between 100hp and 235hp, performance varies significantly: cruising speeds range from 105 mph (170km/hr) for the lowest-powered up to 150 mph (245km/hr) for the 235hp variants. *Country of origin:* France. *Silhouette:* Rallye 100T. *Picture:* Rallye 235G.

Confusion: Rallye   **Aerospace Fletcher FU-24**

Power: 1 × Lycoming piston engine   *Span:* 42ft (12.81m)   *Length:* 31ft 10in (9.70m)

The FU-24 was initially designed by the Sargent-Fletcher company in the USA for agricultural top-dressing work in New Zealand and first flew in 1954. All manufacturing and sales rights were acquired by Air Parts in New Zealand in 1964 after 70 aircraft had been built in the US. Subsequently the type entered quantity production at Hamilton Airport, New Zealand, and more than 250 FU-24s had been completed by the beginning of 1978. Customer countries include Australia, Bangladesh, Iraq, Pakistan, Thailand and Uruguay. Powered by a 400hp Lycoming, the FU-24 has an operating speed of 105–130 mph (170–210km/hr). A new version of the FU-24, the Cresco, is powered by an Avco Lycoming LTP101 turboprop and has many components in common with the standard aircraft. A military utility variant of the Cresco, known as the Pegasus II, is on offer in the USA, where the civil version of the Cresco is designated AgMaster. *Country of origin:* New Zealand.

Beechcraft Skipper *Confusion:* Tomahawk

Power: 1 × Lycoming piston engine   *Span:* 30ft (9.14m)   *Length:* 24ft (7.32m)

The prototype of this two-seat light trainer, designated PD 285, first flew in 1975, fitted at that time with a conventional tail. Production aircraft, designated Model 77, have the now fashionable T-tail. More than 200 Skippers had been delivered, mainly to Beech Aero Centres, by 1981, when production was temporarily suspended. The Skipper bears a marked resemblance to the Piper Tomahawk. *Country of origin:* USA.

Power: 1 × Lycoming piston engine   *Span:* 34ft (10.36m)   *Length:* 23ft 2in (7.06m)

First introduced in 1978, this two-seat trainer follows the new fashion of mounting the tailplane high on the fin. The cabin is also arranged for maximum all-round visibility by cutting down the rear fuselage decking. The Tomahawk bears a marked resemblance to Beechcraft's Skipper, but the Piper aircraft has a more substantial-looking vertical tail and lacks the small dorsal fin fairing of the Beechcraft. Powered by a 112hp Lycoming engine, the Tomahawk cruises at about 125 mph (200km/hr). Other performance figures include a never-exceed speed of 159 mph (256km/hr); maximum level speed at sea level of 126 mph (202km/hr); economical cruising speed at 10,000ft (3,050m) of 97 mph (156km/hr); and maximum sea-level rate of climb of 718ft/min (219m/min). *Country of origin:* USA.

Nord 3202 *Confusion:* Chipmunk

Power: 1 × Potez piston engine   *Span:* 31ft 2in (9.50m)   *Length:* 26ft 8in (8.12m)

The Nord 3202 tandem two-seat primary trainer flew for the first time in 1957. Developed from the Nord 3200 and 3201, it was adopted as a replacement for the Stampe SV.4 trainers of the French Army Air Force. The first 50 of the 100 Nord 3202s built were powered by Potez 4D.32 engines. The second 50 were powered by Potez 4D.34Bs uprated from 240 to 260hp and were fitted with radio compasses. Production of the Nord 3202 ended in 1961. *Country of origin:* France.

Power: 1 × de Havilland piston engine   *Span:* 34ft 4in (10.47m)   *Length:* 25ft 5in (7.75m)

Designed by the Canadian de Havilland company, the tandem two-seat Chipmunk first flew in 1946. Some 220 were produced in Canada for both civil and military users; a further 60 were produced under licence by OGMA in Portugal. Production in the UK consisted of T10s for the RAF and Mk 21s and 23s for civil users; Mk 22s are refurbished ex-RAF aircraft for civil use. The Mk 23 was a single-seat agricultural aircraft and the Mk 22A was a Bristol tourer version with a one-piece blown hood and wheel spats. Powered by a 145hp de Havilland Gipsy Major 10, the Chipmunk has a maximum cruising speed of about 143 mph (230km/hr). Range is 453 miles (730km). *Country of origin:* Canada. *Silhouette and picture:* T10.

HAL HT-2 *Confusion:* Chipmunk, I-115

Power: 1 × Blackburn piston engine   *Span:* 35ft 2in (10.72m)   *Length:* 24ft 8½in (7.53m)

The tandem two-seat HT-2 was the first Indian powered aircraft of indigenous design and first flew in 1951. About 160 have been built, mostly for the Indian Air Force, Navy and civil users. In addition to two aircraft presented to Indonesia and Singapore, twelve were supplied to Ghana. Similar in appearance to the DHC-1 Chipmunk, though with a more angular fin and rudder, the HT-2 is powered by a 155hp Blackburn Cirrus Major III and cruises at about 115 mph (185km/hr). *Country of origin:* India.

AISA I-115

Power: 1 × ENMA piston engine   *Span:* 31ft 3in (9.54m)   *Length:* 24ft 1in (7.35m)

First flown in 1952, the I-115 tandem two-seat trainer was put into production as a standard type for the Spanish Air Force with the designation E.9. Designed as a replacement for the Spanish Air Force's Bucker Bu 131 biplane trainers, the I-115 entered quantity production in May 1954. A total of 450 I-115s were built, and the type has the distinction of being the first aircraft of indigenous design to enter series production for the Spanish Air Force after the war. At the end of their military career most of the 115s were transferred to Spanish flying clubs, although some were retained by the Air Force for liaison and training. Of all-wood construction, the I-115 has a maximum speed of 143 mph (230km/hr), cruises at 126 mph (203km/hr) and has a ferry range of 620 miles. *Country of origin:* **Spain.**

Mudry CAP 10/CAP 20/CAP 21
Confusion: Emeraude

Power: 1 × Lycoming piston engine   *Span* (CAP 10): 26ft 5¼in (8.06m)   *Length* (CAP 10): 23ft 6in (7.16m)

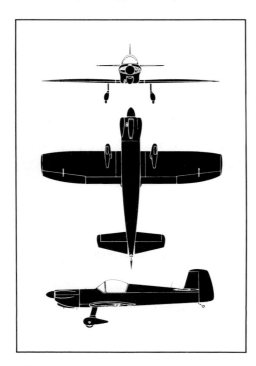

Developed from the Piel Emeraude, the two-seat all-wood CAP 10 is intended for use as a training, touring or aerobatic aircraft. First flight was in 1968, and a total of 89 had been built by mid-1978, including some 30 for the French Air Force. The CAP 20 is essentially a single-seat derivative of the CAP 10, although of almost completely new design. It has been refined considerably since it first flew in 1969, and the latest version, the CAP 20L, is suitable for competition aerobatics. Production was terminated in 1981 to make way for the CAP 21, with a new wing and undercarriage. Powered by a 200hp Lycoming engine, the CAP-20L cruises at about 165 mph (265km/hr), compared with 155 mph (250km/hr) for the 180hp CAP 10B. *Country of origin:* France. *Main silhouette:* CAP 20. *Picture:* CAP 20L.

Piel/Scintex CP 301 Emeraude

Power: 1 × Continental piston engine   *Span:* 26ft 4½in (8.04m)   *Length:* 20ft 8in (6.30m)

Designed by Claude Piel, the two-seat, all-wood Emeraude was first flown in 1952, with the first production aircraft flying the following year. Several versions have been built, commercially and by amateurs, powered by a variety of engines from 65 to 125hp. The Scintex Emeraude is largely similar to the Piel-built aircraft but features a one-piece blown canopy in place of the upwards-opening canopy doors of the latter. The CP 301 was built under licence in small quantities in Britain, where it was known as the Fairtravel Linnet, and in West Germany by Binder Aviatik. The Super Emeraude is a slightly larger version with higher payload and improved performance. Powered by a 90hp Continental piston engine, the CP 301 Emeraude cruises at about 125 mph (200km/hr). *Country of origin:* France. *Main silhouette:* CP 301; *lower side view:* Super Emeraude. *Picture:* Super Emeraude.

Piaggio P.148 *Confusion:* Emeraude

Power: 1 × Lycoming piston engine   *Span:* 36ft 6in (11.12m)   *Length:* 27ft 8½in (8.45m)

The Piaggio P.148 side-by-side two-seat primary trainer was selected for Italian Air Force training schools in 1951. A total of about 100 were ordered and the type first flew in 1951, with production deliveries commencing the following year. In 1962 a small number of ex-Italian Air Force P.148s were delivered to the Somali Air Corps as part of an Italian technical aid programme. The type is also in service in limited quantities with the Zaire Air Force; these are ex-Italian aircraft. Normally flown as a two-seater, the P.148 was certificated as a three-seater, the third position being located centrally behind the side-by-side front seats. The P.148 has many components in common with the P.149. Powered by a 190hp Lycoming engine, the P.148 cruises at about 125 mph (201km/hr). *Country of origin:* Italy.

Power: 1 × Continental piston engine   *Span:* 26ft 11½in (8.22m)   *Length:* 21ft 4in (6.50m)

The D.11, the first two-seat light aircraft in the Jodel series, was developed from the D.9 Bébé. It first flew in 1950. The type has been built extensively by amateurs throughout Europe and North America. The D.112 is more widespread and is a refined version of the D.11. It has been built by Wassmer, SAN and Alpavia, aircraft built by the last two companies being known as D.117s. Amateur-built examples powered by the 95hp Continental C90 are usually designated D.119. There are about 1,500 commercially built aircraft in the series. Cruising speed is approximately 120 mph (195km/hr). *Country of origin:* France. *Silhouette and picture:* D.11.

Jodel DR.1050/DR.1051 Ambassadeur/Sicile *Confusion:* D.11/112

Power: 1 × Continental or 1 × Potez piston engine   *Span:* 28ft 7½in (8.72m)   *Length:* 20ft 10in (6.35m)

Centre Est was formed in 1957 to design and build the Jodel range of light aircraft. First in the series was the DR.100 Ambassadeur, which first flew in 1958. The first DR.1050 with a 100hp Continental was flown in 1959. A further version with a 105hp Potez engine was built in 1960 and designated DR.1051. These aircraft were also built under licence by Société Aéronautique Normande (SAN). In 1963 an improved Ambassadeur was announced, named the Sicile, with either a Continental (DR.1050) or Potez (DR.1051) engine. Last of the series were the DR.1050MM1 and DR.1051MM1 Sicile Record, with swept-back fin and rudder and one-piece elevator. Total production of the DR.100 and its derivatives amounted to more than 800 aircraft. *Country of origin:* France. *Main silhouette:* DR.1050; *upper side view:* DR.1050MM1. *Picture:* DR.1050.

Power: 1 × Continental or 1 × Potez piston engine   *Span:* 33ft 8in (10.27m)   *Length:* 26ft (7.92m)

The Mousquetaire was developed by SAN as an economical four-seat light touring aircraft. It first flew in 1958 and sported a distinctive triangular fin, replaced in later aircraft with a conventional swept assembly. Five versions of the D.140 Mousquetaire were built, the sixth, the D.140R, being designated the Abeille. First flown in 1965, this aircraft was exclusively developed for glider towing and featured an extensively glazed cabin. The D.150 Mascaret is a two-seat light aircraft with a 100hp Continental or 105hp Potez. It is outwardly similar to the D.140 series but slightly smaller. Performance figures for the Mousquetaire include a maximum cruising speed at 7,000ft (2,300m) and 75 per cent power of 149 mph (240km/hr); maximum sea-level rate of climb of 750ft/min (230m/min); and maximum-fuel range of 870 miles (1,400km). *Country of origin:* France. *Main silhouette:* D.140; *lower side view:* D.140B. *Picture:* D.140.

393

Rollason D.62 Condor *Confusion:* Zlin Z 50L

Power: 1 × Continental piston engine   *Span:* 27ft 6in (8.38m)   *Length:* 22ft 6in (6.86m)

The side-by-side two-seat Condor, essentially a much improved version of the amateur-built tandem two-seat Turbi, was built under licence in Britain by Rollason, the first production aircraft flying in 1961. The all-wood Condor is similar in some respects to the Jodel D.112 Club but has a slightly tapered wing without the Jodel's characteristic upturned outer panels. Total production by Rollason reached 51 by early 1974. Powered by a 100hp Rolls-Royce Continental piston engine, the Condor cruises at about 115 mph (185km/hr). *Country of origin:* France/UK.

Power: 1 × Lycoming piston engine *Span:* 28ft 2in (8.58m) *Length:* 21ft 9in (6.62m)

The Zlin Z 50L single-seat fully aerobatic competition aircraft first flew in 1975. The broad wings are of almost constant chord and are symmetrical in section, while the tailplane is braced on the underside. Powered by a 260hp Lycoming engine, the Z 50L cruises at about 170 mph (275km/hr). *Country of origin:* Czechoslovakia.

ICA-Brasov IAR-822/IAR-826/IAR-827 *Confusion:* Pawnee, Ipanema

Power: 1 × Lycoming piston engine   *Span:* 42ft (12.80m)   *Length:* 30ft 10in (9.40m)

Prototype of the IAR-822 single/two-seat agricultural aircraft first flew in 1970, with series production of the first batch of 200 aircraft commencing the following year. Early aircraft were of mixed construction, but in 1973 an all-metal version was introduced, designated IAR-826. Powered by a 290hp Lycoming engine, the IAR-826 has an operating speed of about 75–100 mph (120–160km/hr). The IAR-827A is a developed version of the all-metal IAR-826 with increased payload, a Polish radial engine and improved flying characteristics. Performance figures for the IAR-827 include a cruising speed (agricultural version at maximum take-off weight) of 121 mph (195km/hr) and maximum rate of climb at sea level of 885ft/min (270m/min). *Country of origin:* Romania. *Silhouette:* IAR-826. *Picture:* IAR-827 Turbo.

Power: 1 × Lycoming piston engine   *Span* (Pawnee): 36ft 2in (11.02)   *Length* (Pawnee): 24ft 8½in (7.53m)

The original Pawnee single-seat agricultural aircraft first flew in 1959. The type has become one of the most widely used of all agricultural aircraft and production of the PA-25 version had exceeded 4,250 by 1974. Current production aircraft are the PA-25 Pawnee D, powered by a 235hp Lycoming engine, and the PA-36 Brave, previously known as the Pawnee Brave. Two versions of the Brave are currently in production: the basic Brave 300 powered by a 300hp Lycoming engine and the Brave 375 with 375hp Lycoming. The Brave is externally identifiable by its swept tail assembly, lack of wing bracing and simple sprung-steel undercarriage. *Country of origin:* USA. *Silhouette:* Brave. *Picture:* Pawnee D.

Embraer EMB-201 Ipanema *Confusion:* Pawnee, IAR-822

Power: 1 × Lycoming piston engine   *Span:* 38ft 4in (11.69m)   *Length:* 24ft 4½in (7.43m)

The original version of this single-seat agricultural aircraft was designed to a specification laid down by the Brazilian Ministry of Agriculture and first flew in 1970. The following versions have been built: EMB-200 and EMB-200A, of which 73 were built between 1970 and 1974; EMB-201, the developed version with new wing leading edge and wingtips, of which 188 were built; the current-production EMB-201A, first flown in 1977 with several minor aerodynamic refinements. More than 500 Ipanemas of all versions have been sold. A glider-tug version has also been built, designated EMB-201R. Three examples have been delivered to the Brazilian Air Force. *Country of origin:* Brazil. *Silhouette:* EMB-200. *Picture:* EMB-201.

Power: **1 × PT6A turboprop** *Span:* **50ft 3in (15.32m)** *Length:* **36ft 2in (10.97m)**

First flown in December 1981, the Fieldmaster is the largest agricultural aircraft so far produced in the West and is unusual in having a tricycle undercarriage and a turboprop engine. The Fieldmaster is fitted with a "buddy" seat behind the pilot's position, and features a large titanium chemical hopper forward of the cockpit which is an integral part of the fuselage structure. The spray-dispersal system is incorporated in the wing flaps. Maximum cruise-power speed is 140kt (259km/hr) and range is 700 nautical miles (1,297km). *Country of origin:* UK.

Cessna Ag Wagon/Ag Truck *Confusion:* Basant, Quail, UTVA-65

Power: 1 × Continental piston engine   *Span:* 40ft 8½in (12.41m)   *Length:* 26ft 3in (8m)

The original Model 188 Ag Wagon first flew in 1965, powered by a 230hp Continental, and incorporated a number of components common to the Model 180 high-wing aircraft of that vintage. In late 1971 Cessna introduced a new range of agricultural types, three of which were based on the earlier aircraft. One of them, the Ag Pickup, was discontinued in 1976. The Ag Wagon and Ag Truck are in current production. The Ag Wagon is powered by a 300hp Continental engine and is a conventional agricultural aircraft with strut-braced wings and enclosed cockpit with all-round vision. The Ag Truck is similar to the Ag Wagon, but has a slightly longer wing, a larger hopper and other equipment refinements. Ag Wagon production has now ceased. A turbocharged version of the Ag Truck is called the Ag Husky. *Country of origin:* USA. *Silhouette:* Ag Wagon. *Picture:* Ag Truck.

Power: 1 × Lycoming piston engine   *Span:* 39ft 4½in (12m)   *Length:* 29ft 6¼in (9m)

The HAL HA-31 Basant (Spring) was originally powered by a 250hp Rolls-Royce Continental but was subsequently completely redesigned as the HA-31 Mk II and re-engined with a 400hp Lycoming; it first flew in this form in 1972. A pre-production batch of 20 was built, the first eight of which were handed over to the Indian Ministry of Food and Agriculture in 1974. Series production finished in 1980 after 40 aircraft had been built. The Basant is of conventional design and construction for an agricultural aircraft, with strut-braced wings and a swept fin and rudder. Cruising speed is about 115 mph (185km/hr). *Country of origin:* India.

AAMSA A9B-M Quail *Confusion:* Basant, Ag Truck, Privrednik

Power: 1 × Lycoming piston engine　　*Span:* 34ft 9in (10.59m)　　*Length:* 24ft (7.32m)

In the 1970s the Mexican AAMSA company took over production of the Aero Commander Quail and Sparrow Commander from Rockwell in the USA. The Sparrow Commander is no longer on the line but the Quail continues in production under the designation A9B-M. The Quail has a normal operating speed of 90–100 mph (145–161km/hr) and has a 795lit fertiliser/insecticide hopper. Over 160 Quails have been built. *Country of origin:* **Mexico.**

Power: 1 × Lycoming piston engine *Span:* 40ft 1in (12.22m) *Length:* 27ft 9in (8.46m)

The single-seat UTVA-65 agricultural aircraft first flew in 1965 and combines the basic wings, tail assembly and undercarriage of the four-seat high-wing UTVA-60 with a new all-metal fuselage. In common with most low-winged agricultural aircraft, the UTVA-65 has a high-set, well-protected cockpit located approximately halfway along the fuselage, with a 26.5ft^3 hopper forward of the cockpit. Powered by a 295hp Lycoming piston engine, the UTVA-65 has a maximum speed of about 125 mph (200km/hr). *Country of origin:* Yugoslavia.

WSK-PZL-Mielec M-18 Dromader

Confusion: Kruk, Thrush Commander

Power: 1 × PZL piston engine   *Span:* 58ft 1in (17.7m)   *Length:* 31ft 1in (9.47m)

Significantly larger than the Kruk, which is also made in Poland, the M-18 Dromader first flew in 1976 and is now being produced at the rate of eight aircraft per month. It is attracting foreign sales, particularly as it has a home-built radial engine, a type of powerplant which is out of production in the West. The Dromader has an operating speed of 106–118 mph (170–190km/hr) and a maximum range of 323 miles (520km). *Country of origin:* Poland.

Power: 1 × PZL piston engine   *Span:* 48ft 6½in (14.80m)   *Length:* 29ft 10in (9.10m)

Intended as a replacement for the PZL-101 Gawron, the PZL-101M Kruk (Raven) was designed in the early 1960s. Initially powered by a 260hp Ivchenko engine, the aircraft was progressively refined into the current production version, the PZL-106A. The PZL-106 first flew in 1973, powered by a 400hp Lycoming engine; production aircraft are fitted with a 600hp PZL-35 seven-cylinder radial. Production commenced in 1976, with an anticipated total requirement of some 600 aircraft for the CMEA (Council for Mutual Economic Aid) member countries. The Kruk can carry its maximum chemical payload of 2,205lb (1,000kg) at an operating speed of 75–100 mph (120–160km/hr). A further development is the PZL-106AT Turbo-Kruk, fitted with a PT6A turboprop engine and a Hartzell fully feathering three-blade propeller. The Turbo-Kruk made its first flight in July 1981. *Country of origin:* Poland. *Silhouette:* PZL-106A. *Picture:* PZL-106.

Ayres Thrush/Turbo-Thrush   *Confusion: —*

Power: 1 × R-1340 or 1 × R-1300
piston engine or 1 × PT6A turboprop

Span: **44ft 4in (13.51m)**   *Length:* **29ft 4½in (8.95m)**

Ayres Corporation acquired the manufacturing rights to the Rockwell Thrush Commander-600 in 1977 and has the following versions in production: Thrush-600 with 600hp Pratt & Whitney Wasp radial, and the Turbo-Thrush S-2R, similar to the Model 600 but powered by a 750shp Pratt & Whitney turboprop. The aircraft are being built at the former Rockwell Thrush Commander plant at Albany, Georgia. Working speed of the Model 600 is 105–115 mph (170–185km/hr), that of the Turbo-Thrush S-2R 95–150 mph (153–241km/hr). Both the Thrush and the Turbo-Thrush have as standard a 53 cu ft (1.5m³) hopper capable of holding up to 400 US gal (1,514 lit) of liquid or 3,280lb (1,487kg) of dry chemicals, while the Turbo-Thrush offers a 500 US gal (1,893 lit) hopper as an option. *Country of origin:* USA. *Silhouette and picture:* Thrush-600.

Power: 1 × M462 piston engine   *Span:* **40ft 1¼in (12.22m)**   *Length:* **28ft 0½in (8.55m)**

First flown in 1963, this agricultural and light utility aircraft entered series production in 1965. An improved version, the Z-37A, was introduced in 1971 and is now the standard production model. It features some structural reinforcement and incorporates corrosion-resistant materials. A total of 600 Cmelaks had been delivered by the beginning of 1975, and operators include Bulgaria, Czechoslovakia, Finland, East Germany, Hungary, India, Iraq, Poland, UK and Yugoslavia. Let has also built some 27 examples of a two-seat training version, the Z-37A-2. Powered by a 315hp nine-cylinder radial engine, the Cmelak cruises at about 115 mph (185km/hr) and operates at between 68 and 74 mph (109–119km/hr). *Country of origin:* Czechoslovakia. *Silhouette:* Z-37A. *Picture:* Z-37.

Consisting mainly of touring/light training aircraft, the high-wing/single-engine class also contains a few larger transports and some types used for civil/military roles, such as training, light ground attack and supply-dropping.

The majority have tailwheel undercarriages but a number of the later types have tricycle landing gear. Main points to look for are wing and tail shapes, cabin and undercarriage configuration, and undercarriage shape and position.

Aeritalia AM-3C

The Piper Super Cub and the Autocrat represent the classic older types of light aircraft, the basic design of which did not change for many years. The Aero Boero 150, Citabria and Maule all have cabins faired from the wing at the rear, as does the Skywagon. A number of the others, however, have the cabin rear windows stepped down to the aft fuselage.

Cantilever main undercarriage legs—exemplified by the UTVA-60, Bird Dog and SM.1919—are a clear recognition point. Head-on views are particularly difficult and an overall

de Havilland Canada Beaver

impression of wing struts, undercarriage legs and fuselage cross-section should be gained. A particularly "stalky" type, in both the head-on and side views, is the Brigadyr.

The Beaver, with its very blunt nose and curved fin, stands out, though its family relationship to the larger Otter is quite clear. The Broussard is also in a class on its own, with its high wing, radial engine and twin fins and rudders.

The Gawron also has special characteristics, combining a swept wing with a blunt nose and a rearward-canted main undercarriage. This type contrasts sharply with the Porter, which has a long nose, strutted undercarriage and a very tall, square-cut fin. The Wilga, on the other hand, has a tall, swept fin, small, flat nose and a "double-bend" main undercarriage.

The aircraft of the next group, including the Do 27 and Courier, have no wing or undercarriage bracing struts. The wings with the cabin top appearing above. Their slightly forward-swept wings with cut-outs at the root leading edge are unusual.

Helio Courier

Partenavia Oscar

Stallion has a cantilever wing plus a sharply rearward-canted undercarriage and wingtip tanks.

On the tricycle-undercarriage high-wing singles the student should look for wing, cabin and fin shapes, plus strut layout. Wheel spats can be a help, but care has to be taken because this form of streamlining can be removed.

There is a lot of similarity between the first four tricycle-undercarriage types, the Mescalero through to the Stationair 6, and points of detail must be looked for. The extra length of the Stationair 7 marks it out, while the Centurion has a retractable undercarriage and no struts at all.

The last two types, the Junior and Safari, have shoulder

Piper PA-18 Super Cub *Confusion:* Autocrat

Power: 1 × Lycoming piston engine   *Span:* 35ft 2½in (10.73m)   *Length:* 22ft 7in (6.88m)

The original Super Cub, powered by a 90hp Continental, was first certificated in 1949 and was itself the successor to a long line of Piper light aircraft which began with the Taylor E-2 Cub of 1931. Later aircraft include the J-3 Cub of 1938, the PA-12 Super Cruiser of 1940 and the Vagabond, which was the forerunner of the Tri-Pacer line. Retaining the tandem two-seat arrangement, the current Super Cub is powered by a 150hp Lycoming, giving it a cruising speed of about 105 mph (169km/hr). Most Super Cubs are used for agricultural purposes. By the beginning of 1978 more than 40,000 Cubs of all types had been delivered and large numbers are still flying throughout the world, though most are concentrated in the USA. *Country of origin:* USA. *Silhouette and picture:* Super Cub.

Auster/Beagle Autocrat/Autocar/Terrier

Power: 1 × de Havilland or 1 × Blackburn piston engine   *Span:* 36ft (10.97m)   *Length:* 23ft 8in (7.21m)

The Auster range embraces several types which can still be seen flying throughout the world. The J/1 Autocrat was the first post-war product of the Auster company and was derived from the Taylorcraft Model D spotter aircraft. Most of the range are externally similar and can be recognised by engine differences and by slight variations in the size of the vertical tail. All have V-strut wing bracing and parallel-chord wings. The Beagle A.61 Terrier is a civil conversion of the Auster AOP.6. Early conversions were also known as the Tugmaster. Introduced in 1961, the Terrier has a larger vertical tail and long exhaust pipe and silencer. *Country of origin:* UK. *Main silhouette:* AOP.6; *lower side view:* Terrier. *Picture:* Autocrat.

Aero Boero 95/115/180

Confusion: Citabria

Power: 1 × Continental or 1 × Lycoming piston engine   *Span:* 34ft 2½in (10.42m)   *Length:* 22ft 7½in (6.90m)

This family of three and four-seat light aircraft consists of some eleven different types: the basic AB 95 Standard with 95hp Continental; the AB 95A De Lujo with 100hp Continental; AB 95A Fumigador agricultural version; AB 95B with 150hp engine; AB 95/115 with 115hp engine, wheel fairings and streamlined engine cowling; AB 115 BS with swept-back fin and rudder; AB 180 four-seat version with 180hp Lycoming; AB 180 RV three-seat version with swept-back fin and rudder; AB 180 Condor high-altitude version with modified wingtips. Two lower-powered versions of the AB 180, the AB 150 RV and the RB 150 Ag, have also been built. *Country of origin:* **Argentina.** *Silhouette:* AB 95/115. *Picture:* AB 180.

Power: 1 × Lycoming piston engine   *Span* (Citabria): 33ft 5in (10.19m)   *Length* (Citabria): 22ft 8in (6.91m)

This series of high-wing light aircraft embraces several models of broadly similar appearance but widely differing powerplants and performances. Derived from the Aeronca Champion and Sedan light aircraft of the late 1940s, via the Champion Traveller and Challenger of the 1950s, current aircraft have a squared-off vertical tail and angular fuselage but retain the tandem seating of earlier aircraft. Three versions of the Citabria have been built. Production ceased in 1980. *Country of origin:* USA. *Silhouette:* Citabria. *Picture:* Decathlon.

Maule M-4 Rocket/M-5 Lunar Rocket

Confusion: Citabria

Power: 1 × Continental or
1 × Lycoming piston engine

Span: 30ft 10in (9.40m)

Length: 22ft (6.71m)

Production of the basic Maule M-4 Rocket began in 1963. This design was a conventional four-seat light aircraft with V-strut wing bracing and a rounded vertical tail. Four versions were available: the M-4 Jetasen with 145hp Continental; the M-4 Astro-Rocket with 180hp Franklin engine; the M-4 Rocket with 210hp Continental, which was also available as a seaplane; and the M-4 Strata Rocket, generally similar to the Rocket but powered by a 220hp Franklin engine. The M-5 Lunar Rocket was developed from the Strata Rocket but has a 30% increase in flap area and enlarged tail surfaces. Production is now concentrated on various versions of the M-5. Powered by a 210hp Continental, the M-5 has a cruising speed of about 165 mph (266km/hr). *Country of origin:* USA. *Silhouette:* M-4. *Picture:* M-5.

Confusion: Skywagon, Rocket

HAL HAOP-27 Krishak

Power: 1 × Continental piston engine   *Span:* 37ft 6in (11.43m)   *Length:* 27ft 7in (8.41m)

The Krishak was designed to meet an operational requirement of the Indian Air Force for an air observation post (AOP) light aircraft. It first flew in late 1959 and a total of 68 were ordered, all of which had been delivered by 1969. The Krishak normally carries a crew of two, but there is a swivelling seat for a third person in the rear of the cabin. Evolved from the HUL-26 Pushpak, the Krishak has a similar wing, with the addition of flaps, and has a more pointed vertical tail. Powered by a 225hp Rolls-Royce Continental, it has a cruising speed of about 130 mph (209km/hr). *Country of origin:* India.

Cessna Model 180/Model 185 Skywagon

Confusion: Krishak, UTVA-60

Power: 1 × Continental piston engine   *Span:* 35ft 10in (10.92m)   *Length:* 25ft 9in (7.85m)

This six-seat utility aircraft first flew in 1952 as a four-seater. Throughout its production life the type has retained the tailwheel undercarriage and the upright vertical tail. Two versions are currently in production: the basic Model 180 Skywagon and the Model 180 Skywagon II, which includes a factory-installed avionics package. Production had exceeded 5,800 by the beginning of 1978. The Model 185 Skywagon has been developed from the Model 180 and first flew in 1960. It features a strengthened fuselage and is fitted with a 300hp Continental in place of the Model 180's 230hp unit. A military version, designated U-17 in the US, is also available. Production reached over 6,000 but is now to be terminated. *Country of origin:* USA. *Main silhouette:* Model 180; *lower side view:* U-17. *Picture:* Model 180.

Power: **1 × Lycoming piston engine**   *Span:* **37ft 5in (11.40m)**   *Length:* **27ft 6in (8.38m)**

Derived from the UTVA-56 four-seat utility aircraft of 1959, the UTVA-60 is essentially the production version of the earlier aircraft. Five basic versions have been built, differing in the type of equipment carried for the various roles, which include light transport, air ambulance, agricultural spraying and floatplane. The UTVA-66 was developed from the UTVA-60 and first flew in 1967. Powered by a 270hp Lycoming engine, the UTVA-66 cruises at 143 mph (230km/hr). Both types are in service with the Yugoslav Air Force. *Country of origin:* **Yugoslavia**. *Silhouette:* UTVA-60. *Picture:* UTVA-66.

Cessna O-1 Bird Dog *Confusion:* SM.1019

Power: 1 × Continental piston engine   *Span:* 36ft (10.97m)   *Length:* 25ft 10in (7.89m)

The Bird Dog was developed for the US Army as a light reconnaissance and observation aircraft which could also be used for liaison and training duties. It first flew in 1950 and remained in continuous production until late 1958, by which time more than 3,300 had been built. It briefly re-entered production in 1962 and a further 100 were built. The type is still in large-scale service in many countries throughout the world. The Bird Dog has a tailwheel undercarriage, and nearly all variants have the characteristic rounded fin and rudder. The exception is the O-1C, some 25 of which were built for the US Marine Corps, which has the old-style squared-off tail of the early Cessna 180s and 185s. *Country of origin:* USA.

Power: 1 × Allison 250 turboprop   *Span:* 36ft (10.97m)   *Length:* 27ft 11½in (8.52m)

This tandem two-seat Stol light aircraft is based on the Cessna O-1 Bird Dog but has an extensively modified airframe to meet present-day operational requirements. First flown in 1969, it was put into production for the Italian Army, powered by a 400hp Allison 250-B17 turboprop. Total order was for 100 aircraft. The SM.1019E is stressed for two underwing hardpoints and can carry a variety of operational equipment. Cruising speed is about 185 mph (300km/hr). Other performance figures include a maximum rate of climb at sea level of 1,810ft/min (551m/min); operational ceiling of 25,000ft (7,620m); and a typical operational radius with two rocket launchers of 69 miles (111km). *Country of origin:* Italy.

Aeritalia AM-3C

Confusion: SM.1019

Power: 1 × Piaggio/Lycoming piston engine   *Span:* 41ft 5½in (12.64m)   *Length:* 29ft 4in (8.93m)

The three/four-seat AM-3C was originally designated MB.335 and first flew in 1967. Suitable for forward air control, observation, liaison, passenger and freight transport, casualty evacuation and tactical support, the type has been built in quantity for the Rwanda Air Force and the South African Air Force, in which service it is known as the Bosbok. The AM-3C is stressed to carry a variety of armaments on two underwing pylons. Powered by a Piaggio-built 340hp Lycoming, the AM-3C cruises at about 150 mph (245km/hr). *Country of origin:* Italy.

Power: **1 × Praga Doris piston engine**   *Span:* **45ft 9½in (13.96m)**   *Length:* **28ft (8.54m)**

The L-60 Brigadyr three/four-seat general-purpose aircraft first flew in 1955 and by the time production ended in 1960 more than 400 had been built. Bearing a slight resemblance to the wartime Fieseler Storch, with its long, stalky undercarriage and generous expanse of cabin glazing, the Brigadyr has been used for air observation by the Czech Air Force as well as for agricultural duties. Powered by a 220hp Praga Doris M 208B engine, the L-60 cruises at about 110 mph (177km/hr). *Country of origin:* **Czechoslovakia.**

DHC DHC-2 Beaver

Confusion: Otter, Do 27

Power: 1 × R-985 piston engine or 1 × PT6A turboprop   *Span:* 48ft (14.64m)   *Length:* 30ft 4in (9.24m)

Nearly 1,700 DHC-2 Beaver light utility transports were built, the first flying in 1947. Carrying either seven passengers or freight, the Beaver has proved capable of operating in very rough, remote areas. The Beaver Mk I was produced in both civil and military forms, some 968 of the latter variant going to the US Army/USAF as the U-6A. Beavers have been fitted with floats and skis. A later development is the Turbo-Beaver Mk III, which has the Pratt & Whitney radial engine replaced by a PT6A turboprop. This changes the nose shape significantly. The Mk III can carry 10 passengers, cruises at 157 mph (252km/hr) and has a range of 677 miles (1,090km). *Country of origin:* Canada. *Silhouette and picture:* Mk I.

Power: 1 × R-1340 piston engine   *Span:* 58ft (17.69m)   *Length:* 41ft 10in (12.80m)

First flown in 1951, the 10-seat Otter has been extensively used by the armed forces of USA, Canada, Australia, Ghana and India, and in smaller numbers by several South American nations. A truly utility type, the Otter can be used for carrying passengers or freight, photographic survey or search and rescue. The Otter can be fitted with floats and skis, and has been used in Antarctica. Powered by a 600hp Pratt & Whitney radial engine, the Otter has a cruising speed of about 130 mph (209km/hr) and a maximum level speed of 160 mph (257km/hr). A turboprop conversion of the Otter, powered by a single Pratt & Whitney Aircraft of Canada PT6A-27, has been produced by Cox Air Resources of Edmonton, Canada. Main advantages of the conversion are a reduced empty weight, increased fuel and payload capacity, and a slight improvement in performance. Some 270 piston-engined Otters are still in service. *Country of origin:* Canada.

Max Holste Broussard

Confusion: Beaver

Power: 1 × R-985 piston engine *Span:* 45ft 1in (13.75m) *Length:* 28ft 4½in (8.65m)

The twin-finned Broussard light utility aircraft was developed from the MH 152 experimental observation type and first flew in 1952. Production aircraft are designated MH 1521 and MH 1521A. A modified version, the MH 1522, has also been built with double-slotted wing flaps and full-span leading-edge slots. Total production of the Broussard exceeded 330 aircraft, and operators are based in Argentina, Cameroun, Central African Republic, Chad, Congo, France, Malagasy, Mauretania, Morocco, Portugal and Senegal. Powered by a 450hp Pratt & Whitney Wasp radial, the Broussard cruises at about 150 mph (245km/hr) and has a maximum range of 745 miles (1,200km). *Country of origin:* France. *Silhouette and picture:* MH 1521.

Power: 1 × AI-14R piston engine   *Span:* **41ft 7½in (12.68m)**   *Length:* **29ft 6½in (9m)**

The PZL-101A Gawron (Rook) single–engined agricultural, ambulance and utility light aircraft was developed from the Russian Yak-12M and first flew in 1958. From 1961 the type was approved by a number of Eastern bloc countries as their standard agricultural aircraft, and more than 330 had been built when production ended in 1973. The Gawron has also been sold in Austria, Finland, India, Spain, Turkey and Vietnam. The aircraft is conventional in all major respects, with V-braced high wing and braced tail assembly. Powered by a 260hp AI-14R nine-cylinder radial engine, the Gawron cruises at about 80 mph (130km/hr). *Country of origin:* Poland.

Pilatus/Fairchild PC-6 Porter *Confusion:* Wilga

Power: 1 × Lycoming piston engine or 1 × Astazou turboprop   *Span:* **49ft 8in (15.14m)**   *Length:* **36ft 10in (11.23m)**

The Pilatus Porter Stol utility aircraft was first flown in 1959 and some 50 production aircraft had been delivered by mid-1965, by which time the Turbo-Porter was in quantity production. The Turbo-Porter first flew in 1961 and several variants have been built over the last few years. Current production version is the PC-6/B2-H2 Turbo Porter, powered by a 550shp Pratt & Whitney PT6A turboprop. The type was also manufactured under licence in the USA by Fairchild Industries, the first US-built aircraft flying in 1966. A militarised version with underwing hardpoints is called the AU-23A Peacemaker. The US Army designation for the Turbo-Porter is the UV-20A Chiricahua. By mid-1981 more than 430 PC-6s of all types had been delivered to operators in over 50 countries. *Country of origin:* Switzerland/USA. *Main silhouette:* **Porter**; *lower side view:* **Turbo-Porter**. *Picture:* **Turbo-Porter**.

Power: 1 × Ivchenko piston engine   *Span:* 36ft 5¾in (11.12m)   *Length:* 26ft 6¾in (8.10m)

The Wilga (Thrush) was designed as a successor to the Czechoslovakian L-60 Brigadyr in the agricultural role and first flew in 1962 as the Wilga 1, powered by a 180hp WN-6B engine. The design was modified in 1967 and designated the Wilga 35. Current production versions are the Wilga 35A for club flying, the Wilga 35P light transport, the agricultural 35R and the 35S ambulance version. A further variant is the Wilga 80, some examples of which are fitted with floats. Wilgas can be seen flying in many parts of the world and some 700 have been built. *Country of origin:* **Poland.** *Silhouette:* **Wilga 2.** *Picture:* Wilga 35.

Dornier Do 27 *Confusion:* Super Courier

Power: 1 × Lycoming piston engine   *Span:* 39ft 4½in (12m)   *Length:* 31ft 6in (9.6m)

The Dornier Do 27 six/eight-seat utility aircraft first flew in 1955 in Spain, with large-scale production being undertaken in Germany from 1956. When production ended a total of 680 had been built, including 428 for the West German armed forces and 50 manufactured under licence by Casa in Spain as the Casa C.127. Several versions of the German-built aircraft have been manufactured, the principal differences between variants being engine type and internal fittings for different roles. Powered by a 340hp Lycoming, the Do 27H-2 cruises at about 130 mph (209km/hr). Other performance figures include a maximum rate of climb at sea level of 650ft/min (198m/min); service ceiling of 10,825ft (3,300m); and a range with maximum fuel, no allowances, of 685 miles (1,100km). *Country of origin:* West Germany. *Silhouette:* Do 27. *Picture:* C.127.

Helio Super Courier/Trigear Courier

Power: 1 × Lycoming piston engine   *Span:* 39ft (11.89m)   *Length:* 31ft (9.45m)

Evolved from the two-seat Koppen-Bollinger Helioplane, which first flew in 1949, the original Courier appeared in 1952. The first version to be built in quantity was the H-395 Super Courier, which made its maiden flight in 1958. The two versions most recently built are the H-295 Super Courier and the Trigear Courier Model HT-295. Three military versions are designated U-10A, U-10B and U-10D. All versions have an unbraced cantilever wing and characteristic tall fin. Powered by a 295hp Lycoming, the type has a cruising speed of 150 mph (241km/hr). *Country of origin:* USA. *Silhouette and picture:* H-295.

Helio AU-24A Stallion

Confusion: Super Courier

Power: 1 × PT6A turboprop   *Span:* 41ft (12.50m)   *Length:* 39ft 7in (12m)

Designed as a successor to the Helio Super Courier, the turboprop Stallion first flew in 1964 and has been developed in both civil and military versions. The civil version can carry up to ten people in a high-density layout or up to six passengers in individual seats. The US Air Force acquired 15 of an armed version designated AU-24, 14 of which were subsequently supplied to the Khmer Air Force. The Stallion is easily recognisable by its swept-back main undercarriage legs and long nose accommodating the 680shp Pratt & Whitney PT6A turboprop. Cruising speed is 198 mph (319km/hr). A total of 600 Couriers, Super Couriers and Stallions were built. *Country of origin:* USA. *Silhouette:* AU-24. *Picture:* Model H-600B.

Power: 1 × Lycoming piston engine   *Span:* 42ft 10¾in (13.08m)   *Length:* 30ft 6½in (9.31m)

The C4M Kudu is a six/eight-seat light transport which is capable of operating from unprepared surfaces. The type first flew in 1974. The first military prototype flew in 1975 but no details of production figures are available. The Kudu is a development of the Aermacchi-Lockheed AL.60 Conestoga, which was built in both tricycle and tailwheel forms. The Kudu cruises at 124 mph (200km/hr) and is in civil and military use in South Africa. *Country of origin:* **South Africa.** *Silhouette and picture:* **Kudu.**

Neiva L-42 Regente   *Confusion:* Oscar

Power: 1 × Continental piston engine   *Span:* 29ft 11½in (9.13m)   *Length:* 23ft 1in (7.04m)

The four-seat Regente was first flown in 1961 and entered service with the Brazilian Air Force in 1963. Two versions have been built: the Regente 360C, designated C-42 in Brazilian Air Force service; and the Regente 420L, designated L-42 by the BAF. Main difference between the two is that the L-42 has a stepped-down cabin rear window for improved all-round visibility. When production ended in 1971, 80 C-42s and 40 L-42s had been built. Powered by a 210hp Continental, the L-42 cruises at about 140 mph (236km/hr). The company also developed a civil version of the Regente, the Lanceiro, which first flew in 1970 but did not enter full-scale production. *Country of origin:* Brazil. *Silhouette and picture:* L-42.

Partenavia P.64 Oscar/P.66 Oscar/P.66C-160 Charlie

Power: 1 × Lycoming piston engine   *Span:* 32ft 9in (9.99m)   *Length:* 23ft 9in (7.23m)

The four-seat P.64 Oscar was first flown in 1965, powered by a 180hp Lycoming engine. The following year saw the introduction of an improved version with cut-down rear fuselage decking to improve all-round visibility. A version has also been fitted with a 200hp Lycoming. A small number have been built by AFIC in South Africa as the RSA 200 Falcon. The P.66B Oscar 100 and Oscar 150 are two and three-seat developments of the P.64 and share several major components. More than 270 Oscars of all versions had been built by early 1975. Powered by a 115hp Lycoming engine, the Oscar 100 cruises at about 120 mph (190km/hr). An improved version of the Oscar, the P.66C-160 Charlie, is now in production. *Country of origin:* **Italy.** *Silhouette:* P.64. *Picture:* P.66C-160 Charlie.

Beagle A.109 Airedale

Confusion: Skyhawk

Power: 1 × Lycoming piston engine   *Span:* 36ft 4in (11.07m)   *Length:* 26ft 4in (8.02m)

The four-seat Airedale light touring aircraft, first flown in 1961, was a successor to the famous Auster line of light aircraft. Powered by a 180hp (185km/hr) Lycoming, it cruises at about 115 mph (185km/hr). The Airedale was an unsuccessful attempt at producing a British competitor to the American light aircraft that were beginning to swamp the UK market, and production totalled little more than 40. About 20 remain on the British register, with a handful elsewhere in the world. The Airedale has typically Auster-style parallel-chord wings with squared-off tips and V-type wing bracing struts. *Country of origin:* UK.

Power: 1 × Lycoming or 1 × Continental piston engine   *Span:* 35ft 10in (10.92m)   *Length:* 26ft 11in (8.20m)

First introduced in 1955, the Model 172 was essentially a Model 170 with tricycle undercarriage and revised tail surfaces. The swept-tail 172A was introduced in 1960. Current versions are powered by a 160hp engine giving a cruising speed of about 140 mph (225km/hr). The Model 172E is a more powerful version with a 210hp Continental. Known in the US Army and Air Force as the T-41 Mescalero, the type is used for basic training. It has also been bought by a few South American air forces. Top of the line is the Model R172 Hawk XP, which is also in production in France by Reims Aviation. Power is provided by a 195hp Continental. Total production of Model 172/Skyhawk-series aircraft has exceeded 34,000, including more than 1,000 F 172s built in France. *Country of origin:* USA. *Silhouette:* Skyhawk. *Picture:* T-41.

Cessna Model 150/152 Aerobat

Confusion: Skylane

Power: 1 × Continental or 1 × Lycoming piston engine   *Span:* 32ft 8½in (9.97m)   *Length:* 24ft 1in (7.34m)

This two-seater, first flown in 1957, was intended as a successor to Cessna's earlier tailwheel Models 120 and 140. Several versions of the 150 have been built, the first major change being the introduction of the swept-tail Model 150F in 1966. Production of the basic aircraft ended in 1977 after almost 24,000 had been built, including 1,500+ in France by Reims Aviation. Current production type is the Model 152, which has a more powerful engine than the Model 150 but is otherwise externally similar. The Model 152 Aerobat has certain interior modifications as well as some structural beefing-up to permit simple aerobatics. Maximum cruising speed is 117 mph (188km/hr). *Country of origin:* USA. *Silhouette:* Model 150F. *Picture:* Model 150 Commuter II.

Power: 1 × Continental or 1 × Lycoming piston engine   *Span:* 35ft 10in (10.92m)   *Length:* 28ft 1½in (8.57m)

Derived from the Model 180 utility light aircraft, the Model 182 was introduced in 1956. The swept tail was introduced on 1960 aircraft. Production of the Model 182 was discontinued in 1976 and current production aircraft are the standard Skylane and Skylane II; the latter embodies a factory-installed avionics package. In 1977 Cessna introduced a new retractable-under-carriage version designated Skylane RG (and the Skylane RG II with factory-installed avionics). The RG aircraft were also fitted with the more powerful 235hp Lycoming engine. Total production of all variants exceeds 19,000, including a number built in France by Reims Aviation as the Rocket. Cruising speed is 157 mph (253km/hr). Retractable-undercarriage versions are known as the Skylane RG and Turbo-Skylane RG. *Country of origin:* USA. *Silhouette:* Model 182G. *Picture:* Skylane II.

Cessna Cardinal/Cardinal RG *Confusion:* Skylane

Power: 1 × Lycoming piston engine   *Span:* 35ft 6in (10.82m)   *Length:* 27ft 3in (8.31m)

The original Model 177 four-seat light aircraft, introduced in 1967, was powered by a 150hp engine, later increased to 180hp. The 1978 aircraft were re-designated Cardinal Classic and incorporated many improvements to cabin comfort and basic equipment. The Cardinal RG series was introduced in 1970 and featured hydraulically retractable undercarriage and 200hp Lycoming engine. Cruising speed of the Cardinal Classic is about 150 mph (241km/hr) and that of the Cardinal RG about 170 mph (273km/hr). Other performance figures for the RG include a maximum sea-level speed of 180 mph (290km/hr); economical cruising speed at 10,000ft (3,050m) of 139 mph (233km/hr); maximum rate of climb at sea level of 925ft/min (282m/min); service ceiling of 17,100ft (5,210m); and flaps-down stalling speed of 57 mph (92km/hr). Total production had exceeded 4,000 by early 1978, of which about half were RGs. *Country of origin:* USA. *Silhouette:* **Cardinal**. *Picture:* **Cardinal RG II**.

Power: 1 × Continental piston engine   *Span:* 35ft 10in (10.92m)   *Length:* 28ft 3in (8.61m)

This six-seat light aircraft was introduced in 1962 as the Model 205 powered by a 285hp Continental engine. In 1964 this was superseded by the Model 206 Super Skywagon with more powerful engine and double cargo doors on the starboard side. The aircraft has since been renamed Stationair and Turbo-Stationair. 1978 aircraft were designated Stationair 6 and Turbo Stationair 6, fitted with the 300hp Continental and 310hp turbocharged Continental respectively. The line also includes the de luxe Super Skylane, and a utility version with a single seat and no wheel fairings. By the beginning of 1981 total production of all variants had exceeded 6,600. *Country of origin:* USA. *Silhouette:* Stationair. *Picture:* Stationair 6.

Cessna Stationair 7/Stationair 8   *Confusion:* Stationair 6, Centurion

Power: 1 × Continental piston engine   *Span:* 35ft 10in (10.92m)   *Length:* 31ft 9in (9.68m)

This seven-seat utility aircraft, first announced in 1969, is a stretched version of the Model 206 Super Skywagon. In addition to the longer fuselage, new features included a door for the co-pilot on the starboard side and a separate baggage compartment forward of the cabin. The basic aircraft is powered by a 300hp Continental and cruises at about 165 mph (265km/hr), while the turbocharged aircraft with a 310hp Continental cruises at 185 mph (297km/hr). Production of Model 207s had exceeded 360 by early 1977. The designation was changed to Stationair 7 and Turbo-Stationair 7 for the 1978 aircraft. In 1980 production switched to the eight-seat, slightly longer Stationair 8/Turbo Stationair 8. *Country of origin:* USA. *Silhouette:* Skywagon 207. *Picture:* Stationair 8.

Power: 1 × Continental piston engine *Span:* 36ft 9in (11.20m) *Length:* 28ft 2in (8.59m)

The original Model 210 first flew in 1957 and was the first of the Cessna high-wing range of light aircraft to feature a retractable undercarriage. Later versions also featured an unbraced cantilever wing, as on the Cardinal series. Successive models have introduced enlarged cabin windows, two additional rear windows and increased cabin headroom. In late 1977 Cessna introduced the Pressurised Centurion, generally similar to the standard aircraft but powered by a 310hp Continental engine and with four small windows on each side in place of the panoramic windows. Maximum cruising speed is 188 mph (303km/hr). *Country of origin:* USA. *Silhouette:* Model 210H. *Picture:* Pressurised Centurion.

MFI MFI-9B Trainer/Bolkow BO 208 Junior *Confusion:* Safari

Power: 1 × Continental piston engine   *Span:* 24ft 4in (7.43m)   *Length:* 19ft 2in (5.85m)

The MFI-9B Trainer and MFI-9 Junior are both derivatives of the BA-7 built in the USA by Bjorn Andreasson and first flown in 1958. A total of 25 were built by MFI at Malmo in Sweden. In 1962 Bolkow in West Germany began producing the type under licence from MFI, and by late 1969 production had reached 200 aircraft. Fully aerobatic, the Junior seats two people side-by-side and has a cruising speed of about 125 mph (201km/hr) on its 100hp Rolls-Royce Continental. Other performance figures include a maximum speed of 140 mph (225km/hr); economical cruising speed of 121 mph (195km/hr); and a range of 465 miles (748km). Certified in the normal, utility and glider-towing categories, the MFI-9 is of all-metal construction. The number of Juniors remaining airworthy is dwindling steadily. *Country of origin:* Sweden/West Germany. *Silhouette:* MFI-9B. *Picture:* BO 208.

Power: 1 × Lycoming piston engine   *Span:* 29ft 0½in (8.85m)   *Length:* 22ft 11½in (7m)

The two-seat Saab Safari (formerly known as the MFI-15) basic trainer and utility aircraft first flew in 1969, powered by a 160hp engine. Originally flown with a low-set tailplane, the type now has a near T-tail. Although designed with a tricycle undercarriage, the type may be seen with an optional tailwheel arrangement. A military version is also available, known as the Supporter. Externally similar to the Safari, the Supporter is stressed to carry stores on six underwing stations. Supporters have been delivered to Denmark, Pakistan and Zambia. Powered by a 200hp Lycoming, both versions cruise at about 130 mph (210km/hr). *Country of origin:* Sweden. *Silhouette and picture:* Supporter.

This section covers three very diverse groups of flying vehicles, all of them significantly different from the types which have gone before.

The amphibians have the floats and hydrodynamic hulls which mark their association with the water. The biplanes unmistakeably have two wings, one above the other, and the twin-boom aircraft have a trademark which makes it impossible to confuse them with conventional types.

The first two amphibians, the Lake Buccaneer and Teal, have their own marked differences. One has a pusher propeller and the other a tractor, wing aspect ratios are very dissimilar, and one is T-tailed while the other is not.

There is a layout similarity between the Goose, Widgeon and Albatross, but detail separates the first two and a two-step hull and inboard floats distinguish the third. The CL-215 has a very broad-span tailplane and extremely tall fin. Strut bracing is distinctive on the Catalina, as is the broad cross-section of the fuselage. The Mail has characteristics which are all its own: gull wing, fore and aft protuberances (radar and MAD boom), and twin fins. The PS-1/US-1 is the only current amphibian with four engines and a T-tail.

Shin Meiwa PS-1

de Havilland Tiger Moth

The first two of the biplanes, the Tiger Moth and SV.4, are remarkably similar. Curved-tip wings versus square-cut, and tall versus squat fins are the main keys. The Sports Trainer has a somewhat ungainly look compared with the compact streamlining of the Pitts Special, while the Jungmann/Jungmeister have very long undercarriage legs but very different engine installations. Of the three agricultural/general-purpose aircraft, the Colt is in a size and shape class on its own.

The Vampire and Venom are the only twin-boom jets. There should be no difficulty in deciding between the Cessna 337 and the Arava, which has a coned rear fuselage, endplate fins and fixed undercarriage.

The Noratlas and Boxcar are similar except for their wingtips, wing head-on shape and boom thickness, while the Argosy has four engines.

The Bronco could be mistaken for the Noratlas at very long range; the high-mounted slab tailplane is the point to look for. Finally, the M-15 and the Airtruk are so bizarre in outline as to be virtually unmistakable.

Power: 1 × Lycoming piston engine   *Span:* 38ft (11.58m)   *Length:* 24ft 11in (7.60m)

The LA-4 Buccaneer four-seat light amphibian is the production develop-ment of the C-1 Skimmer, which first flew in 1948. Powered by a 150hp Lycoming, the three-seat Skimmer was built originally by the Colonial Aircraft Corporation before manufacturing rights were acquired by Lake in 1959. The first Lake-built aircraft, slightly larger than the Skimmer and designated LA-4, first flew in 1960. Current production version is the LA-4-200, which was certificated in 1970. A total of over 1,000 LA-4s of all versions have been built. Powered by a 200hp Lycoming, the LA-4-200 has a cruising speed of 150 mph (241km/hr). Maximum rate of climb at sea level is 1,200ft/min (366m/min), service ceiling 14,700ft (4,480m), and range with maximum fuel at maximum cruising speed is 650 miles (1,046km). *Country of origin:* USA. *Silhouette and picture:* LA-4-200.

Schweizer TSC-1 Teal *Confusion:* Lake Buccaneer

Power: 1 × Lycoming piston engine   *Span:* 31ft 11in (9.73m)   *Length:* 23ft 7in (7.19m)

The two-seat all-metal Teal amphibian was developed originally by Thurston Aircraft and first flown in 1968. Design and production rights were acquired by Schweizer in 1972. Production of the Teal I ran to 15 aircraft. The Teal II incorporates several minor design changes. The entire Teal programme was transferred to Teal Aircraft Corporation at St Augustine, Florida, in the spring of 1976. Last production versions were the Teal II and the improved Teal III, which has a more powerful Lycoming engine and can accommodate up to four people. The standard Teal II cruises at about 115 mph (185km/hr). *Country of origin:* USA. *Silhouette and picture:* Teal II.

Power: 2 × PT6A turboprops   *Span:* 50ft 10in (15.49m)   *Length:* 39ft 7in (12.07m)

The original six/seven-seat Grumman G-21 first flew in 1937, powered by a pair of 450hp Wasp Junior radials. In the conversion, carried out by McKinnon Enterprises of Oregon, the radial engines are replaced by a pair of 680shp turboprops giving a maximum speed of about 220 mph (354km/hr). Other changes include the fitting of retractable wingtip floats, longer nose, dorsal fin and larger cabin windows as well as numerous interior and equipment changes. The first Turbo-Goose conversion was flown in 1966. There is accommodation for 9 to 12 people. The company subsequently became McKinnon-Viking and moved to Canada. Conversion work has now ceased. *Country of origin:* USA. *Main silhouette:* Turbo-Goose; *upper side view:* G-21. *Picture:* Turbo-Goose.

McKinnon Super Widgeon   *Confusion:* Turbo-Goose

Power: 2 × Lycoming piston engines   *Span:* **40ft (12.9m)**   *Length:* **31ft 1in (9.47m)**

The original G-44 Widgeon was a four-seat light amphibian and first flew in 1940. Although designed as commercial transports the 176 Widgeons built during the Second World War were used as three-seat anti-submarine patrol aircraft. Subsequent civil aircraft were five-seaters, and a number were built in France as the SCAN 30. The McKinnon Super Widgeon is an executive conversion with the original Ranger in-line engines replaced by two 270hp Lycomings, giving a cruising speed of about 180 mph (290km/hr). The company converted more than 70 aircraft, a number of which have retractable wingtip floats. Other features include picture windows, a modern instrument panel, improved soundproofing and an emergency escape hatch. Three or four passengers can be carried over a maximum-fuel range of 1,000 miles (1,600km). *Country of origin:* USA. *Main silhouette:* Super Widgeon; *upper side view:* G-44. *Picture:* Super Widgeon.

Grumman HU-16 Albatross

Power: **2 × R-1820 piston engines**   *Span:* **96ft 8in (29.46m)**   *Length:* **63ft 7in (19.38m)**

The twin-engined Albatross was originally designed to meet a US Navy requirement for a utility transport and air-sea rescue amphibian and first flew in 1947. The type was subsequently adopted by the US Air Force as its standard air-sea rescue amphibian under the designation HU-16A, and production ran to more than 300. The HU-16B is an improved version with a modified wing. The US Navy equivalent was the HU-16D and that for the US Coast Guard the HU-16E. The Albatross has served widely throughout the world, particularly in South America and South-east Asia. With a crew of three (five in the SAR role) and up to 22 passengers, the Albatross cruises at about 225 mph (362km/hr). *Country of origin:* USA. *Silhouette and picture:* HU-16B.

Canadair CL-215 *Confusion:* Albatross

Power: 2 × R-2800 piston engines   *Span:* 93ft 10in (28.60m)   *Length:* 65ft 0½in (19.82m)

The Canadair CL-215 twin-engined amphibian first flew in October 1967 and is intended mainly for firefighting. Carrying ground-loaded fire-retardants, the CL-215 can also scoop up water from any stretch of lake or ocean, filling its tanks in 10–16sec. Operators include Canada, France, Spain, Greece and Thailand; the Thai aircraft are equipped for search and rescue. Cruising speed is about 180 mph (290km/hr) and power is provided by a pair of 2,100hp Pratt & Whitney R-1800 18-cylinder radial engines. Some 70 CL-215s have been completed. *Country of origin:* Canada.

Power: 2 × R-1830 piston engines *Span:* **104ft (31.69m)** *Length:* **63ft 10in (19.50m)**

Originally intended for the maritime reconnaissance role, the few Catalinas remaining in military service are almost entirely used for transport and air-sea rescue. Most surviving examples serve with commercial companies, particularly in South America. More than 2,700 of all variants were built in the USA and Canada during the Second World War, but the number of survivors can now be measured in tens. The Catalina cruises at about 130 mph (209km/hr). *Country of origin:* USA.

Beriev Be-12 Mail *Confusion:* PS-1/US-1

Power: 2 × Ivchenko turboprops   *Span:* 97ft 6in (29.70m)   *Length:* 107ft 11¼in (32.90m)

The twin-engined Be-12 maritime patrol amphibian is in current service with the Soviet Naval Air Force. A successor to the Be-6, it was displayed publicly for the first time at Moscow Tushino in 1961. The Mail is the holder of several class records for speed with varying payloads and has a normal operating speed of about 200 mph (322km/hr). Armament is carried in an internal bomb bay and there is provision for two stores pylons underneath each wing. About 100 Be-12s are thought to have been built. The Be-12 holds every one of the FAI world records in its class, no fewer than 38 in all. These marks include an average speed of 343 mph (552km/hr) over a 500km closed circuit, and a closed-circuit distance of 1,592 miles (2,562km). *Country of origin:* USSR.

Power: **4 × T64 turboprops**   *Span:* **108ft 9in (33.15m)**   *Length:* **109ft 9¼in (33.46m)**

Developed to fill a Japan Maritime Self-Defence Force requirement for an anti-submarine (PS-1) and search and rescue (US-1) type, this aircraft, which carries the company designation SS-2 (SS-2A for the amphibious version), first flew in October 1967. Twenty-three PS-1s, including two prototypes, were delivered. The first US-1 flew in 1974 and seven had been delivered at the time of writing, with an eighth scheduled to complete the batch. One PS-1 has been converted into a water bomber for firefighting duties. Cruising speed is about 265 mph (426km/hr). *Country of origin:* Japan. *Silhouette and picture:* SS-2A.

de Havilland D.H.82 Tiger Moth *Confusion:* SV.4

Power: 1 × de Havilland piston engine   *Span:* 29ft 4in (8.94m)   *Length:* 23ft 11in (7.29m)

Probably the most famous training aircraft of all, the Tiger Moth first flew in 1931. When production ended more than 7,000 had been built in Britain, Canada, Australia and New Zealand. Relatively few are still airworthy, with only about 120 on the British register, but several of these have been extensively rebuilt and should be flyable for many years to come. Its distinctive de Havilland-style tail and swept-back wings make the Tiger Moth fairly easy to recognise. Powered by a 130hp Gipsy Major engine, the Tiger Moth cruises at about 90 mph (145km/hr) over a range of 300 miles (483km). *Country of origin:* UK.

Power: 1 × Renault or 1 × de Havilland piston engine   *Span:* 27ft 6in (8.38m)   *Length:* 22ft 10in (6.96m)

The SV.4 tandem two-seat light biplane was first flown in 1933, powered by a 130hp Gipsy III engine. Used originally as a primary trainer by the Belgian Air Force, it has since been much sought after as a sporting aircraft by virtue of its excellent aerobatic qualities. Before the advent of the Pitts and Zlin the Stampe SV.4 was the mainstay of British competition aerobatics. Bearing a superficial resemblance to the Tiger Moth, the Stampe may be recognised by its rounded fin and rudder, rounded wingtips, and ailerons on both upper and lower wings. Powered by the 130hp Gipsy Major, the SV.4 cruises at about 110 mph (177km/hr). *Country of origin:* Belgium. *Silhouette:* SV.4. *Picture:* Single-seat conversion of SV.4.

Power: 1 × Lycoming piston engine   *Span:* 26ft 8in (8.13m)   *Length:* 20ft 4in (6.20m)

The original Model 2T-1 tandem two-seat light biplane was built in substantial quantities by the Great Lakes Aircraft Co between 1929 and 1932 and was fitted with a variety of engines ranging in power from 95 to 200hp. The company was taken over in 1972 and subsequently the Great Lakes Sports Trainer was put back into production, initially powered by a 140hp Lycoming. Current production aircraft are fitted with 180hp engines. *Country of origin:* USA. *Silhouette and picture:* Sports Trainer.

Power: 1 × Lycoming piston engine   *Span:* **17ft 4in (5.28m)**   *Length:* **15ft 5½in (4.71m)**

Designed by Curtis Pitts and first flown in single-seat form in 1944, the Pitts Special has become the best-known competition aerobatics aircraft. Originally designed for amateur construction only, the type is now in production by Pitts Aerobatics in Wyoming as the S-1S. Powerplant is a 180hp Lycoming giving the type a top speed of about 175 mph (282km/hr). A two-seat version, the S-2A Special, is also available. *Country of origin:* USA. *Main silhouette:* S-1S; *lower side view:* S-2A. *Picture:* S-1S.

Power: 1 × Hirth (Jungmann) or
1 × Siemens piston engine (Jungmeister)

Span (Jungmann): 24ft 3¼in (7.40m)

Length (Jungmann): 21ft 8in (6.60m)

The tandem two-seat Jungmann was first flown in 1934 and several remain in use throughout the world. The type has been licence-built in several countries, including Czechoslovakia, Switzerland and Spain, with production in the latter country resuming in 1956 with the manufacture of 55 aircraft by Casa. The single-seat Jungmeister was introduced in 1935 as an advanced aerobatic biplane and, like the Jungmann, the type was licence-built in Spain and Switzerland. Limited production was restarted in 1968 by Aero Technik Canary in West Germany, the aircraft being standard apart from the wheels and instruments. *Country of origin:* West Germany. *Main silhouette:* Jungmeister; *lower side view:* Jungmann. *Picture:* Jungmeister.

Power: 1 × R-1820 piston engine   *Span:* **41ft 8in (12.70m)**   *Length:* **30ft (9.14m)**

The first Emair MA-1 was built by Air New Zealand engineers under contract to a Hawaiian company and first flew in 1969. Subsequently 25 were produced in Texas by Emair. Production of the MA-1 ended in 1976 and a new version, the MA-1B Diablo 1200, was put into production, 48 being built before the line was closed in 1980. Powerplant is a 1,200hp Wright R-1820 radial derated to 900hp, giving a cruising speed of about 115 mph (185km/hr). As in most agricultural aircraft, the cockpit is raised well above the level of the fuselage top decking and incorporates a hefty roll-bar. The chemical hopper is built into the front fuselage and has two outlets. *Country of origin:* USA. *Silhouette:* MA-1. *Picture:* MA-1B.

Schweizer Super Ag-Cat *Confusion:* MA-1B

Power: 1 × R-985 or 1 × R-1340 piston engine   *Span:* 35ft 11in (10.95m)   *Length:* 24ft 4in (7.42m)

The original Ag-Cat agricultural biplane first flew in 1957 and was manufactured by Schweizer under licence from Grumman; Schweizer has since taken over all rights to the Ag-Cat. The Super Ag-Cat was first certificated in 1966 and was fitted with a 600hp Pratt & Whitney. Several versions of the Super Ag-Cat have been built, with a variety of power options; the B and C versions are also slightly larger. The Turbo Ag-Cat D has a very long nose housing a Pratt & Whitney PT6A turboprop. All Ag-Cats have the distinctive square fin and rudder and are considerably shorter than the other US-built agricultural biplane, the Emair MA-1B. *Country of origin:* USA. *Silhouette:* Ag-Cat. *Picture:* Super Ag-Cat.

Power: 1 × Shvetsov radial   *Span:* **59ft 8½in (18.18m)**   *Length:* **41ft 9½in (12.74m)**

Designed originally for agricultural duties under the designation SKh-1, the An-2 first flew in 1947. It has since been used by the Soviet Air Force for light utility roles. Several variants have been produced over the years with numerous minor design changes, but the overall shape has remained identifiable throughout. No longer produced in the USSR, the An-2 is now manufactured under licence in Poland by PZL-Mielec. Over 9,000 Colts have been built in Poland in addition to the more than 5,000 produced in the USSR. There are 11 Polish variants, including the An-2M floatplane and the An-2 Geofiz survey version. Cruising speed on the power of the 1,000hp nine-cylinder radial is about 115 mph (185km/hr). *Country of origin:* Poland/USSR. *Main silhouette:* **An-2**; *upper side view:* **An-2M**. *Picture:* **An-2R**.

de Havilland Venom/Vampire   *Confusion:* Skymaster

Power: 1 × Ghost turbojet   *Span:* 41ft 8in (12.7m)   *Length:* 31ft 10in (9.7m)

First flown in 1949, the Ghost-powered Venom fighter-bomber was a successor to the earlier Goblin-powered Vampire, which it closely resembles. Some Vampires still remain in use in Switzerland, Africa (the Zimbabwe Air Force has six FB9s and four T55s) and South America (the air force of the Dominican Republic operates half a dozen). The Venom has been phased out by all operators except the air force of Switzerland, where the type was built under licence. Four 20mm cannon are fitted in the nose, and auxiliary fuel tanks, bombs or rockets can be carried on two underwing pylons. The Venom has a top speed of 597 mph (961km/hr). Other performance figures include a service ceiling of 37,000ft (11,285m) and a range with external tanks of 1,000+ miles (1,610km). Over 70 of the 250 Venom F4s originally acquired by the Swiss Air Force remain in service, operating in the ground attack and photo-reconnaissance roles. *Country of origin:* UK. *Silhouette:* Venom. *Picture:* Vampire FB6.

Power: 2 × Continental piston engines   *Span:* 38ft 2in (11.63m)   *Length:* 29ft 9in (9.07m)

This all-metal four/six-seater is unusual in having a 210hp Continental mounted at each end of the fuselage nacelle. First flown in 1961, it entered series production as the fixed-undercarriage Model 336 Skymaster in May 1963. A military version, designated O-2, has also been delivered to the USAF and Iranian Air Force for forward air controller and psychological warfare missions. Military deliveries totalled 513. The Model P337 is a pressurised version distinguished by having four instead of three fuselage cabin windows. Deliveries of all variants had totalled 2,993 by the time production was terminated in 1980. Performance figures for the P337 include a maximum level speed of 250 mph (402km/hr), maximum cruising speed of 236 mph (380km/hr), and a range at economical cruising speed of 1,330 miles (2,140km). *Country of origin:* USA. *Main silhouette:* Model P337; *upper side view:* O-2. *Picture:* Model P337.

IAI 101/102/201 Arava *Confusion:* Noratlas

Power: 2 × PT6A turboprops   *Span:* **68ft 9in (20.96m)**   *Length:* **42ft 9in (13.03m)**

The Arava was designed to fulfil a requirement for a light Stol transport for civil and military use. First flight was in late 1969. Four versions have been announced to date. Three of these are externally similar: the IAI 101, the first civil version; the IAI 102, the second civil version, based on the original 101 and able to accommodate up to 20 passengers; and the IAI 201, the military transport version. Based on the original 101, the 201 first flew in 1972. Latest variant is the IAI 202, distinguished by its wingtip winglets. An electronic-warfare version of the IAI 201 is reported to be in service with the Israeli Air Force. Operators outside Israel are mainly South American armed forces. *Country of origin:* Israel. *Silhouette:* IAI 202. *Picture:* IAI 201.

Power: 2 × Hercules piston engines   *Span:* **106ft 7½in (32.50m)**   *Length:* **72ft 0½in (21.96m)**

The twin-engined, twin-boom Noratlas was the standard medium tactical transport of both the French and West German air forces, which received 211 and 188 respectively. The type is currently in service further afield as the major users have sold off surplus aircraft; Chad, Greece, Israel, Niger and Portugal are listed as operators. Accommodation is for a crew of five and up to 45 troops. Alternatively, up to 15,000lb of freight may be carried. Similar in size to the Fairchild C-119 Flying Boxcar, the Noratlas has squared-off rudders and narrower wings; the nose is also more rounded. Powered by two 2,090hp Snecma-built Bristol Hercules engines, the Noratlas cruises at about 200 mph (322km/hr). *Country of origin:* **France.**

Fairchild C-119 Flying Boxcar

Confusion: Argosy, Noratlas, Arava

Power: 2 × R-3350 piston engines   *Span:* 109ft 3in (33.30m)   *Length:* 89ft 5in (27.25m)

The C-119 is a development of the C-82 Packet, which first flew towards the end of the Second World War. Retaining the twin-engine, twin-boom arrangement of the Packet, the Flying Boxcar has a longer and slimmer fuselage. When production ended in 1955 some 1,100 C-119s had been built. Although no longer used in quantity by US forces, the type is still in limited service with Taiwan, India and Ethiopia. Powered by two 3,400hp Wright R-3350 radials, the C-119 cruises at about 200 mph (320km/hr). Maximum payload is 20,000lb (9,070kg), which can be carried over a range of 990 miles (1,595km). Ferry range with four 500 US gal overload tanks is 3,460 miles (5,570km). Variants currently in service include the AC-119 gunship and the Indian Air Force's C-119 Jet Pack, fitted with an auxiliary Orpheus turbojet. *Country of origin:* USA.

Power: **4 × Dart turboprops**   *Span:* **115ft (35.05m)**   *Length:* **46ft 10in (14.27m)**

Designed by the former Armstrong Whitworth company to meet a requirement for a large-capacity civil and military passenger and freight transport, the Argosy first flew in 1959. Currently the only four-engined twin-boom aircraft flying, the Argosy is in small-scale service in Europe and the USA. Only half a dozen are now on the UK civil register, the type having been withdrawn from RAF service. With an economical cruising speed of 280 mph (451km/hr), the Argosy can carry its 32,000lb (14,515kg) maximum payload over a range of 485 miles (780km). Alternatively, range with maximum fuel and 18,000lb (8,165kg) payload, plus allowances for a 230-mile diversion and 45min reserve, is 1,760 miles (2,835km). *Country of origin:* **UK.** *Silhouette:* Argosy. *Picture:* Argosy C1.

Rockwell OV-10 Bronco

Confusion: —

Power: 2 × T76 turboprops   *Span:* 40ft (12.19m)   *Length:* 41ft 7in (12.67m)

The Bronco was North American's winning entry in the US Navy's Light Armed Reconnaissance Aircraft (LARA) competition and the first prototype flew for the first time in mid-1965. The OV-10A, the basic production aircraft, is in service with the USAF, US Navy and US Marine Corps. This variant has also been delivered to Thailand, Venezuela, Indonesia and South Korea; these aircraft carry the designations OV-10C, E, F, and G respectively. The OV-10B is used for target towing, while the OV-10B(Z) is equipped with an auxiliary turbojet mounted above the fuselage nacelle. The OV-10D is the Night Observation Gunship System (NOGS) with increased armament, including a 20mm gun turret beneath the rear fuselage. *Country of origin:* USA. *Silhouette:* OV-10A. *Picture:* OV-10D.

Power: 1 × Ivchenko turbofan   *Span:* 73ft 6in (22.40m)   *Length:* 41ft 9in (12.72m)

Produced as a result of an anticipated Soviet requirement for up to 3,000 large agricultural aircraft, the Polish-built M-15 Belphegor first flew in 1973. The full-chord interplane struts are used as streamlined chemical hoppers, while the 3,306lb-thrust turbofan is mounted in a pod on top of the fuselage. The single pilot is accommodated in the extreme nose of the aircraft and there is a cabin to the rear of the cockpit for two extra people during ferry flights. A tandem two-seat trainer version has been built, and an improved standard version is under development. Firefighting and cargo variants are also being studied. *Country of origin:* Poland.

Transavia PL-12/T-320 Airtruk *Confusion: —*

Power: 1 × Continental piston engine   *Span:* 39ft 3½in (11.98m)   *Length:* 20ft 10in (6.35m)

This single–engined agricultural aircraft has one of the most distinctive layouts imaginable, the twin-boom arrangement having been adopted to keep the tails clear of chemicals and also to permit rapid loading from a vehicle. After a first flight in 1966, production had reached 116 by the beginning of 1981 for customers in Australia, Denmark, India, Malaysia, New Zealand, Thailand and Africa. A utility version designated the PL-12-U has also been built. This variant can carry one passenger on the upper deck behind the pilot's position and another four on the lower deck. The T-320 Airtruk differs principally in having a 325hp Continental Tiara in place of the PL-12's 300hp Rolls-Royce Continental. A development is the T-300 Skyfarmer with an Avco Lycoming engine. Cruising speed ranges from about 110 mph (177km/hr) for the PL-12 to 130 mph (209km/hr) for the T-320. *Country of origin:* Australia. *Silhouette and picture:* PL-12.

In learning to recognise helicopters the student must concentrate on features completely different from those used to identify fixed-wing aircraft. With the rotor in motion, the fuselage shape becomes much more important, as does the position of the tail rotor. With few exceptions, engines are in or on the fuselage, so that there is little help to be had from wing/engine shapes. Undercarriage arrangements are often distinctive, and head-on views need very careful study.

The first three designs in this section are very simple and have the minimum of structure. While the Bell 47 and Alouette II both have open tail booms, the French type is distinguished by its turbine powerplant, mounted prominently behind the rotor mast. The third type in this class, the piston-engined Hiller UH-12, has a faired-in tail boom.

The Alouette III combines the engine installation and tail bumper of the Alouette II with a faired tail boom, enclosed cabin and tricycle undercarriage. The Gazelle has a "fenestron"—a vertical annular fan buried within the tail structure—instead of a conventional tail rotor. This is repeated in the Dauphin, which also has a spatted main undercarriage.

Bell AH-1S HueyCobra

The Wasp and Scout have stepped cockpits, compared with the fully glazed noses of the previous types. The next five aircraft are from Bell and they all bear the hallmarks of that company, displaying distinctive tadpole-shaped fuselages in the underside view. The Bell 206 and 216 are the only members of the family with major differences, particularly in fuselage width and nose streamlining.

Westland Lynx

The Lynx is characterised by a deep windscreen and a long nose, while the tail arrangement is significantly different from that of the Bell 216. Despite its brand-new fuselage the Westland 30 shows clear signs of having been developed from the Lynx.

The Augusta 109 and Bell 222 are similar in outline except for the faired-in engine and small stub wings of the latter. The Kaman Seasprite is squat and has a tall rotor boom, while the next two types, the BO 105 and Hughes 500, are essentially rounded in outline.

Fairchild-Hiller's 1100 has a humped back, contrasting

Bell UH-1D Iroquois

Bell AH-1G HueyCobra

Hughes Defender

with the two Brantly-Hynes helicopters, which have straight-line fuselage tops. So too does the Enstrom Shark, but this type's nose is up-swept.

The Silvercraft SH-4 combines an Ecureuil-style nose profile with a corrugated tail boom similar to that of the Hiller UH-12, while the Mi-1 has a rounded underside to the rear fuselage and a distinctive upward-curved nose.

The Bell AH-1 assault helicopter is distinguished by its tandem crew positions and under-nose cannon. The Hughes 300, with its bubble cockpit and tightly grouped engine and fuel tanks, is unlike any of the other designs in this chapter. The Mi-2/Swidnik has S-62-style intakes over the cockpit but a completely different fuselage shape. The Mi-2's nosewheel retracts while the main undercarriage is fixed.

Hiller UH-12/Model 360/H-23 Raven

Power: 1 × Franklin or 1 × Lycoming piston engine   *Rotor dia:* 35ft 5in (10.80m)   *Length:* 28ft 6in (8.69m)

The UH-12 was first produced in 1948 and was followed in 1950 by the UH-12A with a semi-enclosed cockpit. The UH-12B was the military variant and the UH-12C introduced the "goldfish bowl" cabin. The Models A, B and C were all powered by 200hp or 210hp Franklin engines. The Model 12E was powered by the 305hp Lycoming engine. Hiller Aviation was reformed in 1973 and has put the Model 12E back in production, the current designation being UH-12E for the basic three-seat version and UH-12E-4 for the four-seat version powered by a 400shp Allison turboshaft engine. The H-23 Raven is a military version of the Hiller 12. Performance figures for the Model 12E/Raven include a maximum speed of 96 mph (154km/hr), cruising speed of 90 mph (145km/hr), sea-level range of 225 miles (362km/hr) and service ceiling of 15,200ft (4,360m). *Country of origin:* USA. *Silhouette and picture:* Hiller 12E.

Bell Model 47/H-13 Sioux/AH1 Sioux *Confusion:* Raven, Alouette II

Power: 1 × Lycoming piston engine   *Rotor dia:* 37ft 1½in (11.32m)   *Length:* 31ft 7in (9.63m)

The basic Bell Model 47 first flew in 1945, and the first production models were ordered for service with the US Army and Navy. Many versions have subsequently been built for military service in a variety of countries, and a large number are used by civil operators. The Model 47 has also been built under licence in Italy as the Agusta-Bell 47 series, and in Britain by Westland as the Sioux AH1. All models from the 47D onwards have the familiar "goldfish bowl" cabin and open tail-boom. Subsequent variants had engines of differing powers, but the main design change came with the Model 47H and Model 47J Ranger, which had a fully enclosed fuselage and cabin. These changes apply also to Agusta-built aircraft. *Country of origin:* Italy/UK/USA. *Silhouette:* Bell 47G2. *Picture:* Sioux AH1.

Power: 1 × Lycoming piston engine   *Rotor dia:* 25ft 2in (7.67m)   *Length:* 28ft 9in (8.76m)

Over 800 Robinson R22 light utility helicopters have been ordered and the production rate was expected to be two per day in 1982. One of the cheapest two-seaters on the market, the R22 has a top speed of 116 mph (187km/hr) and cruises at 108 mph (174km/hr). Maximum range is 240 miles (386km). The prototype R22 first flew in 1975. The current production model has a higher-powered engine and in this form it is known as the R22HP. *Country of origin:* USA.

Aérospatiale Alouette II *Confusion:* Bell 47, Alouette III

Power: 1 × Artouste   *Rotor dia:* **36ft 1¾in (11.02m)**   *Length:* **33ft 8in (10.26m)**
or 1 × Astazou turboshaft

All the helicopters in this family are basically similar and differ principally in their powerplants. The prototypes were built as SE.3120s and powered by a Salmson 9 engine; production types were designated SE.3130 and subsequently SE.313B Alouette II. Production totalled more than 900. The Astazou-powered SA.318C first flew in 1961 and when production ended in 1975 more than 350 had been built. The SA.315B Lama is an Artouste-powered version built to an Indian requirement, while the Cheetah is a licence-built version produced by HAL for the Indian Army. The Lama has been sold to operators in more than 20 countries. *Country of origin:* France. *Main silhouette:* SA.318C; *lower side view:* SE.313B. *Picture:* SA.318C.

Power: 1 × Artouste
or 1 × Astazou turboshaft

Rotor dia: **36**ft 1¾in (11.02m) *Length:* **32**ft 10¾in (10.03m)

The Alouette III series was derived from the Alouette II, offering a larger cabin, more powerful engine and improved performance. The type first flew in 1959 as the SE.3160, and later production aircraft were designated SA.316B. More than 1,500 Alouette IIIs of all versions have been sold to a number of operators in more than 70 countries. The SA.316B has also been built under licence in India as the Chetak, and in both Switzerland and Romania. The SA.319B, a direct development of the SA.316B, is powered by a 870shp Turboméca Astazou engine. First flown in 1967, the type is still in production. Powered by an 870shp Turboméca Artouste turboshaft, the SA.316B cruises at 115 mph (185km/hr), while the SA.319B cruises at about 120 mph (190km/hr). *Country of origin:* **France**. *Main silhouette:* SA.316B; *lower side view:* SA.319B. *Picture:* **Chetak**.

Aérospatiale SA.341/342 Gazelle *Confusion:* Alouette III, Dauphin

Power: 1 × Astazou turboshaft   *Rotor dia:* 34ft 5½in (10.50m)   *Length:* 39ft 3½in (11.97m)

This five-seat light helicopter first flew in 1967, powered by an Astazou III engine. The first production aircraft flew in 1971, differing from the prototype in having a longer cabin, larger tail unit and uprated Astazou IIIA. Ten versions of the Gazelle have been built to date: the SA.341B, 341C, 341D and 341E for the British armed forces; the SA.341F for the French Army; the SA.341G and SA.342J for civil operators; SA.341H military export version; and the SA.342K, 342L and 342M military versions. Under an Anglo-French agreement signed in 1967, Gazelles are produced jointly with Westland Helicopters and are also built under licence in Yugoslavia. Total sales have exceeded 1,000 units. *Country of origin:* **France**. *Silhouette:* SA.341. *Picture:* Gazelle HT2.

Power: 1 × Astazou turboshaft (SA.360 and SA.361) or
2 × Arriel turboshafts (SA.365)

Rotor dia: 37ft 8¾in (11.50m) *Length:* 43ft 3½in (13.20m)

Developed as a replacement for the Alouette III, the SA.360 Dauphin first flew in 1972 powered by a 980shp Turboméca Astazou XVI turboshaft. Production aircraft are powered by the 1,050shp Astazou XVIIIA. The SA.361H Dauphin is similar in most respects to the SA.360 but is powered by a 1,400shp Astazou XXB. The SA.365C Dauphin 2 is marginally larger than the standard Dauphin and differs principally in having two 650shp Turboméca Arriel engines and accommodation for up to 13 persons. Cruising speed for both versions is about 170 mph (275km/hr). *Country of origin:* **France.** *Silhouette:* Dauphin 2. *Picture:* SA.360

Aérospatiale SA.365N Dauphin 2 *Confusion:* SA.365C, Gazelle

Power: 2 × Arriel turboshafts   *Rotor dia:* 39ft 1in (11.93m)   *Length:* 37ft 6in (11.44m)

Confusing because it is also called Dauphin 2, the 365N is in fact a major redesign compared with the 365C, with extensive use of composite materials and a retractable undercarriage. The 365N is a 10–14-seat transport, 365M a military utility vehicle and 365F a maritime version for anti-shipping and search and rescue. The SA.366, with two Avco Lycoming turboshafts, has been ordered by the US Coast Guard for short-range recovery. In this form it has the US designation HH-65A Dolphin. The 365N has a maximum cruising speed of 172 mph (278km/hr) and a maximum range of 546 miles (880km). *Country of origin:* **France.** *Silhouette:* SA.365F. *Picture:* SA.365N.

Power: 1 × Nimbus turboshaft   *Rotor dia:* **32ft 3in (9.83m)**   *Length:* **30ft 4in (9.24m)**

Derived from the Saunders-Roe P.531, which first flew in 1958, the Scout army helicopter is fitted with a skid undercarriage. The British Army took delivery of about 150 Scouts and the type is also in service with Australia. The Wasp naval version, distinguished by its wheeled undercarriage, was first delivered to the Royal Navy in 1963. Wasps are also operational in Brazil, the Netherlands, New Zealand and South Africa. Powered by a 710shp Rolls-Royce Nimbus turboshaft, the Scout cruises at about 120 mph (210km/hr) and the Wasp at about 110 mph (175km/hr). *Country of origin:* **UK**. *Main silhouette:* **Scout**; *lower side view:* **Wasp**. *Picture:* **Scout**.

Bell Model 204/UH-1 Iroquois

Confusion: Scout/Wasp, Bell 205, Bell 212

Power: 1 × T53 turboshaft   *Rotor dia:* 44ft (13.41m)   *Length:* 38ft 5in (11.70m)

The Model 204 and UH-1 Iroquois belong to a family of commercial utility and military general-purpose helicopters derived from the XH-40, which first flew in 1956. The civil and military versions are essentially similar in external appearance and differ principally in their internal equipment. A licence-built version, the Agusta-Bell 204B, was in production in Italy between 1961 and 1974. Italian-built aircraft were fitted with the Rolls-Royce Gnome turboshaft. *Country of origin:* USA/Italy. *Main silhouette:* Bell 204; *lower side view:* Agusta-Bell 204B. *Picture:* Agusta-Bell 204B.

Power: 1 × PT6T turboshaft   *Rotor dia:* 48ft 2¼in (14.69m)   *Length:* 42ft 4¾in (12.92m)

The Model 212 Twin Two-Twelve 15-seat military/civil utility helicopter first flew in 1968. Military aircraft are designated UH-1N in the USA and CH-135 in Canada. Powerplant is a 1,290shp Pratt & Whitney of Canada PT6T-3 Turbo Twin-Pac, comprising two PT6 turboshafts coupled to a combining gearbox. The Agusta-Bell Model 212ASW was produced in Italy by Agusta for the Italian Navy, Turkey, Iran and a number of other countries, including Peru and Venezuela. Main external difference is the large cylindrical radome mounted on top of the forward cabin roof. Armament options include two homing torpedoes or depth charges for the anti-submarine role, and up to four AS.12 air-to-surface wire-guided missiles for use against ships. *Country of origin:* USA/Italy. *Main silhouette:* Bell 212; *lower side view:* 212ASW. *Picture:* 212ASW.

Power: 1 × T53 turboshaft   *Rotor dia:* 48ft (14.63m)   *Length:* 41ft 10¾in (12.77m)

The Model 205 military general-purpose helicopter first flew in 1961. Basically similar to the earlier Model 204 Iroquois, it has a longer fuselage, an additional cabin window and equipment improvements. The Model 205A-1 15-seat commercial utility version of the Model 205 is powered by a 1,250shp Lycoming turboshaft. Both versions are also built under licence in Italy by Agusta. Cruising speed for all versions is about 125 mph (200km/hr). *Country of origin:* USA. *Main silhouette:* UH-1D. *Picture:* Model 205A.

Bell Model 214A/214B BigLifter

Power: 1 × T55 turboshaft   *Rotor dia:* 50ft (15.24m)   *Length:* 42ft 4¾in (12.92m)

Initially produced in quantity for Iran as the Isfahan, the Bell 214A military utility helicopter was developed from the Bell 205 and first flew in 1974. Iran also ordered the 214C version for search and rescue. The civil version is the 214B BigLifter, which carries 14 passengers or can be used for cropspraying or firefighting. The latter version, known as the BigFighter, can carry a maximum of 800 US gal (3,025lit) of water or fire suppressant. Bell claims that the 214 has more lift capability than any other medium-sized commercial helicopter. Typical internal load is 4,000lb (1,814kg), while up to 7,000lb (3,175kg) can be slung externally. The BigLifter differs from the 214A in having a fire-extinguishing system, push-out escape windows and commercial avionics. Agusta has also built the 214A. Cruising speed is 161 mph (259km/hr) and range 300 miles (483km). *Country of origin:* USA. *Main silhouette:* Model 214; *lower side view:* Model 214B. *Picture:* Model 214A.

Power: 1 × Allison 250 turboshaft   *Rotor dia:* 33ft 4in (10.16m)   *Length:* 31ft 2in (9.50m)

This general-purpose and light observation helicopter first flew in 1962. The original Model 206A JetRanger remained in production until 1972, when 660 had been built. Deliveries of the Model 206B JetRanger II, powered by a 400shp Allison turboshaft, began in 1971. A total of 1,619 were delivered. Current production model is the Model 206B JetRanger III, which has an uprated engine of 420shp, an enlarged tail rotor mast and other detail improvements. Deliveries began in 1977. The Kiowa is the military variant of the JetRanger, from which it differs in having a main rotor of slightly greater diameter and equipment changes for its military role. More than 6,000 of the Model 206 series have been built. *Country of origin:* USA. *Silhouette and picture:* Kiowa.

Power: 2 × LTS101 turboshafts   *Rotor dia:* 36ft 1in (11m)   *Length:* 42ft 8in (13m)

A joint development by West Germany and Japan, the BK 117 seats seven passengers in executive form and up to eleven in high-density transport form. With a range of 339 miles (545km), the BK 117 has a cruising speed of 145 mph (234km/hr). The first prototype flew in Germany in May 1979, followed by a second in Japan. Over 150 of these helicopters have been ordered and there are two production centres, at Gifu in Japan and Munich in Germany. Production deliveries began in the first half of 1982. *Country of origin:* Japan/West Germany.

487

Power: 2 × Gem turboshafts   *Rotor dia:* 42ft (12.80m)   *Length:* 39ft 6¾in (12.06m)

One of the three helicopters covered by the Anglo-French agreement of 1967, the Lynx first flew in 1971. Two main versions have been built, one for naval use and the second for the British Army. Equipped with a skid undercarriage, the Lynx AH1 entered British Army service in 1977. Naval versions are the Lynx HAS2, 60 of which have been ordered for the Royal Navy, and variants for the French Navy, the Royal Netherlands Navy and the navies of Argentina, West Germany and Brazil. The type has also been ordered by Qatar, Denmark and Norway. All naval aircraft are equipped with a wheeled undercarriage. Powered by two 750hp Rolls-Royce Gem turboshafts, the Lynx has a cruising speed of about 130 mph (210km/hr). *Country of origin:* UK/France. *Main silhouette:* AH1; *lower side view:* HAS2. *Picture:* HAS2.

Power: 1 × Allison 250 turboshaft   *Rotor dia:* 37ft (11.28m)   *Length:* 33ft 3in (10.13m)

The Model 206L LongRanger seven-seat general-purpose helicopter first flew in 1974. Developed from the Model 206B JetRanger II, it has a longer fuselage with an additional pair of cabin windows. First deliveries were in 1975. Current production version is the LongRanger II. Double doors on the port side of the cabin provide an opening 5ft (1.52m) in width, permitting the straight-in loading of stretchers or cargo. Two stretchers and two walking patients can be carried in the ambulance role, while an optional executive interior accommodates four passengers. Powered by a 420shp Allison turboshaft, the LongRanger cruises at about 130 mph (210km/hr) over a sea-level range of 342 miles (550km). Service ceiling is 19,500ft (5,945m). The type is also being licence-built in Italy by Agusta. Under development are the LongRanger III and IV, the latter with a four-blade rotor. *Country of origin:* USA. *Silhouette and picture:* Model 206L.

Agusta A.109 *Confusion:* Bell 222

Power: 2 × Allison 250 turboshafts   *Rotor dia:* 36ft 1in (11m)   *Length:* 42ft 10in (13.05m)

The Agusta A.109A high-speed twin-engined helicopter is available in both civil and military versions. First flown in 1971, the type entered production in 1976. The A.109 is powered by two 420shp Allison turboshafts and features a fully retractable undercarriage. Military versions, under construction for the armies and navies of several nations, are externally similar to the civil model, varying only in the armament and equipment carried. An improved Mk II version is now on the line. The military Mk II can perform the utility, ECM, ambulance, scout/attack/air defence and anti-tank roles, armed with various combinations of machine guns, rocket pods and Hot or Tow anti-tank missiles. *Country of origin:* Italy.

Power: 2 × LTS101 turboshafts   *Rotor dia:* 39ft (11.89m)   *Length:* 36ft 0¼in (10.98m)

The Model 222 eight-seat light commercial helicopter first flew in 1976. The first commercial light twin-engined helicopter to be built in the USA, the Model 222 has a fully retractable undercarriage accommodated in two short-span sponsons set low on each side of the fuselage. The tailplane, mounted midway along the rear fuselage, is fitted with endplate fins. The type is produced in three versions: the basic Model 222, the 222 Executive and the 222 Offshore. Externally alike, these variants are distinguished by equipment differences, notably an emergency flotation system and auxiliary fuel tanks on the 222 Offshore. Powered by two 600shp Avco Lycoming turboshafts, the Model 222 cruises at about 165 mph (265km/hr). *Country of origin:* USA.

Kaman H-2 Seasprite *Confusion:* Westland 30

Power: 2 × T58 turboshafts   *Rotor dia:* **44ft (13.41m)**   *Length:* **38ft 4in (11.68m)**

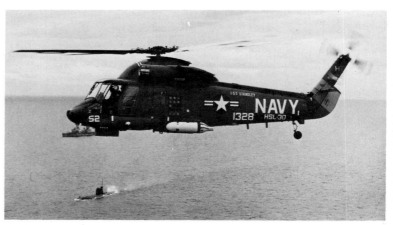

The H-2 Seasprite anti-submarine, anti-missile defence, search and rescue, observation and utility helicopter first flew in 1959. The original series was single-engined and, as the UH-2A, entered service with the US Navy in 1963. Few remain in service, although some have been converted to twin-engine standard. Current versions are the HH-2D for coastal and geodetic survey; NHH-2D test aircraft for the Lamps programme; SH-2D Lamps anti-submarine and utility aircraft; and SH-2F, a developed Lamps version. All SH-2Ds are being upgraded to SH-2F standard. Powered by two 1,350shp General Electric turboshafts, the SH-2F cruises at about 150 mph (240km/hr). *Country of origin:* USA. *Silhouette:* SH-2F. *Picture:* SH-2D.

Power: 2 × Gem turboshafts   *Rotor dia:* 43ft 8in (13.31m)   *Length:* 47ft (14.33m)

A combination of the Lynx rotor and powerplant with a new transport fuselage, the Westland 30 seats 17 passengers to airliner standards and up to 22 in high-density layout. The type is also available as a multi-role military helicopter. First flown in April 1979, the Westland 30 is in full production and is in service with British Airways Helicopters. The prototype is known as the 30 Series 100, the present production machines with Gem 41 engines are designated Series 200, and a developed version with uprated Gem 60 engines will be the Series 300. Cruising speed is 150 mph (241km/hr) and range with seven passengers is 426 miles (686km). *Country of origin:* UK.

Hughes Model 500 *Confusion:* BO 105

Power: 1 × Allison 250 turboshaft   *Rotor dia:* 26ft 4in (8.03m)   *Length:* 23ft (7.01m)

The Model 500 series is the commercial and foreign military counterpart of the US Army's OH-6 Cayuse. The Model 500 and Model 500C are identical apart from the installation of the uprated 400shp Allison turboshaft in the Model 500C. The Model 500D and Model M-D are fitted with the 420shp Allison turboshaft and are distinguished by a small T-tail and five-blade rotor. The Model 500D is the basic commercial version, while the 500M-D Defender multi-role military variant is in production for South Korea, Colombia and Mauretania and has been ordered by Israel. First flown in 1963, the basic Model 500 cruises at about 145 mph (235km/hr). *Country of origin:* USA. *Main silhouette:* Model 500D; *lower side view:* Defender. *Picture:* Defender.

Power: 2 × Allison 250 turboshafts   *Rotor dia:* 32ft 3½in (9.84m)   *Length:* 38ft 11in (11.86m)

The MBB BO 105 five-seat light utility helicopter first flew in 1967. A number of different versions have been built, but all are essentially similar in external appearance. Original standard production model was the BO 105C, powered by two 400shp Allison turboshaft engines. This was succeeded in 1975 by the BO 105CB, powered by two 420shp Allison turboshaft engines and incorporating strengthened rotor gearing. Other versions currently in production are the BO 105CBS with longer fuselage and increased seating capacity; BO 105D for the UK market; BO 105M (PAH 1) military version armed with six Hot missiles; and the BO 105M (VBH) light observation helicopter for the German Army. Cruising speed is about 145 mph (235km/hr). *Country of origin:* **West Germany.** *Main silhouette:* BO 105CB; *middle side view:* BO 105M; *bottom side view:* BO 105CBS. *Picture:* BO 105C.

Aérospatiale AS.350 Ecureuil/Astar/Twinstar   *Confusion:* FH-1100

Power: 1 × Arriel or 1 × LTS101
or 2 × Allison 250 turboshafts

Rotor dia: 35ft 0¾in (10.69m)   *Length:* 35ft 9½in (10.91m)

Intended as a successor to the Alouette II, the Ecureuil (Squirrel) first flew in 1975 as the Arriel-powered AS.350B. The Lycoming-powered AS.350C Astar is intended for the US market alone, with the AS.350B available elsewhere. Accommodation is provided for six people in bucket seats in the front of the cabin and two rows of bench seats behind. Performance of the two versions is similar, cruising speed being about 145 mph (235km/hr). A twin-engined version, known as the Twinstar (AS.355E) in the USA and the Ecureuil 2 (AS.355F) elsewhere, is now in production. *Country of origin:* France. *Silhouette:* Ecureuil. *Picture:* AS.355F.

Power: 1 × **T63** turboshaft *Rotor dia:* **35ft 4¾in (10.79m)** *Length:* **39ft 9½in (9.08m)**

The FH-1100 utility helicopter, the first American light turbine-powered helicopter to enter the market, evolved from the Hiller OH-5A, which first flew in 1963. The FH-1100 was developed by Fairchild Industries, which had taken over Hiller, and first deliveries began in 1966. Production eventually reached about 250, for both civil and military operators, and the type remains in small-scale service with the armed forces of a number of South American nations. Powered by a 317hp Allison turboshaft, the FH-1100 cruises at about 120 mph (195km/hr). *Country of origin:* USA.

Brantly-Hynes B-2   *Confusion:* Brantly-Hynes 305

Power: 1 × Lycoming piston engine   *Rotor dia:* 23ft 9in (7.24m)   *Length:* 21ft 9in (6.62m)

The Model B-2 two-seat light helicopter was first flown in 1953, though deliveries did not begin until 1959. The B-2A is an updated version with redesigned cabin and improved equipment. Main production version is the B-2B, which differs in having a fuel-injected engine for improved performance. Powered by a 180hp Lycoming piston engine, the B-2B has a cruising speed of about 90 mph (145km/hr). Other performance figures include a maximum speed at sea level of 100 mph (161km/hr); maximum sea-level rate of climb of 1,900ft/min (580m/min); service ceiling of 10,800ft (3,290m); and maximum-fuel range of 250 miles (400km). *Country of origin:* USA. *Silhouette:* B-2B. *Picture:* B-2.

Power: 1 × Lycoming piston engine   *Rotor dia:* 28ft 8in (8.74m)   *Length:* 24ft 5in (7.44m)

The Model 305 five-seat light helicopter first flew in 1964. Similar in configuration to the Model IB-2B, the Model 305 is larger in all respects. Accommodation consists of two front seats side-by-side, with a rear bench seat for three persons. The Model 305 can be fitted with skid, wheel or float undercarriage. Powered by a 305hp Lycoming flat-six piston engine, the Model 305 cruises at about 110 mph (175km/hr). Other performance figures include a maximum speed at sea level of 120 mph (193km/hr); maximum sea-level rate of climb of 975ft/min (297m/min); service ceiling of 12,000ft (3,660m); and range with maximum fuel and maximum payload, plus 15min reserves, of 220 miles (345km). *Country of origin:* USA.

Enstrom F-28/Model 280 Shark

Confusion: SH-4

Power: 1 × Lycoming piston engine   *Rotor dia:* 32ft (9.75m)   *Length:* 29ft 4in (8.94m)

The original three-seat F-28 first flew in 1962 and entered production in 1965. During 1973 an advanced version of the basic Model F-28A was developed. Known as the Model 280 Shark, it is generally similar to the F-28A but has improved cabin contours and some small modifications to the tail area. There are a number of production versions: the F-28A powered by a 205hp Lycoming; Model 280 Shark; F-28C with turbocharged 205hp Lycoming; Model 280C; F-28C-2; and Models 280F and 280L Hawk. The last-named is a four-seater which first flew in 1978. *Country of origin:* USA. *Silhouette and picture:* Model 280.

Power: 1 × Franklin piston engine   *Rotor dia:* 29ft 7½in (9.03m)   *Length:* 25ft 1¼in (7.65m)

The SH-4 is a three-seat light helicopter designed for pilot training, utility, agricultural and similar roles. First flown in 1965, the type entered full-scale production in 1967 and a total of 50 were completed. Two versions were built: the standard SH-4 and the SH-4A agricultural version fitted with spraybars and two chemical tanks. Powered by a 235hp Franklin engine derated to 170hp, the SH-4 cruises at about 81 mph (130km/hr). Other performance figures include a maximum level speed at sea level of 100 mph (161km/hr); economical cruising speed of 73 mph (117km/hr); maximum sea-level rate of climb of 1,180ft/min (360m/min); and a range of 200 miles (320km). *Country of origin:* Italy. *Silhouette:* SH-4. *Picture:* SH-4A.

Mil Mi-1 Hare *Confusion:* —

Power: 1 × Ivchenko piston engine   *Rotor dia:* 47ft 1in (14.35m)   *Length:* 39ft 8½in (12.10m)

The first helicopter to enter series production in the USSR, the Mi-1 first flew in 1948 under the designation GM-1; delivery of production aircraft began in 1951. The type remained in production until 1964 and several versions were built. A version built in Poland by WSK-Swidnik is designated SM-1. Powered by a 575hp Ivchenko radial engine, the Mi-1 has a cruising speed of about 90 mph (145km/hr). Maximum level speed at sea level is 106 mph (170km/hr), and maximum range at economical cruising speed and 3,280ft (1,000m) altitude is 370 miles (600km). Maximum climb rate at 5,070lb (2,300kg) all-up weight is 1,043ft/min (318m/min). Built in both civil and military versions, the type is still in widespread service, particularly in Third World countries. *Country of origin:* USSR. *Silhouette and picture:* Mi-1.

Power: 1 × T53 or 1 × T400 turboshaft   *Rotor dia:* **44ft (13.41m)**   *Length:* **44ft 7in (13.59m)**

The Model 209 HueyCobra armed attack helicopter first flew in 1965. Four single-engined versions have been built to date: AH-1G, the original version for the US Army; AH-1Q anti-armour version with eight Tow missiles; AH-1R, as AH-1G but with a more powerful engine; and the AH-1S advanced version equipped with Tow missiles and featuring a flat-plate canopy. Some 690 AH-1Gs will ultimately be modified to AH-1S standard. AH-1S has a cruising speed of about 140 mph (225km/hr). The twin-engined versions of the HueyCobra are the AH-1J SeaCobra, operated by the US Marine Corps, and the AH-1T Improved SeaCobra. The AH-1J is essentially a modified version of the AH-1G with Marine avionics; the first pre-production aircraft flew in 1969. Improved SeaCobra is a modification of the AH-1J with a dynamic system similar to that of the Bell 214. *Country of origin:* USA. *Silhouette:* AH-1G. *Picture:* AH-1J.

503

Hughes Model 269/Model 300/Model 300C/TH-55A Osage *Confusion:* —

Power: 1 × Lycoming piston engine   *Rotor dia:* 25ft 3½in (7.71m)   *Length:* 21ft 11¾in (6.80m)

Design and development of the original Model 269 two-seat light helicopter began in 1955, with the first aircraft flying the following year. Production aircraft were designated Model 269A and by early 1968 nearly 1,200 had been built for both civil and military operators. The Model 300 was developed under the designation Model 269B, with production commencing in 1964. In 1964 the Model 269A was selected by the US Army as a light helicopter primary trainer and designated TH-55A Osage. Nearly 800 were built, with deliveries completed by the end of 1969. *Country of origin:* USA. *Silhouette:* Model 300. *Picture:* TH-55A.

Power: 2 × Isotov turboshafts   *Rotor dia:* 47ft 6¾in (14.50m)   *Length:* 57ft 2in (17.42m)

The Mi-2 twin-engined development of the Mi-1 was first announced in late 1961. Under an agreement signed in 1964, production and marketing were assigned exclusively to Poland and production began in 1965. Several thousand have since been built, mainly for export, with more than 2,000 being delivered to the USSR. The type is used by both civil and military operators and can be fitted out for a variety of roles, including ambulance, search and rescue, agricultural work, freight and transport of up to eight passengers. Mi-2s of the Polish Air Force have been fitted with unguided rocket pods and air-to-surface missiles on pylons on each side of the fuselage. *Country of origin:* USSR.

The classes of helicopters in this section differ widely in shape and role. There are airliners, assault transports, anti-submarine types, gunships and flying cranes.

The long-serving Mi-4 Hound is distinguished by its blunt fuselage and rear loading doors. The next four, the Whirlwind, S-55, S-58 and Wessex, all have a clear family resemblance, though the last two have continuous fuselage lines, lacking the pole-like tail booms of the first two.

The Puma and Super Frelon come from the same stable but differ in length, sponson size and undercarriage. The S-61L/N can be confused with Super Frelon, and the nose and boat-shaped hull of the S-61L/N should be noted.

The S-62's very bulbous sponsons show up, particularly in the head-on view, and this type also has an engine intake directly above the cockpit. S-62/SH-3 and the Sea King have a common design base; the latter's dorsal radome is unusual.

Mil Mi-24 Hind-D

Sikorsky S-76 Spirit

Sikorsky S-61 Sea King

The S-61R has a longer fuselage with large stub wings which can carry streamlined fuel tanks, and a horizontal stabiliser mounted on the starboard side of the tail boom. The Mi-8 Hip now has a naval counterpart, the Mi-14 Haze. Like some US types, the Mi-14 has a boat hull.

Hind is in a class on its own, with its long wings, twin cockpits and multiplicity of guns and other weapons. Sikorsky's S-76 has much sleeker lines which compare with those of the S-70, although the latter has a fixed under-carriage. The much larger S-65A is extensively streamlined, and has a seven-blade rotor and a curious tail arrangement in

Sikorsky UH-60A Black Hawk

rotors mounted one above the other, four undercarriage legs and a multiplicity of bumps, aerials and blisters. The latest Kamov design, code-named Helix, has only two fins but retains the coaxial rotor system.

Boeing Vertol CH-47 Chinook

the head-on view: compound tailplane dihedral balanced by a canted tail rotor.

The CH-53E can easily be mistaken for the S-65A but is larger. Mi-6 Hook is big and has intakes over the cockpit, long wings, and underbelly loading doors. The top line of the Harke's fuselage is similar to that of the Hook. But there the similarity ends, as Harke has a flat-bottomed fuselage and a very long undercarriage. Its American flying-crane counterpart, the S-64, is much smaller and is virtually a cockpit mounted at one end of a boom carrying engines, stub wings and tail rotor. Care should be taken, however, because the attachment of a containerised load to the S-64 completely changes this type's lines.

Among the twin-rotor types, the Ka-25 and Ka-25K look like recognition cartoons come to life, with triple fins, two

Like the S-64, the Ka-26 can look very different when a load pod is added to its basic crane-like structure. Once again, this Soviet type has a four-wheel undercarriage.

The Kaman Huskie combines twin pylons carrying intermeshing rotors, a very squat fuselage with square-cut rear end, and four fins on a long, slim tailplane.

507

Mil Mi-4 Hound *Confusion:* Whirlwind

Power: 1 × Shvetsov piston engine   *Rotor dia:* 68ft 11in (21m)   *Length:* 55ft 1in (16.80m)

The Mi-4, code-named Hound, was first put into production in 1952 and several thousand examples have been built for military and civil work. Exports have been widespread throughout the Soviet sphere of influence and to countries such as Egypt and India. Fourteen troops can be carried in the military version, while freight can be loaded through the rear clamshell doors. A military close-support variant is armed with a machine gun in an underfuselage pod, plus air-to-surface rockets. The anti-submarine version is fitted with magnetic anomaly detection gear and an undernose search radar. The civil version is the 11-passenger Mi-4P and the agricultural variant is the Mi-4S. China built the type under licence. Economical cruising speed is 99 mph (160km/hr) and maximum range is 370 miles (595km). *Country of origin:* USSR. *Silhouette:* Mi-4P. *Picture:* Mi-4 (military).

Power: 1 × Gnome turboshaft   *Rotor dia:* 53ft (16.15m)   *Length:* 44ft 2in (13.46m)

The Whirlwind, a licence–built version of the Sikorsky S-55, first flew in 1952. Series 1 and 2 aircraft were powered by piston engines; only a few remain in service (with Cuba and Yugoslavia). The Series 3 Whirlwind was extensively modified, the installation of a 1,050shp Rolls-Royce Gnome turboshaft necessitating a change in the nose shape. The type is still in limited service in Brazil, Nigeria and Qatar. *Country of origin:* UK. *Silhouette:* Series 3. *Picture:* Whirlwind HAR10.

Sikorsky S-55/H-19/S-55T *Confusion:* Whirlwind, S-58

Power: 1 × R-1300 piston engine   *Rotor dia:* 53ft (16.15m)   *Length:* 42ft 3in (12.88m)

The S-55, the first American helicopter to be certificated for commercial operation, first flew in 1949. The type has been sold to civil and military operators all over the world and has also been licence-built in Japan by Mitsubishi and in Britain by Westland as the Whirlwind. The military version is designated H-19 Chickasaw in US service use and is still operated by a number of South American countries as well as Greece and Turkey. More than 1,200 were built. Powered by an 800hp Wright R-1300 piston engine, the S-55 has a cruising speed of about 90 mph (145km/hr). US company Helitec has produced a turbine-powered version, the S-55T. *Country of origin:* USA. *Main silhouette:* S-55; *lower side view:* S-55T. *Picture:* S-55T.

Power: 1 × R-1820 piston engine or   *Rotor dia* (S-58T): 62ft (18.9m)   *Length* (S-58T): 54ft 9in (16.69m)
1 × PT6T turboshaft

A general-purpose 18-passenger piston-engined military/civil helicopter, the S-58 has been operated all over the world and production totalled 1,821. US Army designations are CH-34A to CH-34D Choctaw. In marinised form the type is known as the UH-34D, VH-34D and UH-34E Seahorse, and the name Seabat is used for anti-submarine variants (SH-34G and SH-34J). The S-58B, C and D are civil transports. First flown in 1970 with two PT6 turboshaft engines, the S-58T was eventually offered as new or in the form of a conversion from the piston-engined version. *Country of origin:* USA. *Main silhouette:* S-58; *lower side view:* S-58T. *Picture:* S-58T.

Westland Wessex *Confusion:* S-55, S-58

Power: 2 × Gnome turboshafts   *Rotor dia:* 56ft (17.07m)   *Length:* 48ft 4½in (14.74m)

A general-purpose and anti-submarine helicopter first flown in 1958, the Wessex was originally powered by a Gazelle engine but was later fitted with Rolls-Royce Gnomes. Used by the RAF and Royal Navy, the Wessex has been built in various versions, including the HC2 transport/ambulance for the RAF and the HAS1 anti-submarine and HU5 commando assault transport for the Royal Navy. The Wessex carries a crew of two and ten passengers. Range is 334 miles (538km). *Country of origin:* UK. *Silhouette:* HAS1. *Picture:* HU5.

Power: 2 × Turmo turboshafts   *Rotor dia:* 49ft 2½in (15m)   *Length:* 46ft 1½in (14m)

Originally a French product which first flew in 1965, the SA.330 Puma was later adopted as part of a joint Franco-British programme under which production was shared between the two countries. The RAF and the French Army use the type as a transport and over 560 have been ordered for military and civil applications in many countries. Early versions were the 330B (French Army), 330C (export), 330E (RAF), 330F and G (civil) and 330H (military). Current models are the 330J (civil) and 330L (military). Sixteen troops or up to 20 passengers can be carried at a cruising speed of 159 mph (257km/hr). *Country of origin:* France/UK. *Silhouette:* SA.330. *Picture:* Puma HC1 (SA.330E).

Aérospatiale SA.332 Super Puma   *Confusion:* Puma, Wessex, Super Frelon

Power: 2 × Makila turboshafts   *Rotor dia:* 49ft 6in (15.08m)   *Length:* 48ft 8in (14.82m)

A much modified version of the Puma, the 332 Super Puma has a lengthened nose, new undercarriage and higher-powered engines. The five versions of the 332 on offer are the military 332B seating 20 troops; civil 332C seating 17; 332F for ASW/search and rescue and other naval duties; 332L with 2ft 6in (0.76m) fuselage extension, four more seats and two extra windows; and 332M with the same extension for military use. More than 100 Super Pumas have been ordered, of which 35 332Ls, named Super Tigers, are for Bristow Helicopters. The 332L has a maximum speed of 184 mph (296km/hr) and range at cruising speed of 527 miles (848km). *Country of origin:* France.

Power: 3 × Turmo turboshafts   *Rotor dia:* 62ft (18.9m)   *Length:* 75ft 7in (23m)

First flown in 1962, the three-engined SA.321 Super Frelon is used as a military and civil transport and for anti-submarine work. Civil versions are the 321F and 321J, the former designed to carry 34/37 passengers. The 321G for the French Navy is amphibious, has radar and carries torpedoes and other military equipment. The 321H army/air force variant accommodates 27–30 troops or cargo. The Super Frelon has been built in large numbers and sold to eight countries, including Israel. Cruising speed is 155 mph (250km/hr) and range 509 miles (820km). *Country of origin:* France. *Silhouette:* SA.321F. *Picture:* SA.321K.

Sikorsky S-61L/S-61N

Confusion: Super Frelon, S-62

Power: 2 × CT58 turboshafts   *Rotor dia:* 62ft (18.9m)   *Length:* 72ft 10in (22.2m)

A widely used helicopter airliner, the S-61L/N can seat up to 28 passengers. The S-61L is non-amphibious, while the N has stabilising floats and a sealed hull for use on water. British Airways Helicopters is the largest single operator of this type. The S-61L first flew in 1960 and the S-61N in 1962. The undercarriage is retractable and the nose carries a thimble radome containing weather radar. Range is 495 miles (796km) and cruising speed 138 mph (222km/hr). *Country of origin:* USA. *Main silhouette:* S-61L; *lower side view:* S-61B. *Picture:* S-61N.

Power: 1 × T58 turboshaft   *Rotor dia:* 53ft (16.16m)   *Length:* 44ft 6½in (13.58m)

The first amphibious helicopter to be built by Sikorsky, the S-62 first flew in 1958 and has been used in both military and civil forms. As an airliner it carries 12 passengers or cargo. The original S-62A was licence-built by Mitsubishi in Japan, the S-62B had the main rotor system of the S-58 instead of that of the S-55, and the S-62C was the last commercial version. The US Coast Guard took delivery of 99 S-62s, designating them HH-52A. Maximum cruising speed is 98 mph (158km/hr) and range 474 miles (764km). *Country of origin:* USA. *Silhouette and picture:* HH-52A.

Sikorsky SH-3/S-61 *Confusion:* Sea King, S-61R

Power: 2 × T58 turboshafts   *Rotor dia:* 62ft (18.9m)   *Length:* 54ft 9in (16.69m)

The multi-purpose S-61 is used for anti-submarine work, transport and search and rescue. As the S-61 the type can carry 26 troops. In the anti-submarine role it is known as the Sea King and carries weapons, including homing torpedoes. US Navy designation is SH-3 and there are a number of variants, from SH-3A through to SH-3H. The SH-3 is known as the CH-124 in the Canadian Armed Forces. The SH-3 has been widely exported and is standard equipment in Japan and Italy, where it is built by Agusta. The SH-3 first flew in 1959. Range is 625 miles (1,005km) and cruising speed 136 mph (219km/hr). *Country of origin:* USA. *Silhouette:* SH-3H. *Picture:* SH-3D.

Westland Sea King/Commando

Power: 2 × Gnome turboshafts   *Rotor dia:* 62ft (18.9m)   *Length:* 55ft 10in (17.01m)

Developed under licence from the American S-61D, the Sea King is the Royal Navy's standard anti-submarine helicopter under the designations HAS1 and 2. The HAR3 is used by the RAF for search and rescue. The Sea King has been exported to West Germany, India, Norway, Pakistan, Egypt, Australia and Belgium. Capable of fully all-weather operations, the Sea King can carry depth charges and homing torpedoes. The Commando military transport version can seat 30 troops and has no amphibious capability. Commando Mks 1 and 2 are in service. The Commando Mk 1 differs minimally from the Sea King, while the Mk 2, the main production version, can be used for tactical troop transport, logistic support, casualty evacuation, air-to-surface strike, and search and rescue. Sea King cruising speed is 131 mph (211km/hr) and range 937 miles (1,507km). *Country of origin:* UK. *Silhouette:* HAS2. *Picture:* Mk 41.

Sikorsky S-61R/CH-3E/HH-3F Pelican

Confusion: Sea King, SH-3/S-61

Power: 2 × T58 turboshafts   *Rotor dia:* 62ft (18.9m)   *Length:* 57ft 3in (17.45m)

Developed from the S-61 Sea King, the S-61R has a rear loading ramp and retractable undercarriage. It is used for transport, assault and search and rescue. The first S-61R flew in 1963 and the type is used by the USAF as the CH-3E and HH-3E and by the US Coast Guard as the HH-3F Pelican, with a nose radome. The HH-3E has armour, defensive armament and an in-flight refuelling probe on the starboard side. Up to 30 troops can be carried and a hoist is fitted. Agusta in Italy has built a version of the Pelican for the Italian Air Force. Cruising speed is 144 mph (232km/hr) and range 465 miles (748km). *Country of origin:* USA. *Silhouette:* HH-3F. *Picture:* HH-3E.

Power: 2 × Isotov turboshafts   *Rotor dia:* 69ft 10in (21.29m)   *Length:* 61ft (18.3m)

A replacement for the Mi-4 Hound, the Mi-8 is a twin-turbine helicopter seating up to 32 passengers. As with other Soviet medium helicopters, the Hip is used by both the Soviet services and Aeroflot. The military versions have round windows and are code-named Hip-C to Hip-F. Hip-E carries a gun and massive rocket-projectile armament. The transport has rectangular windows and no radome. Range is 232 miles (375km) and maximum cruising speed 140 mph (225km/hr). *Country of origin:* USSR. *Silhouette and picture:* Mi-8.

Mil Mi-14 Haze *Confusion:* Hip, S-61

Power: 2 × Isotov turboshafts   *Rotor dia:* 69ft 10in (21.29m)   *Length:* 59ft 7in (18.15m)

Developed from the Mi-8, the Mi-14 Haze is a shore-based Soviet Navy anti-submarine helicopter. A boat hull is incorporated, there is a radome under the nose, and a magnetic anomaly detector is mounted under the tailboom. The undercarriage is fully retractable. Haze is in full production and in large-scale service with the Soviet Naval Air Force. About 80 have been delivered, with production continuing at a rate of approximately 25 per year. A few are reported to have been delivered to Bulgaria in 1979. Anti-submarine weapons are certain to be carried, although the weapons bay is not visible. Dimensions and dynamic components are generally similar to those of the Mi-18, while the powerplant is a pair of Isotov TV3-117 turboshafts of the kind fitted to the Mi-24 gunship. Maximum speed is approximately 142 mph (230km/hr). *Country of origin:* USSR.

Power: 2 × Isotov turboshafts   *Rotor dia:* **55ft (16.76m)**   *Length:* **55ft 6in (16.9m)**

A heavily armed assault and gunship helicopter, the Mi-24, code-named Hind, is in service in the Soviet Union in very large numbers. Hind-A carries eight troops and has stub-wing-mounted missiles and a nose gun, while Hind-D has separate cockpits for pilot and weapon operator and a four-barrel machine gun in a chin mounting. Hind-C has no nose gun or under-nose sighting system. Hind-E carries tube-launched anti-tank missiles. Early Hinds had the tail rotor on the starboard side, while later versions have it on the port side. Cruising speed is 140 mph (225km/hr) and range 300 miles (480km). *Country of origin:* USSR. *Silhouette and picture:* Hind-D.

Sikorsky S-76 Spirit

Confusion: S-70

Power: 2 × Allison 250 turboshafts   *Rotor dia:* 44ft (13.41m)   *Length:* 44ft 1in (13.44m)

A commercial transport seating 14 passengers, the Sikorsky S-76 first flew in 1977. Though it is a completely new design not related to a military type, the S-76 is also suitable for service operators. Over 450 S-76s have been ordered and the type can be fitted with long-range tanks, cargo hook and hoist. The S-76 is classified as an all-weather helicopter. Maximum cruising speed at a gross weight of 8,400lb (3,810kg) is 178 mph (286km/hr). Range with eight passengers, auxiliary fuel and offshore equipment is 691 miles (1,112km), reducing to 461 miles (742km) with 12 passengers and standard fuel. *Country of origin:* USA.

Power: 2 × T700 turboshafts   *Rotor dia:* 53ft 8in (16.23m)   *Length:* 51ft 1in (15.26m)

First flown in 1974, the Sikorsky S-70 Black Hawk, military designation UH-60A, was the winner of the US Army's Utility Tactical Transport Aircraft System (Uttas) competition and is now in full-scale production. Ultimately 1,000 Black Hawks may be acquired. Eleven fully equipped troops can be carried, and alternative loads include cargo and stretchers. Up to 8,000lb (3,629kg) can be carried externally on a hook. An electronic counter-measures variant is known as the EH-60A, and five prototypes of the EH-60B are being built; this version is the basis for the Stand-Off Target Acquisition System (SOTAS). The US Army plans eventually to acquire 75-100 SOTAS Black Hawks for battlefield target-spotting. Endurance is up to three hours and maximum cruising speed 169 mph (272km/hr). *Country of origin:* USA. *Silhouette and picture:* UH-60A.

Sikorsky SH-60B Seahawk

Confusion: Black Hawk, S-76

Power: 2 × T700 turboshafts   *Rotor dia:* 53ft 8in (16.36m)   *Length:* 50ft 1in (15.26m)

Developed from the Black Hawk, the three-crew SH-60B Seahawk was the winner in the US Navy's Light Airborne Multi-Purpose System (LAMPS) Mk III competition. The Seahawk will be used for anti-submarine warfare and ship surveillance/ship targeting from cruisers, destroyers and frigates. Sophisticated detection and processing equipment and anti-submarine torpedoes are carried. Deliveries will start in 1983 and the US Navy requirement is for 204, to be followed by a less complex version, the SH-60C. *Country of origin:* USA.

Sikorsky S-65A/CH-53 Sea Stallion

Power: 2 × T64 turboshafts   *Rotor dia:* 72ft 3in (22.02m)   *Length:* 67ft 2in (20.47m)

A heavy assault transport, the S-65A first flew in 1964 and incorporates many S-64 components. Fitted with rear loading doors, the type can carry vehicles, guns or 55 troops. The US Marines and Iran use the CH-53A Sea Stallion, while the USAF has the HH-53B/C. An improved US Marine Corps version is the CH-53D, and the CH-53G is licence-built in Germany. The S-65 (MCM), designated RH-53D in the US Navy, is used for mine countermeasures and has a tow boom. Austria bought two S-65-Oes for rescue work in the Alps. Range is 257 miles (410km) and maximum cruising speed 173 mph (278km/hr). *Country of origin:* USA. *Silhouette:* CH-53G. *Picture:* S-65.

Sikorsky CH-53E Super Stallion *Confusion:* S-65A/CH-53

Power: 3 × T64 turboshafts   *Rotor dia:* 79ft (24m)   *Length:* 73ft 5in (22.38m)

Developed from the S-65/CH-53A/B/D Sea Stallion, the CH-53E Super Stallion three-engined amphibious assault transport helicopter is used by both the US Navy and US Marines. Up to 56 troops can be accommodated, and very large loads, such as aircraft, can be slung externally. The first prototype flew in 1974 and production deliveries of 49 machines started in 1980. Maximum cruising speed is 173 mph (278km/hr). *Country of origin:* USA.

Power: 2 × Soloviev turboshafts　　*Rotor dia:* 114ft 10in (35m)　　*Length:* 108ft 10½in (33.18m)

When it first appeared in 1957 the Mi-6, code-named Hook, was the world's largest helicopter. Basically a military design, of which over 800 have been built, the type has also been employed by Aeroflot as a specialised civil transport. Military Hooks have been exported to Egypt, Bulgaria and Vietnam. Equipment, including missiles, can be loaded through the rear clamshell doors and heavy loads can be carried externally. A total of 65 passengers can be accommodated. Maximum cruising speed is 155 mph (250km/hr) and range 404 miles (650km). At one time the Mi-6 held a total of 14 FAI-recognised records. Those still standing include a speed of 211 mph (340km/hr) over a 100km closed circuit; a speed of 186 mph (300km/hr) with payloads of 1,000kg and 2,000kg over a 1,000km circuit; and a speed of 176 mph (284km/hr) with a payload of 5,000kg over a 1,000km closed circuit. *Country of origin:* USSR.

Mil Mi-26 Halo *Confusion:* Hook

Power: 2 × Lotarev turboshafts   *Rotor dia:* 105ft (32m)   *Length:* 110ft 8in (33.7m)

The heaviest helicopter built anywhere in the world, the Mi-26, Nato code-named Halo, is the first to have an eight-blade rotor. Initially flown in 1977 and now in full-scale production, the Mi-26 can carry 44,090lb (20,000kg) of internal payload or up to 70 troops. Capable of operating in extreme winter conditions in the Soviet Union in the civil role, the Mi-26 also has a variety of military applications. The Mi-26 made its first public appearance at the 1981 Paris Show, where it aroused major interest. The Mi-26's top speed is 183 mph (295km/hr) and range 497 miles (800km). *Country of origin:* USSR.

Power: 2 × Soloviev turboshafts   *Rotor dia:* 114ft 10in (35m)   *Length:* 107ft 10in (32.86m)

Developed from the Mi-6, the Mi-10 Harke is a very large flying crane which first flew in 1960. Bulky loads can be carried between the long main undercarriage legs and the cabin accommodates up to 28 passengers. The Mi-10 is used by both the Soviet armed forces and Aeroflot. The Mi-10K has the same fuselage, plus a short undercarriage and a gondola under the nose housing a second pilot. A closed-circuit television system, with cameras scanning forwards from under the rear fuselage and downwards through the sling hatch, is used to monitor Mi-10 payloads. The pilot also uses this system as a touchdown reference. The Mi-10K was first publicly demonstrated in 1966. Range of the Mi-10 is 155 miles (250km) and cruising speed 112 mph (180km/hr). *Country of origin:* USSR. *Silhouette:* Mi-10K. *Picture:* Mi-10.

Sikorsky S-64 Skycrane/CH-54 Tarhe *Confusion:* Harke

Power: 2 × JTFD12 turboshafts   *Rotor dia:* 72ft (21.9m)   *Length:* 70ft 3in (21.41m)

A flying crane designed to lift heavy bulk loads, the S-64 first flew in 1962 and was adopted by the US Army as the CH-54A Tarhe. Special standardised containers can be slung under the fuselage boom. With a maximum loaded weight of 20,000lb (9,072kg), these pods can accommodate 45 combat-equipped troops, 24 stretchers, cargo or other equipment. They can also be adapted in the field to act as surgical units or command and communications posts. A variant with more power and modified rotor system is known as the CH-54B. Civil versions are designated S-64E and S-64F. Range is 230 miles (370km) and maximum cruising speed 127 mph (204km/hr). Production has now ceased. *Country of origin:* USA. *Silhouette and picture:* S-64.

Power: 2 × Glushenkov turboshafts   *Rotor dia:* 51ft 8in (15.74m)   *Length:* 32ft (9.75m)

Produced in large numbers, the Ka-25 Hormone is the Soviet Navy's standard shipborne anti-submarine helicopter. Distinguished by a large chin radome, it carries depth charges, torpedoes and guided missiles. Twin main rotors are mounted on a single shaft. A transport version seats 12, while Hormone-B carries special electronics equipment. The Ka-25K, with the radome replaced by a glazed gondola, is a commercial version for crane and general duties. Cruising speed is 120 mph (193km/hr) and range 250 miles (402km). *Country of origin:* USSR. *Silhouette:* Ka-25K. *Picture:* Ka-25.

Kamov Ka-32 Helix *Confusion:* Hormone, Hoodlum

Power: 2 × turboshafts   *Rotor dia:* 54ft 10in (16.75m)   *Length:* 39ft 5in (12m)

First observed aboard a Soviet cruiser in 1981, this latest Kamov helicopter is believed to be designated Ka-32 and is Nato code-named Helix. The layout of Helix is similar to that of Hormone but the former is significantly larger and heavier, with a longer fuselage, increased rotor diameter and two instead of three fins. Helix is basically an anti-submarine helicopter, with two pilots and three sensor operators, although it is also understood to be under development as a marine/civil transport. One Helix has been observed bearing Aeroflot markings. The type will be able to lift heavy loads by means of a belly hook. *Country of origin:* USSR.

Power: 2 × Vedeneev piston engines *Rotor dia:* 42ft 8in (13m) *Length:* 24ft 5in (7.75m)

First flown in 1956, the Ka-26, Nato code-named Hoodlum, is a light transport and agricultural helicopter in large-scale service in the Eastern Bloc and exported to such countries as West Germany, Sweden and Sri Lanka. Payloads are interchangeable by the use of specialised fuselage pods designed for the transport, ambulance, cropdusting/spraying and geophysical survey roles. A lifting hook can be fitted. Some Hoodlums are employed on military work. Carrying seven passengers, Hoodlum has a range of 248 miles (400km). *Country of origin:* USSR.

Kaman H-43 Huskie   *Confusion:* Hormone

Power: 1 × T53 turboshaft   *Rotor dia:* 47ft (14.33m)   *Length:* 25ft 2in (7.67m)

Originally piston-engine-powered, the Huskie was first used by the US Navy and USAF in the 1950s. The initial turbine-powered version was the HH-43B, first flown in 1956 and ordered by the USAF, Burma, Colombia, Morocco, Pakistan and Thailand. A later development was the HH-34F, built for the USAF and Iran. The US Navy uses a drone version designated QH-43G. Up to ten passengers, a firefighting/rescue team, or stretchers and medical personnel can be carried. Range is 504 miles (811km) and cruising speed 110 mph (117km/hr). The Huskie is unusual in having twin rotor masts and intermeshing rotors. *Country of origin:* USA. *Silhouette and picture:* HH-34F.

Power: **2 × T55 turboshafts**   *Rotor dia:* **60ft (18.29m)**   *Length:* **51ft (15.54m)**

Many hundreds of tandem-rotor Chinook helicopters have been built. In addition to US production, the type is made under licence in Italy. Initial variant was the CH-47A, followed by the uprated CH-47B. The current production model is the CH-47C with more range and better performance. The US Army is upgrading all its Chinooks to -47C standard. The RAF operates the Chinook as its standard medium-lift helicopter, and there have been exports to other countries. Up to 44 troops can be carried in the cabin and large loads can be slung. The commercial passenger version, the Model 234, is now in service with British Airways Helicopters. Mission radius of action is 115 miles (185km) and cruising speed 158 mph (254km/hr). *Country of origin:* USA. *Silhouette and picture:* CH-47C.

Boeing Vertol H-46 Sea Knight/Model 107 *Confusion:* Chinook

Power: 2 × T58 turboshafts   *Rotor dia:* 51ft (15.54m)   *Length:* 44ft 10in (13.66m)

The Sea Knight operates as a shipboard and land-based assault transport carrying 25 troops or freight. First flown in 1958, the Sea Knight has been built in a variety of versions: the CH-46A, -46D, -46E and -46F for the US Marines, and the UH-46A and -46D for the US Navy. Canada operates the type under the designations CH-113 and CH-113A, while Sweden bought some Rolls-Royce Gnome-powered HKP-4s. The commercial version is the Model 107, now solely built by Kawasaki, which also supplies a military KV-107 to the Japanese forces. Range is 633 miles (1,022km) and cruising speed 154 mph (248km/hr). *Country of origin:* USA/Japan. *Main silhouette:* H-46; *lower side view:* Kawasaki KV-107. *Picture:* KV-107/II-5.

aerofoil section Cross-section through an aircraft wing or helicopter rotor blade.

afterburner Gives a jet engine greatly increased thrust by burning fuel in the exhaust gas stream. Also called reheat.

aileron Wing-mounted lateral control surface.

airbrake Retractable "door" mounted on the fuselage or wing and used to slow the aircraft down or steepen descent angle.

AI Airborne intercept radar.

all-up weight Fully loaded weight of an aircraft or helicopter.

amphibian Aircraft capable of alighting on both land and water.

anhedral Angle at which a wing slopes down from the horizontal in the head-on view. Opposite of dihedral.

antenna Any form of aerial for the transmission/reception of radio/radar signals.

arrester hook Underfuselage hook designed to engage wires on an airfield or a carrier deck in order to stop the aircraft.

aspect ratio The ratio between the span and chord of a wing. Derived by dividing span by chord.

ASV Air-to-surface-vessel radar. Used by maritime aircraft.

balance tab Part of an aileron, elevator or rudder which moves into the opposite sense to the main control surface.

bank/banking Manoeuvre in which the aircraft is rolled to left or right.

bicycle undercarriage Two main wheels in tandem under the fuselage. Usually with outrigger wheels on the wings.

bogie undercarriage Four or more wheels on each undercarriage leg.

camber Curvature of an aerofoil section.

canard Aircraft with its tailplane mounted forward of the wing.

canopy Transparent cockpit cover.

cantilever Wing or undercarriage without bracing struts.

c of g Centre of gravity.

chord Measurement from the leading edge to the trailing edge of a wing or rotor blade, parallel with the fuselage centreline.

contrail White vapour trail caused by the condensation of the water in engine exhaust gases at certain altitudes.

contra-rotating propellers Two propellers mounted on one shaft and rotating in opposite directions.

crescent wing Sweptback wing with varying degrees of sweep on the leading edge.

delta Triangular wing or tailplane.

dihedral Angle at which a wing slopes up from the horizontal in the head-on view. Some wings have dihedral on the outer sections only. Opposite of anhedral.

dogtooth Notch in a wing leading edge, visible in the plan view. Also known as a sawtooth.

dorsal fin Extension of the main fin along the top of the fuselage.

drag The resistance offered by the air to an aircraft or part of an aircraft passing through it.

drone Pilotless aircraft used for reconnaissance, electronic warfare or as a target. Also known as a remotely piloted vehicle (RPV).

droop Means of increasing the camber and therefore the lifting capacity of a wing by mechanically extending and lowering the leading edge.

ECM Electronic countermeasures. Means of jamming or distorting radio or radar signals.

ECCM Electronic counter-countermeasures. Means of overcoming ECM.

ejection seat Seat designed to fire aircrew clear of the aircraft in an emergency.

elevator Tailplane-mounted surface used to control an aircraft in the vertical plane.

elevon Combined elevator and aileron; used on delta-wing aircraft.

fence Vertical metal strips mounted chordwise on a wing upper surface to contain spanwise airflow.

fenestron Multi-blade tail rotor mounted in a duct.

fin Fixed part of a vertical tail.

flap Surface mounted at the wing trailing edge and deployed to increase lift for take-off and landing.

flaperon Trailing-edge surface combining the functions of flap and aileron.

flat four Horizontally opposed four-cylinder piston engine. Also flat twin and flat six.

flight refuelling Means of passing fuel from one aircraft to another in the air. Under the British system the "tanker" aircraft trails a hose with a drogue at the end, into which a probe on the receiving aircraft is inserted. The American system is based on a "flying boom" which can be directed to a receiving point on the aircraft which is being refuelled.

flying tail Tailplane which has no fixed portion and moves in its entirety to give vertical control.

foreplane Forward control surface on a canard aircraft.

fuselage Main body of an aircraft or helicopter.

gull wing A wing with dihedral on the inner sections only. An inverted gull wing has anhedral on the inner sections.

hardpoint Reinforced point, usually on the wings, to which external stores can be attached.

JATO Jet-assisted take-off. Technique under which auxiliary rocket packs are mounted on the aircraft to shorten the take-off run. Also known as RATO (rocket-assisted take-off).

leading edge The front edge of a wing, tail or rotor blade.

lift The upward force which keeps an aircraft flying.

Mach number The ratio between the speed of an aircraft and the speed of sound at a particular height. At sea level the speed of sound is 720 mph, so that an aircraft travelling at 720 mph would be flying at Mach 1; 576 mph under the same conditions would be equivalent to Mach 0.8. The speed of sound decreases with altitude up to 36,600ft; thereafter it stays constant at 660.6 mph.

mass balance Weight mounted internally or externally on a control surface to prevent damaging oscillation.

monocoque Aircraft structure in which the outer skin takes most of the load.

nacelle Streamlined structure housing engines, radar or other equipment.

parasol Monoplane with wings mounted on struts above the fuselage.

payload Paying load of a transport, i.e. passengers or freight.

pitot tube Instrument which detects ram-air pressure. This is compared with static pressure to find airspeed.

pod Separate nacelle attached to fuselage or wing and carrying an engine, radar or other equipment.

pressurisation The maintenance of pressure inside an aircraft so that passengers and crew can breathe without personal oxygen supplies at high altitude.

pylon Wing or fuselage-mounted structure carrying engine pods, auxiliary fuel tanks or weapons.

radome Dome-shaped fairing over a radar aerial.

refuelling probe Used to receive fuel from an airborne tanker.

reheat See *afterburner*.

rotor blade Helicopter lifting and control surfaces. A rotor is made up of two or more blades. The main rotor generates lift and creates propulsive thrust. The vertically mounted tail rotor balances out the torque which makes the fuselage tend to rotate in the opposite direction to the main rotor.

rudder A fin-mounted vertical surface which provides directional control.

servo tab Moving surface on aileron, elevator or rudder which when moved causes the main control surface to deflect in the opposite direction.

slat Section of wing leading edge which moves forward to produce a slot between itself and the wing. Increases lift and improves control at low speeds.

slot Spanwise gap at the wing leading edge (see *slat*).

slotted flap Flap which creates a slot between itself and the wing trailing edge.

sonobuoy Listening device dropped from an aircraft to detect submarines.

split flap Flap which is hinged forward of the wing trailing edge, so that the wing upper surface is unchanged when the flap is lowered.

spoiler Retractable wing-mounted surface deployed to create drag and reduce lift. Used to slow the aircraft and control its descent path.

sponson Stub wing carrying undercarriage or other equipment.

spring tab Small control surface which acts as both balance tab and servo tab.

stabiliser Tailplane (US).

STOL Short take-off and landing.

subsonic Speeds below that of sound, i.e. less than Mach 1.

supercharger Compressor used to boost the power of a piston engine. Also called a turbocharger.

supersonic Speeds in excess of that of sound, i.e. above Mach 1.

sweepback Plan-view angle between the wing and the fuselage centreline.

taileron Tailplane used as a primary control surface in both pitch and roll.

tailplane Horizontal surface at the rear of an aircraft which normally carries the elevators.

taper The decrease in wing chord from root to tip.

thickness/chord ratio Ratio of the thickness of the wing section to the chord at a given point. Usually expressed as a percentage.

thrust The force that moves an aircraft forward. Also used to express the power of a jet engine.

thrust reverser System which turns the thrust of a jet engine forwards for braking purposes.

transonic Speeds just above and below Mach 1.

trim tab Adjustable tab on a control surface.

turbofan A jet engine with a large fan on the front which passes air round the core of the engine and also gives more impetus to the compressor.

turbojet An engine in which the hot gases expelled at the rear provide all the propulsive thrust.

turboprop A gas turbine engine in which the shaft is geared to drive a propeller.

turboshaft A gas turbine in which the power is transmitted to a shaft, usually to drive a helicopter rotor.

vortex generators Small protruding plates fitted to wing, tail or fuselage to change the airflow pattern.

wing loading Aircraft loaded weight divided by wing area.

SILLOGRAPH PROFICIENCY TEST

Test your aircraft-recognition skill by identifying these sillograph outlines of well known aircraft. Tackle the whole test in one go, and write down your answers. The solution is on page 559.

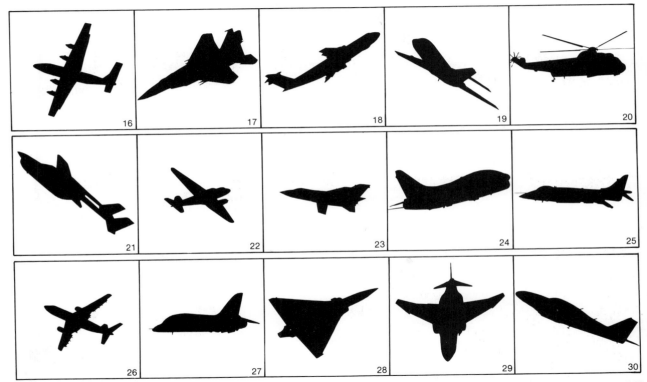

INDEX

544

INDEX

INDEX

INDEX

INDEX

INDEX

Test answers (see page 542)

1 Concorde
2 Do 28
3 Buffalo
4 Cessna 152
5 Jetstream
6 Tomcat
7 Baron
8 Flogger
9 F.27
10 Trident
11 A-10
12 Islander
13 One-Eleven
14 Backfire
15 F-16

16 Dash 7
17 Eagle
18 Galaxy
19 Falcon 20
20 Sea King
21 Skymaster
22 DC-3
23 Tornado
24 Two-seat Corsair II
25 Sea Harrier
26 Airbus A300
27 Hawk
28 Mirage 2000
29 Phantom
30 Aztec